WRITING IN THE CENTER

TEACHING IN A
WRITING CENTER SETTING

Third Edition

Irene L. Clark Ph.D.
University of Southern California

KENDALL/HUNT PUBLISHING COMPANY
4050 Westmark Drive   Dubuque, Iowa 52002

# CONTENTS

Preface to the Third Edition   *v*

Introduction for Tutors   *vii*

1 Writing and the Writing Center: History and Theory   1

2 Preparing for Tutoring: Remembering, Reflecting, Anticipating   23

3 Working with Students: Interpersonal Communication   43

4 Interpreting Assignments, Developing Ideas   65

5 Purpose, Thesis, Audience   93

6 Helping Students Revise: Global and Surface Level Revision   111

7 Dealing with Learning Disabilities in the Writing Center   147
Julie Neff-Lippman, University of Puget Sound

8 Working With Computers in the Writing Center   165

9 Special Assignments: The Research Paper and the Literary Essay   181

10 Working With Non-native and Dialect Speakers in the Writing Center   203
John R. Edlund, California State University, Los Angeles

A   Are Writing Centers Ethical?   235
Irene L. Clark, Dave Healy

B   Leading the Horse: The Writing Center and Required Visits   253
Irene L. Clark

Index   *259*

PREFACE TO THE THIRD EDITION

Writing centers are flourishing. Twelve years have passed since the first publication of *Writing in the Center*, and during that time, writing centers have attained even greater credibility within the academic community and have proliferated across the country, in high schools as well as in colleges and universities. The National Council of Teachers of English and the Conference on College Composition and Communication now regularly hold an exciting array of workshops and panels concerned with writing centers, and the National Writing Centers Association, once an inconspicuous get-together in a corner of a conference room, now hosts its own national conference and requires a large hall to house its many regional divisions. Composition historians, such as Peter Carino, are tracing the history of writing centers; subscriptions to the *Writing Lab Newsletter* continue to grow, and the *Writing Center Journal* has become an established, well-respected journal. Now, when I mention my profession both within and beyond academic circles, I am less frequently asked "What is a writing center?" and I have learned of the existence of writing centers in Australia, New Zealand, Mexico, Canada, and Japan. Happily, as Gary Olson observed several years ago, "although writing centers have always been diverse in their pedagogies, philosophies, and physical makeups, the writing center's period of chaotic adolescence is nearly over. Center directors are slowly articulating common goals, objectives, and methodologies, and writing centers are beginning to take on a common form to evolve into a recognizable species" (vii).

Part of this professional credibility can be traced to an increased understanding of the suitability of writing centers for implementing composition theory. As the romantic concept of writing as a solitary act has been replaced by the idea of writing as a social process, writing centers are recognized as an appropriate environment for students to receive their first introduction to the academic discourse community. Thus, although writing centers remain eminently practical, flexible, and student oriented, they have moved beyond the realm of the makeshift and the "whatever works" mentality. In fact, one might say that the writing center has now become a pedagogical concept as well as an actual place.

Writing centers' enhanced professional status may also be traced to the growing recognition that everyone, good writers as well as poor ones, can benefit from insightful feedback and that even professional writers experience writing block, write multiple revisions, and seek audience response. This realization means that writing centers are now less frequently tainted with the stigma of "remediation" with its accompanying overemphasis on mechanical correctness. As a result, the image of the writing center as a dreary place for remedial students to work on "skill and drill" activities has been replaced by a vital one of lively student/tutor interactions and meaningful discoveries, a true center for writers.

Validated on both a theoretical and pedagogical level, writing centers have thus achieved new status, and accordingly, this third edition addresses recent theoretical connections as well as provides additional practical suggestions and resources. In preparing this third edition, I have discovered that my pedagogical precepts have not changed drastically from those I advocated in the first and second editions, although this edition emphasizes the role that writing centers play in working with an increasingly diverse population of students, incorporates my own interest in genre theory, and provides updated examples and dialogues, as well as additional strategies and models. The new edition also contains chapters written by two of my colleagues who have particular areas of expertise, the chapter on working with non-native speakers written by John Edlund at the California State University, Los Angeles, and the chapter concerned with learning disabilities written by Julie Neff, at the University of Puget Sound. I am deeply grateful for their insights, which have significantly enriched this book. I have also included previously published articles, "Are Writing Centers Ethical?" written in collaboration with Dave Healy at the University of Minnesota and "Leading the Horse: The Writing Center and Required Visits." These articles are intended to stimulate discussion about several critical writing center issues, in particular, the controversy over directive, versus non-directive tutoring and the question of whether or not writing center visits should be mandated.

Aside from these additions, I have tried to preserve the aim and spirit of the first and second editions, that is, I continue to view *Writing in the Center* as a work for new writing center tutors who want to understand what tutoring writing is about and as a resource for writing center directors for training and guidance. Most importantly, I hope that this third edition conveys my continued enthusiasm for the work I do and my firm belief that writing centers provide the liveliest, as well as the most effective, arena for helping students learn to write.

⬤ INTRODUCTION FOR TUTORS ———

Since the publication of the first edition of *Writing in the Center* in 1985, writing centers have been flourishing, not only in the United States, but in many other countries as well. So important have writing centers now become that in a recent on-line discussion concerned with the teaching of writing, I learned that a few institutions of higher learning are considering a proposal that would assign all writing instruction to writing centers, thereby eliminating the need for writing classes. Whether this suggestion ever becomes a reality or is, in fact, desirable, there is no question that writing centers are proliferating. Whatever physical (or even virtual) manifestations they assume, and whether the people who work there are called "tutors," "consultants," "advisors," or "assistants," writing centers continue to be lively, energetic places that are playing an increasingly important role in helping students of all levels learn to write.

Why have writing centers become so important, when in the past, many people managed to learn to write without them? The concept of a writing center derives primarily from research in Composition that has established what writers have always known—that teaching students to write does not involve lecturing or assigning "how-to" books; rather, that one learns to write by *writing, talking* about writing, getting *feedback* on one's writing, and then rewriting and rewriting, preferably in a comfortable, non-threatening setting. This process is especially well-suited to the flexible environment of the writing center where instruction is individualized and where students can obtain help with their writing at any stage in the composing process. Students find them comfortable, non-threatening places for working on their writing; tutors find them a satisfying place to help students learn to write.

If you are about to become involved in the tutoring of writing, either in a writing center or as part of a teacher preparation class, then perhaps you may be feeling a bit anxious about your prospective new role. Some of you may envision that first tutorial session with a certain amount of trepidation. You may wonder how you ought to begin, what you should say to students to put them at ease. Should you imitate teachers and tutors you yourself have had acquaintance with in the past? Do you know enough about Composition theory or about how to diagnose a student paper, so that you will be able to do a good job? After all, a writing center conference sometimes lasts only about a half hour, perhaps an hour at most. And sometimes the papers students write need a lot more work than you can cover in that amount of time. How will you know which skill to target? How will you insure that students will learn something that they will be able to apply to their next paper? How will you inspire confidence in your students if you have had so little experience?

In the past, most people who worked in writing centers were given little preparatory training. Somehow it was assumed that once a potential tutoring staff became conversant with a bit of rhetorical theory and was provided with the names of a few reputable textbooks, that it would somehow "sense" the best method of conducting a conference. Often, new tutors were merely given a brief lecture about conferencing and then simply thrust into a conference session. Learning to tutor, presumably, took place on the job.

Today, however, it is recognized that learning to be a good tutor requires a self-examination and professional training beyond that which had been customarily provided and that successful writing conferences do not simply "happen" (at least not usually). More often, they occur because tutors have become experts in the field—they plan their tutoring time, determine a sequence of instruction based on a theoretically grounded diagnosis, and then focus the conference toward the accomplishment of specific goals.

This book is designed to present you with some fundamental concepts of tutoring writing that will enable you to approach your conferences with greater insight and confidence. If you have never tutored in a writing center before, I think you will find it an interesting and rewarding enterprise—each student is an individual, each paper contains its own strengths and weaknesses, and every conference is a new challenge. And unlike teaching writing in a traditional classroom, tutoring in a writing center frees both students and tutors from the pressure of grades. Both are free to experiment with a variety of approaches and styles.

Of course, tutoring, like teaching or painting or performing, is an art as well as a profession, and some of you are going to feel naturally more comfortable in the tutorial role and to be intuitively better tutors than others. Moreover, becoming an effective tutor is a function of experience and practice, and no amount of reading about tutoring can substitute for spending many hours actually tutoring students and evaluating the quality of that tutoring. A book, though, can generate ideas about a process before that process is actually begun. In thinking and reading about tutoring, you have begun an important part of your preparation.

WRITING AND THE WRITING CENTER: HISTORY AND THEORY

t the beginning of each school year, I distribute writing center brochures at a Campus Resource Fair for new students, who wander about collecting information about various university services. As might be expected, when these students come to the table marked "Writing Center," at least some of them usually ask what a writing center is and what sort of help writing centers provide. However, over the past few years, I have noticed that fewer students are asking these questions and that most seem quite familiar with the concept of a writing center. Glancing at the "Writing Center" sign, they take a brochure, look it over briefly, stuff it into their back packs, and nod their heads enthusiastically. Sometimes they say, "This is what I need!" or "You'll see me there a lot."

Writing Centers are now established all over the United States, and a few exist in other countries as well, although sometimes they are called by other names, such as writing "labs," writing "rooms," or writing "places." Their physical settings also vary considerably. At the present time, I work in a newly refurbished writing center with attractive, well-lit study spaces, modular tables and chairs, and state of the art computers. But before the remodeling, less than two years ago from the time I am writing, my writing center was like many others, distinctly shabby—a converted classroom with a few battered tables and chairs, a faded old sofa, a sprinkling of posters and plants serving as tokens of welcome and cheer. But no matter what they are called or how upscale or shabby they might be, writing centers are currently recognized as playing a significant role in helping students learn to write. In fact, some people feel that they fulfill this function more efficiently, effectively, and pleasantly than does the traditional writing classroom.

This chapter presents a brief overview of why and how writing centers have become so prominent in the field of composition and summarizes several theories that will help you tutor with greater insight and self-awareness. Although as a new tutor, you may be more concerned with practical matters than about theoretical ones (most new tutors are concerned primarily about what to say and do and about how to avoid looking like a fool), your tutoring will be more effective if it is based on a coherently thought out concept of how students learn to write, and you will gain greater confidence as well. If tutors are not acquainted with theories of writing and learning, they will simply be **guessing** about what is likely to be effective when they work with students in the writing center. An important idea behind this book is that although writing centers address practical concerns, effective writing center tutoring is based on a firm theoretical foundation.

Having said this, however, I will introduce the writing center approach with a practical illustration, embodied in the following two scenarios:

Scenario #1

You are a novice skier, and suddenly you find yourself riding a chairlift, heading inexorably up a steep snowy slope. All alone, close to panicking, you feel the chair climb higher and higher. Suddenly, the top of the slope is upon you, and you slide off, as best you can, fear in your throat, tumbling about until you gain your balance. Upright once again, you attempt to get down the hill as best you can, stumbling over your skis, losing control, standing for hours paralyzed by fear. When you finally do get to the bottom of the slope, you are cold, frightened, and bruised. You have only a vague idea of how you managed to get down and are absolutely terrified of trying again.

Scenario #2

You are a novice skier, but as you move up the snowy slope, a supportive and well-trained instructor is with you to provide instruction and assistance, one step at a time. The instructor accompanies you on the chairlift and calms your fears as you push off and begin moving down the slope. As you complete each maneuver, you receive feedback on what you did properly and advice about how to improve. Once you get down the slope, you feel encouraged to try again, knowing you can always ask for help if you need it. You haven't only gotten to the bottom of the slope; you have also become a better skier!

These two scenarios depict the approach to writing on which the concept of a writing center is based—that is, it is possible to learn to ski or to write by stumbling around, making mistakes and getting hurt, but the learning will be neither efficient nor agreeable. Moreover, some people will be so frightened by the experience that they may *never* learn. A better alternative, as scenario #2 illustrates, is to learn under benevolent and informed guidance, receiving feedback as needed. Writing centers provide this sort of guidance, and they are important because they effectively facilitate student learning. They do not simply provide a "quick-fix" for flawed student papers; instead, they are centers for individualized writing instruction, enabling students at all levels to become *better writers*.

What is a Writing Center?

Broadly defined, a Writing Center is a facility where writers of all kinds, from a first semester freshman to a faculty member, can come for an individualized writing conference with a knowledgeable, well-trained tutor (I will use the word "tutor" throughout this book, although sometimes tutors have other titles, such as "writing consultants," "writing advisors," or "writing assistants"). Writing center tutors work with papers at all stages of the writing process—papers that are in the process of being formulated, as well as rough drafts, or relatively polished efforts that need only slight additional editing. Frequently, students come to the writing center to discuss a writing topic before they have written anything at all, or they may come in with outlines or rough drafts. Talking about writing, working with drafts in progress, and helping writers develop workable approaches to and strategies for writing are considered the most useful writing center activities, although some students also work with writing center materials such as books or handouts, or computers.

Writing Centers and the History of Writing Instruction

Although it is now recognized that writing centers play an important role in helping students learn to write, one might question why writing centers have gained such pedagogical prominence, when not too long ago they were virtually unknown in the

United States and are still unknown in many other countries. Writers have been writing throughout the ages, yet writing centers and labs have proliferated only during the last twenty-five years or so. Why is there now a need for writing centers when it seems that people once learned to write without them?

Of course, one might respond that there are many approaches and techniques currently being used in education that did not exist in the past—computers, tape recorders, and films, to cite only a few examples. One explanation is to point out that writing centers exist simply because they are now recognized as pedagogically effective—most students find that writing centers help them not only to write better papers but also to become better **writers** (North 438). But the historical explanation is that the development of writing centers is closely correlated with the interest in writing and the teaching of writing that began in the United States in the latter part of the nineteenth century and continued throughout the next century. Those who study the history of writing maintain that the special field of "written rhetoric," which came to be called "Composition," grew out of the more established practice and teaching of oral rhetoric, which has its roots in antiquity. But during the nineteenth century, a number of political and technological developments occurred which had the effect of focusing attention on the importance of writing in English as opposed to Latin and Greek. The establishment of land grant colleges in 1867 resulted in a new population of university students from less privileged backgrounds, students who had not studied classical languages as part of their education, and therefore had to write in the vernacular—that is, in English. Then, a number of inventions and developments facilitated the use of writing in a wide variety of settings and situations—the invention of the mechanical pencil (1822), the fountain pen (1850), the telegram (1864), the typewriter (1868) plus the increasing availability of inexpensive and durable paper. As writing became more important, the task of teaching writing was assumed by various institutions, which were viewed as "a device for preparing a trained and disciplined workforce" and for assimilating "huge numbers of immigrants into cultural norms defined in specifically Anglo-Protestant terms (Berlin 1996, 23). In 1874, Harvard University introduced an entrance exam that featured a writing requirement, and when the English faculty received the results, they were profoundly shocked by the profusion of error of all sorts—punctuation, capitalization, spelling, and syntax.

The Freshman Writing Course and the Use of Handbooks

The realization that so many students had difficulty with the mechanics of writing led to the establishment of a college entrance exam at Harvard, which, apparently, more than half the students did not pass, and ultimately to the creation of a required Freshman composition course that was then replicated at other universities. However, the creation of a writing course did not solve the problem, at Harvard or anywhere else; moreover, it was soon recognized that teaching writing was a complex activity that involved a great deal of work if one were going to read and respond to student writing, a great deal more work than many faculty had anticipated. But by the turn of the century, a presumed solution to this difficulty came into vogue. That solution was the "handbook," in which all of the rules and conventions of writing could be written and to which teachers could refer in the margins of student papers. The premise was that teachers had only to skim a student paper for errors, circle those errors in red, and cite rule numbers that students would be able to find in their handbooks. Soon every publisher had developed a handbook, then a workbook, the goal of both being to remove all but the most mechanical work from beleaguered English teachers. Yet, not surprisingly, problems with teaching students to write continued, nor had student writing improved.

The difficulties encountered by those involved in the teaching of writing at the beginning of the twentieth century are recounted in the lead article of the first issue of the *English Journal* published in 1912. The title of that article is "Can Good Composition Teaching Be Done Under Present Conditions?" and the first word of that article is "No!" Then, after a few sentences, the article goes on as follows:

> Every year teachers resign, breakdown, perhaps become permanently invalided, having sacrificed ambition, health, and in not a few instances, even life, in the struggle to do all the work expected of them.
>
> *(Hopkins 1)*

Certainly, this is not an encouraging portrait of an emerging field!

Moreover, the Composition course was a problem not only for teachers; it was a nightmarish experience for students as well. Lad Tobin in his essay "How the Writing Process Was Born—and Other Conversion Narratives," recalls it like this:

> Once upon a time, in an age of disciplinary darkness and desolation, say about 1965 or so, writing students were subjected to cruel and inhuman punishments. They were assigned topics like "Compare Henry Fleming from *The Red Badge of Courage* to one of the characters in the *Iliad*; make sure to consider the definition of an anti-hero" or "Write about your most humiliating moment." They were told, with a straight face, that no decent person ever wrote without outlining first, that there is a clear distinction between description, narration, exposition, and argument; that grammatical errors were moral and mortal sins, and that teachers' evaluations of student essays were always objective, accurate and fair. . . .
>
> In that dark period of our disciplinary history, teachers rarely explained anything about the process of writing (unless you count "outline, write, proofread, hand in) as the student's process . . . Or they would explain some of the rules governing good writing. But they would say nothing about invention, about how to get started, what to do in the middle, or what to do when the middle turned back into the start, and so on. (Tobin 2-3)

The Reemergence of Rhetoric and the "Process" Movement

Presumably the discouraging situation described by Tobin pertained through the 1950's and 1960's. But then, in 1963, at the Conference of College Composition and Communication, a reinvigoration occurred in the field of rhetoric, and with this revival was born the "process" approach to composition and a research area that focused on understanding how people write and learn to write. As a result, a number of process-oriented methods and techniques were developed— staged writing, conferencing, various strategies for invention and revision—and as the process movement caught fire, writing teachers all over the country changed their way of thinking, tossing out their handbooks and grammar style sheets and experimenting with new techniques to help students develop a more effective writing "process."

Early Writing Centers

Where do writing centers fit into this history? As Peter Carino points out in his article, "Early Writing Centers: Towards a History," concern with helping students learn to write led to the creation of a classroom format known as the "laboratory method" that enabled teachers to provide individual help through conferencing and peer editing groups. As early as 1904, reports of the success of the laboratory method began appearing in the journals, although at this point, writing "labs" were housed in classrooms and were nothing more than a classroom approach. But eventually a few separate writing labs were formed, among them the early writing labs at the University of Minnesota and the State University of Iowa in 1934. During the 1940's, three articles in *College English* describe a program within the Armed Forces to provide young officers with the equivalent of two years of training in English in just two semesters using a free standing laboratory. And in Wisconsin, at Stephens College, "the writing 'clinic' was set up for [t]he student who finds it very difficult to spell correctly or who makes gross errors in English usage. Here causes are determined, exercises under supervision are given, and practical applications to everyday writing are made" (Wiksell 1945, cited in Carino 108)."

The Seventies and Open Admissions

A few stand alone writing labs were in existence before 1970. However, writing centers gained significantly in importance about twenty-five years ago, when a policy of open admissions resulted in a rapid increase in many underprepared students attending colleges. Products of their culture, many of these students were familiar with the media and were relatively articulate; however, most of them had done little reading and virtually no writing, in school or elsewhere. Naturally, these students were terribly anxious at the thought of having to write papers for their college classes. And the papers they wrote made their instructors anxious as well!

After a few years of confusion and speculation about the "decline in standards" and the need to reestablish what was termed the "basics," the needs of this new group of students generated academic interest in how one "learns" to write and in how writing can best be "taught." At first, perhaps because of an underlying persistent cultural conviction that writing is a mysterious process, a virtually unteachable "natural" talent, teachers of writing did not attempt to deal with anything that occurred between the conception of an idea and the completion of a first draft. Teaching writing meant simply the teaching of editing skills: grammar, punctuation, and usage, something like the "handbook" approach of the past. Students were assigned a topic and went home and wrote their papers, which they then submitted to the instructor for evaluation. The instructor marked the paper up in red, occasionally wrote scathing comments, and assigned grades. Such was the teaching of composition—tedious for instructors, terrifying for students.

Eventually, though, the pragmatic needs of the new student population and the theoretical reorientation born of the process movement resulted in a concern with pedagogical strategies for intervening in the writing process at all stages. This type of instruction is particularly well-suited to the flexible structure of writing centers, where instruction is individualized and where students can obtain help with their writing at any stage in the composing process. Writing centers, then, were considered particularly appropriate for the new composition pedagogy. Students found them comfortable, non-threatening places for learning; teachers found them a satisfying setting for teaching. As Steve North says, the concept of a writing center

> represents the marriage of what are arguably the two most powerful contemporary perspectives on teaching writing: first, that writing is most usefully viewed as a process; and second, that writing curricula need to be student-centered. This new writing center, then, defines its province not in terms of some curriculum, but in terms of the writers it serves (438).

For Writing and Discussion

1. Write a 2-3 page paper explaining how the teaching of writing was approached in the schools you attended. Were you taught by a "process" approach? Was much emphasis placed on surface correctness? What sort of comments did your teachers write on your papers? Did you use a handbook?

2. If you have relatives or friends who are a generation older than you, ask them how writing was approached in the schools they attended. Was

there a concern with correctness? Did they receive papers back marked in red? Are they familiar with grammar?

Theories That Have Impacted Writing Center Pedagogy

The development of writing centers closely parallels the rise of the process movement. However, writing center pedagogy has been also been affected by theories of language development, learning, and reading, as well as by various philosophical approaches to writing, including social constructionism and genre theory. This section presents a brief overview of these theories in terms of their influence on writing centers.

Writing Centers and Theories of Language Development

Writing center pedagogy has been strongly influenced by what linguists and psychologists have discovered about language development. Jean Piaget, studying the stages of learning through which children pass from birth to late adolescence, points out that the young child begins perceiving the world totally from his own perspective—that is, his vision is egocentric and his attempts to communicate are through "egocentric speech," whereby he "talks for himself," although he "thinks he is talking for others and is making himself understood" (Piaget 8). A young child, for example, introduced to a stranger, might being discussing something about which the stranger could have no previous information. The child might say, "I fixed the car all by myself," without explaining what car, what wheel, or the problem it had in the first place.

Building upon Piaget's work, L.S. Vygotsky points out that egocentric speech evolves eventually into "inner speech," a mature process of thought, a dynamic "fluttering between word and thought" (*Thought and Language* 249). Written language is perceived by Vygotsky as developed inner speech, "whose predication and condensation give way in writing to fully developed syntax and word specificity" (Foster 13). Vygotsky maintains that the composing process "reflects the process by which inner speech becomes external speech. In the process of communication, reflection in language (inner speech) becomes communication through language (external speech)" (Foster 13).

This concept of stages in writing growth is well suited to writing center pedagogy, where tutors can work individually with students at whatever level in their writing abilities they happen to be. The writing center environment also enables students to receive immediate audience feedback on their work, feedback that enables them to become aware of when they are writing "ego-centrically" or, as Linda Flower terms it "writer-based prose," defined as an "unretouched and underprocessed version" (Flower, "Writer-Based Prose" 1979) of the writer's own thought. Writing centers, then, enable teachers of writing to apply what psychological and linguistic theory has discovered about the writing process.

Writing Centers and Theories of Learning

Because effective tutoring is based on conditions that are likely to facilitate learning, writing centers also utilize insights gained from learning theories. Well-known learning theorist, Jerome Bruner, maintains that students learn best when they are active participants in the learning process, not passive recipients of information and that "to instruct someone in [a] discipline is not a matter of getting him to commit results to mind. Rather it is to teach him to participate in the process that makes possible the establishment of knowledge . . . Knowledge is a process, not a product" (72). Bruner points out that all learning must be viewed as

> a provisional state that has as its object to make the learner or problem solver self-sufficient. Any regimen of correction caries the danger that the learner may become permanently dependent on the tutor's correction. The tutor must direct his instruction in a fashion that eventually makes it possible for the student to take over the corrective function himself. Otherwise, the result of instruction is to create a form of mastery that is contingent upon the perpetual presence of the tutor (53).

Bruner's approach to learning suggests that students who learn by discovery are likely to acquire a sense of adequacy, whereas too much reliance on lectures, texts, or programs tend to make students dependent on others and minimizes the likelihood of their seeking answers or solving problems on their own.

The idea of learning by discovery is also consistent with *attribution theory*, a learning theory maintaining that the allocation of responsibility (that is, the particular reason to which one attributes the cause of an event or accomplishment) manifestly guides subsequent behavior. Attribution theory contends that "within achievement related contexts" (Weiner 185), affect is maximized when success and failure are attributed to the internal element of ability and effort, rather than to the external element of luck or change, and that "causal attributions influence the likelihood of undertaking achievement activities, the intensity of work at these activities, and the degree of persistence in the face of failure" (Weiner 195). According to this theory, in order for students to improve in their writing, they must attribute their success to their own efforts and abilities, not to the skill of the tutor. Thus, writing center ideology stresses the importance of encouraging students to be active participants in their conferences, not disciples sitting in humility at the feet of a mentor.

Approaches to Composition: Theories and Models

In addition to incorporating theories of learning and language acquisition, writing centers implement several approaches to the teaching of writing derived from recent theoretical perspectives on composition. These approaches may be defined according to which element in the act of writing they emphasize: the writer, the prospective reader, or the community or context. Of course, when writing occurs, all of these elements impact one another, functioning interdependently; however, for instructional purposes, each can be examined separately. In this section, I shall focus on four principal approaches to composition pedagogy: **process theory, reading theory, social constructionist theory, and genre theory.**

Process Theory

The process approach to composition emphasizes the **writer**; it is concerned primarily with the activities writers engage in when they create and produce a text. This approach evolved as a reaction to the dominance of the product-centered pedagogy discussed earlier in this chapter, one that focused on error correction and formulaic patterns of organization. In contrast, the process approach is concerned with **how** writers produce texts and with helping writers develop an effective writing process.

The concept of viewing writing as a process became prominent through the early work of Wallas and the later refinements of Winterowd, and of Young, Becker, and Pike. Their work resulted in a model based on several overlapping and recursive stages: starting point, exploration, incubation, illumination, composing, reformulation, and editing. The starting point is the point at which the writing task is perceived as a problem to be solved. The *exploration* stage includes all the preparatory work—collecting data, doing research, brainstorming for relevant memories and experiences, focusing on the problem to be solved. During *incubation*, the conscious mind withdraws from concentration on the problem, so that the subconscious mind may take over. "Creative figures in many disciplines have attested to the necessity of this conscious withdrawal—and withdrawal from consciousness—from the task at hand in order to free our less understood creative forces" (Freedman 4). The *illumination* is the moment when our ideas take shape. What had been a formless mass of information is now focused on a particular purpose.

Composing takes place either before, during, and after the moment of illumination. Reformulation involves the reworking of the thesis in terms of language and meaning. Editing involves core technical matters of mechanics, punctuation, and spelling, or, as Winterowd writes, " the adjustment of the 'surface' of the text so that it approximates . . . Edited Standard English" (163).

Janet Emig, having observed the composing process of twelfth graders, similarly describes the writing process as consisting of prewriting, planning, starting, and reformulating. Britton, Burgess, MacLeod, and Martin emphasized three elements in the writing process: *conception*, which ends when the writer knows he is going to write and has some idea of what is expected of him, *incubation*, and finally *production*. Britton and his colleagues say, too, that when a writer takes on a task as soon as it is set, the three elements are likely to be concurrent.

In all of these process oriented models, words such as "prewriting," "writing," and "rewriting" may suggest that writing is a linear process that can be divided into distinct sequential steps. However, it is now recognized that the writing process is *recursive*, that is, cyclical and fluid, rather than linear and stage-bound (USC Orientation Notebook). As the writing process model presented here indicates, most writers shift back and forth in composing and may use all elements of the process at different moments, maybe at the same time. As Graser describes it,

> Think of three separate metal rings, interlocked, each able to move in its own plane, but not separable. As you twirl one ring backward and forward, for the moment you let the other two slip out of your attention; yet moving one ring, you may reveal a previously unseen aspect of the others. You know that moving one will cause the others to move, but you look at each separately for a clearer view. We may name one *prewriting*, another *writing*, and the third *rewriting*. We can look at them one at a time, but we can't separate them. Writers may be concerned with any or all of them in any sequence (5).

Concerned with avoiding models that suggest that the writing process is linear, Flower and Hayes set up a cognitive theory based on four points:

1. The process of writing is best understood as a set of distinctive think processes that writers orchestrate or organize during the act of composing.

2. These processes have a hierarchical highly embedded organization in which any process can be embedded within any other.

3. The act of composing itself is a goal-directed thinking process, guided by the writers' own growing network of goals.

4. Writers create their own goals in two key ways: by generating both high-level goals and supporting sub-goals that embody the writer's developing sense of purpose, and then, at times, by changing major goals or even es-

tablishing new ones based on what has been learned in the act of writing (Flower and Hayes 366).

Cultural Influences on Process Theory

The early process movement was developed in reaction against the product approach to the teaching of writing, and, in some ways the movement can be viewed "as a kind of political-pedagogical protest. . . . It was the power we loved to hate" (Marshall 47). However, although this movement was of great pedagogical importance and was propelled by considerable intellectual, and even moral energy, it did not address the issue of how gender, race, class and culture influence writers' goals, standards, and methods, or even the concept of literacy itself. More recently, scholars such as Denny Taylor and Catherine Dorsey-Gaines have examined how the concept of "process" is influenced by race, and Nancie Atwell and Julie Neff have written about how a process approach must be specially tailored to the needs of the learning disabled. Mike Rose, in *Lives on the Boundary: The Struggle and Achievements of America's Underprepared* (1989), and Shirley Brice Heath in *Ways with Words: Language, Life, and Work Communities and Classrooms* (1983), have discussed the impact of social class on the acquisition of literacy.

The Process Approach and the Writing Center

The writing center provides an ideal setting for implementing a process approach to the teaching of writing. In the writing center, tutors can work with students throughout the composing process, changing and rearranging goals and subgoals. As they discover new directions for their texts, students can return to invention strategies even after they have written a first draft, engaging in additional brainstorming, and developing additional material. Thus, the process approach in the writing center enables students to learn experimentally that writing is a process of rethinking, and that writing means rewriting.

The writing center also implements process by providing opportunities for students to practice different kinds of writing strategies. They can work with invention, planning, organization, and revision strategies that will not only improve the paper they are working on, but can also be applied to a subsequent writing task.

Reading Theory and the Writer-Reader Transaction

While process theory emphasizes the writer, reading theory, emphasizes the *reader,* in particular, the relationship between the writer and the reader, the text serving as the means of creating a dialogue between the two. Reading theory envisions the writer as a person engaged in a dialogue with an audience, a dialogue impacted by the role of world knowledge and the reader's expectations. Reading theorists, such Kenneth Goodman or Frank Smith, "conceive of reading not as the passive decoding of information but as the active construction of meaning by a reader within a cultural and cognitive context" (Freshman Writing Orientation Notebook).

Reading theory points out that readers bring world knowledge to a text; that is, they bring a great deal more information than the text itself supplies, and that information affects how that text will be understood or interpreted. A successful writer, then, must consider what sort of knowledge the reader is likely to bring to the text, and to provide background material, when necessary.

The role of knowledge and reader expectation in the creation of a text is embodied in two terms coined by Linda Flower: *writer-based prose* and *reader-based prose*. Writer-based prose, like Vygotsky's ego-centric speech discussed above, refers to prose that only the writer can understand, because he or she has not adequately considered the needs of the reader. Writer-based prose is associated with early drafts of a text, in which the writer is simply throwing out ideas, without providing adequate "cueing" or signalling devices to aid the reader. Through revision, however, the writer can convert writer-based prose into reader-based prose, that is, writing that provides adequate background information and cueing strategies, so that the text can be understood by a reader.

This idea that a writer engages in a dialogue with the reader supports the importance of talking through a paper before beginning to write. Britton points out that "the relationship of talk to writing is central to the writing process" (29) in that talk permits "the expression of tentative conclusions and opinions . . . The free flow of talk allows ideas to be bandied about, and opens up new relationships, so that explaining the whole thing to oneself may be much easier" (30).

The Reader-Writer Transaction and the Writing Center

Writing centers are extremely well-suited for clarifying the transaction between the reader and the writer, since by assuming a non-evaluative, non-threatening role, writing center tutors can act as receptive readers. Connections between reader and writer are easily established in the writing center, because the writing center tutor responds not in the form of written comments in margins, a technique that reinforces distance between reader and writer, but rather in the form of questions, which call for immediate student response. When a tutor indicates that he or she has misread the text or is lacking some important information, students easily understand the necessity of including the necessary information or textual clues and can easily provide them on the spot.

Viewing text in terms of the reader-writer transaction provides an important foundation for writing centers, in that talking is a vital component of the writing center approach. Talking through a paper enables students to probe further into their topics, conversational banter often leading to serious exploration and discovery.

Social Constructionism and the Discourse Community

Writing process theory emphasizes the *writer*. Reading theory emphasizes the *reader* and the interaction of the writer with the reader. Social constructionist theory emphasizes the importance of the *context* or *community* for which the text is being written. The principle idea of social constructionist theory is that all knowledge is social knowledge, derived from our surroundings. According to Bakhtin, language

> lies on the borderline between oneself and the other. The word in language is half someone else's. It becomes 'one's own' only when the speaker populates it with his own intentions, his own accent, when he appropriates the word, adapting it to his own semantic and expressive intention. Prior to this moment of appropriation, the word does not exist in a neutral and personal language . . . but rather it exists in other people's mouths, in other people's contexts, serving other people's intentions; it is from there that one must take the word and make it one's own (cited in Ede, 5).

The research of Marilyn Cooper, Ann Gere, Patricia Bizzell, and Kenneth Bruffee is concerned with viewing writing as "an activity through which a person is continually engaged with a variety of socially constructed systems" (Cooper 36).

An important idea in social constructionist theory is the term "discourse community," which may be defined as a community of knowledgeable peers who share common assumptions, goals, methods of communication, and conventions. According to this definition, an important function of education is to help students become an accepted member of an academic discourse community.

Social Constructionism and the Writing Center

In her essay "Writing as a Social Process: A Theoretical Foundation for Writing Centers?" Lisa Ede points out the relevance of social constructionist theory for the collaborative approach to writing characteristic of writing centers. Citing the work of Hawkins, Bruffee, and others, Ede emphasizes the importance of replacing the deeply ingrained romantic concept of writing as a solitary individual act with the idea of viewing writing as a social process, a view that involves collaboration and recognizes the importance of context. Ede stresses that this view of writing is vital to establishing the centrality of what occurs in writing centers and she calls for those who work in writing centers to "do case studies, or even more detailed ethnographic analyses" (11) to gain a better understanding of collaborative learning.

Social constructionist theory becomes particularly relevant to writing center tutoring in terms of helping students learn the conventions of the academic discourse community. Student essays are often flawed because students do not understand what is meant by an academic argument or how to support their arguments plausibly—in the writing center, tutors can focus on helping students become aware of these conventions. Social constructionist theory also becomes relevant when tutors help students develop a sense of appropriate academic style and tone. This also includes increasing student sensitivity to grammar, spelling, and mechanics, errors which immediately label the student as an outsider to the academic discourse community and consequently can seriously impede the effectiveness of the text.

Genre Theory

Genre theory emphasizes the purpose and generic features of various types of texts or *genres,* focusing on how such features enable a genre to achieve its purpose. The premise of this theory is that genre awareness enables writers to approach a writing task with greater insight into the nature of that task and therefore offers new possibilities for helping students understand the expectations of their college writing assignments. Although in the past, the word "genre," was associated with notions of form and text classifications, in particular with describing the formal features of a literary work, the concept of genre has been reconceptualized in terms of **function.** While recognizing that genres can be characterized by regularities in textual form and substance, current thinking about genre looks at these regularities as surface traces of a different kind of underlying regularity. The work of Freedman and Medway (1994) and Swales (1990) among others, views such regularity as deriving from "typical ways of engaging rhetorically with recurring situations" and perceives similarities in textual form and feature as evolving from an effective response to situations that "writers encounter repeatedly" (Devitt 576). Because genres arise as a result of writers' responding in suitable ways to recurring rhetorical situations, the new concept of genre perceives generic conventions as deriving from suitability and appropriateness, rather than from arbitrary traditions and conventions.

I first became acquainted with genre theory and its implications for teaching writing when I was teaching writing to Ph.D. candidates in the field of geography at the university of Utrecht in Holland in 1989 and 1993. Looking for new approaches to help these students, I was pleased to discover the work of John Swales who applied genre theory to what he terms the characteristic "moves" within a scientific article. In his 1990 book, *Genre Analysis,* Swales defined genre primarily by its common communicative purposes, maintaining that these purposes and the role of the genre within its environment have generated specific textual features—that is, form derives from purpose and context, not the other way around. Swales feels that a genre centered approach to teaching would enable students to understand why a particular genre has acquired characteristic features, thereby enabling them both to produce it more effectively as well as to make informed decisions about deviating from it. In either case, Swales maintains, awareness of genre will enable students to gain insight into the nature of the texts they are assigned to produce, thereby providing them with a significant advantage.

Genre Theory and the Writing Center

In the writing center, genre awareness can be of great assistance to students who are often unfamiliar with the purpose, form, and context of academic writing, because, as the title of an article by Joseph Williams and Greg Colomb argues, "What You Don't Know Won't Help You." Genre theory can help students become aware of the generic features of the texts they are assigned to produce and to understand how genre requirements influence other facets of college writing, such as the writer, as he or she appears in the essay, the audience for whom the essay is intended, the topic selected, the approach to the topic, the type of support and evidence used, and the assumptions underlying the main idea. Using genre analysis, writing center tutors can work with students to examine text structure the way archaeologists examine artifacts—that is, to try to understand function and to recreate the strategies implicit in the structure in terms of purpose. Form then can be perceived as "fossilized rhetorical processes." (Coe 160).

Writing center tutors can help students become aware of the generic features of the texts they are assigned to produce by asking the following genre based questions:

1. In completing this assignment, are you expected to use a particular genre?

2. What purpose does this genre serve?

3. What are the features of this genre?

4. How do its particular generic features serve its purpose?

☞ For Writing and Discussion: Applying Theory to Practice

Alison has come to the writing center with the assignment and paper reproduced below. In small groups, discuss what you feel are the strengths and weaknesses of the paper and the sort of revisions you would suggest for Alison. Then write a paper discussing how you could apply process theory, reading theory, social constructionist theory, and genre theory to work with her.

Alison's Assignment

Background

The term "political correctness" or PC refers to a particular view of the world that its proponent maintain should be actively promoted both in school and in the workplace. This view perceives Western culture as having always been oppressive to women and racial minorities and emphasizes that in order for such oppression to end, an atmosphere of sensitivity to others should be maintained through mandating acceptable boundaries for speech and behavior. The label "politically correct" is often applied to statements, programs, or policies that foster this position and to people whose opinions are in accord with it.

Although proponents of the PC movement view it as simply another way of requiring people to "do the right thing"; others perceive it as a potential threat to the preservation of democracy and culture. These critics are concerned that the notion of requiring PC language will endanger the right of free speech and lead ultimately to a society in which people use one language in private and another in public and where thought is mandated as well, a move in the direction of an Orwellian Big Brother society.

Based on the readings assigned above, write an argumentative essay in response to the following question:

Is the PC movement likely to benefit or harm society?

In responding to this question, be sure to qualify your position by defining your terms and specifying the extent to which the harm or benefit is likely to occur.

 ## Alison's Paper/PC is Ridiculous!

A debate has scourged the United States for several decades regarding the issue of "PC." The abbreviation is often confused with several different meanings, such as Personal Computer, President's Choice, but instead I am addressing the coined term "Political Correctness." Everyday the debate about PC becomes a more prominent topic in the classroom, the newspapers, and casual conversation and people are getting sick of it.

The truth of the matter is actually simple. No matter what Stanley Fish might claim, political correctness stifles free speech and will ultimately lead to a completely repressive society. Even now, students are afraid to open their mouths and say what they really think because they are afraid of being labeled "racist" or "sexist. Is this what education is about? Isn't it time we stopped being afraid of telling the truth?

Political correctness has been taken to an extreme. People can't say that someone is "short" anymore. They have to say they are "vertically challenged." It is now considered insulting to refer to a female person as a "girl" because we now have to say "woman." This is just ridiculous! Anyone who gets insulted from such trivial statements can't be very intelligent.

Our country was founded on the Bill of Rights and the first amendment to that document guarantees freedom of speech. If the P.C. people continue to make policy in our colleges and universities, free speech will no longer be a guaranteed right for students. Are students supposed to be considered second citizens? Isn't the university a place where people can speak freely? The P.C. movement has gotten completely out of hand and all policies concerned with it on campus ought to be eliminated.

For Writing and Discussion: Assessing Your Own Process

Think about papers you have written for classes, and write an essay describing your own writing process. Include in your discussion an analysis of how process, reading, social constructionist theory, and genre theory could help you understand your own process.

Writing Center Scholarship

This chapter provided a brief overview of several theories pertaining to writing and learning and the relationship of these theories to the kind of teaching that occurs in the writing center. Tutors may also find it useful to read more recent publications concerned with writing centers, in particular, *The Writing Lab Newsletter* and the *Writing Center Journal*, addresses for which are listed at the end of this chapter, if you wish to subscribe. *The Writing Lab Newsletter* is filled with useful suggestions and discussions of practical tutoring strategies, while the *Writing Center Journal* focuses on more theoretical concerns. Both of these publications will enable you to approach tutoring with greater insight.

For Further Exploration: Suggested Sources

Books About Writing Centers

Flynn, Thomas and Mary King. *Dynamics of the Writing Conference: Social and Cognitive Interaction.* Urbana, Illinois: NCTE, 1993.

Harris, Muriel. *Teaching One-to-One: The Writing Conference.* Urbana, Illinois. NCTE, 1986.

Kinkead, Joyce A., and Jeanette G. Harris. *Writing Centers in Context: Twelve Case Studies.* Urbana, Illinois. NCTE, 1993.

Meyer, Emily, and Louise Z. Smith. *The Practical Tutor.* New York: Oxford University Press, 1987.

Mullin, Joan, and Ray Wallace. Eds. *Intersections: Theory and Practice in the Writing Center.* Urbana, Illinois. NCTE, 1994.

Murphy, Christina, and Joe Law. Eds. *Landmark Essays on Writing Centers.* Davis, CA.: Hermagoras Press, 1995.

Stay, Byron, Christina Murphy and Eric H. Hobson. Eds. *Writing Center Perspectives.* Emmitsburg, Maryland: NWCA Press, 1995.

Writing Process Theory

Atwell, Nancie. "A Special Writer at Work." In *Understanding Writing: Ways of Learning, Observing, and Teaching K-8.* 2nd ed. Edited by Thomas Newkirk and Nacie Atwell. Portsmouth, New Hampshire: Heinemann, 1988.

Britton, James et al. *The Development of Writing Abilities (11-18)* London: Macmillan Education Ltd, 1975.

Elbow, Peter. *Embracing Contraries: Explorations in Learning and Teaching.* New York: Oxford University Press.

Emig, Janet. *The Composing Processes of Twelfth Graders.* Urbana, Illinois: NCTE, 1971. *The Web of Meaning: Essays on Writing: Teaching, Learning, and Thinking.* Montclair, New Jersey: Boynton/Cook, 1983.

Graser, Elsa. *Teaching Writing: A Process Approach.* Dubuque, Iowa: Kendall/Hunt Publishing Company, 1983.

Heath, Shirley Brice. *Ways With Words: Language, Life, and Work in Communities and Classrooms.* New York: Cambridge University Press, 1983.

Newkirk, Thomas, and Lad Tobin. Eds. *Taking Stock: The Writing Process Movement in the '90s.* Portsmouth: Boynton/Cook, 1994.

Taylor, Denny, and Catherine Dorsey-Gaines. *Growing Up Literate: Learning From Inner-City families.* Portsmouth, New Hampshire: Heinemann, 1988.

Winterowd, W. Ross. "Developing a Composition Program." *Reinventing the Rhetorical Tradition.* Ed Aviva Freedman and Ian Pringle. Conway Arkansas: L&S Books, 1980.

Young, Richard E., Alton L. Becker, and Kenneth L. Pike. *Rhetoric: Discovery and Change.* New York: Harcourt, 1970.

Reading Theory

Britton, Bruce K. and Arthur C. Graesser. Eds. *Models of Understanding Text.* Mahwah, N.J.: Lawrence Erlbaum Associates, 1996.

Dillon, Goerge L. *Constructing Texts: Elements of a Theory of Composition and Style.* Bloomington, Indiana: Indiana University Press, 1981.

Gibson, Eleanor J. and Harry Levin. *The Psychology of Reading.* Cambridge, Mass.: MIT Press, 1980.

Goodman, Kenneth S. "A Psycholinguistic Guessing Game." *Journal of the Reading Specialist* 6 (1967): 126–135.

Smith, Frank. *Writing and the Writer.* New York: Holt, Rinehart and Winston, 1982.

Social Constructionist Theory

Bruffee, Kenneth. "Collaborative Learning and the 'Conversation of Mankind.'" *College English* 46 (1984): 635–652.

———"Social Construction, Language, and the Authority of Knowledge: A Bibliographical Essay." *College English* 48 (1986): 773–790.

Ede, Lisa. "Writing as a Social Process: A Theoretical Foundation For Writing Centers." *The Writing Center Journal* 9.2 (1989): 3–15.

Gillam, Alice. "Collaborative Learning Theory and Peer Tutoring Practice." in *Intersections: Theory-Practice in the Writing Center,* Edited by Joan A. Mullin and Ray Wallace. Urbana: NCTE, 1994, 39–53.

Murphy, Christina. "TheWriting Center and Social Constructionist Theory." in *Intersections: Theory-Practice in the Writing Center,* Edited by Joan A. Mullin and Ray Wallace. Urbana: NCTE, 1994, 25–38.

Petraglia, Joseph. "Interrupting the Conversation: The Constructionist Dialogue in Composition." *Journal of Advanced Composition* 11, 37–55.

Genre Theory

Bakhtin, Mikhail. "The Problem of Speech Genres." In *Speech Genres and Other Late Essays.* edited by Caryle Emerson and Michael Holquist and translated by Vernon W. McGee. Austin, Texas: University of Austin Press, 1986. 60–102.

Bazerman, Charles. *Shaping Written Knowledge: The Genre and Activity of the Experimental Article in Science.* Madison, Wisconsin: University of Wisconsin Press, 1991.

Devitt, Amy J. "Generalizing About Genre: New Conceptions of an Old Concept." *College Composition and Communication* 44 (1993):573–86.

Freedman, Aviva, and Peter Medway. Eds. *Learning and Teaching Genre.* Portsmouth New Hampshire: Boynton/Cook Publishers, 1994.

Miller, Carolyn. "Genre as Social Action." *Quarterly Journal of Speech* 70 (1984): 151–167.

Swales, John. *Genre Analysis.* Cambridge: Cambridge University Press, 1990.

Williams, Joseph, and Gregory G. Colom. "The Case for Explicit Teaching: Why What You Don't Know Won't Help You." *Research in the Teaching of English* 27.3 (1993): 252–264.

Works Cited

Berlin, Jamess. *Rhetorics, Poetics, and Cultures: Refiguring English Studies.* Urbana, Illinois: NCTE, 1996.

Britton, James et al. *The Development of Writing Abilities.* 11-8. London: Macmillan, 1975.

Bruner, Jerome. *Toward a Theory of Instruction.* Cambridge, Mass.: The Belknap Press of Harvard University Press, 1966.

Carino. Peter. "Early Writing Centers: Toward a History." *Writing Center Journal.* 15.2 (Spring 1995): 103–115.

Coe, Richard. "Teaching Genre as Process." in *Learning and Teaching Genre,* Eds. Aviva Freedman and Peter Medway. Portsmouth, New Hampshire: Bognton/Cook Publishers, 1994: 157–169.

Comb, Arthur C. and Donald Snygg. *Individual Behavior,* revised edition (Harper: New York, 1959).

Cooper, Marilyn. "The Ecology of Writing. *College English* 48 (1986):364–75.

Devitt, Amy. "Generalizing About Genre: New Conceptions of an Old Concept." *College Composition and Communication* 44 (1993):573–86.

Ede, Lisa. "Writing as a Social Process: A Theoretical Foundation For Writing Centers." *The Writing Center Journal* 9.2 (1989): 3–15.

Emig, Janet. *The Composing Process of Twelfth Graders. Research Report No. 13.* Urbana: NCTE, 1971.

Flower, Linda. "Writer-Based Prose: A Cognitive Basis for Problems in Writing." *College English* 41 (September 1979): 19–38.

Flower, Linda and John Hayes. "A Cognitive Process Theory of Writing." *College Composition and Communication* 32 (1981): 365–388.

Foster, David. *A Primer for Writing Teachers.* Upper Montclair, Boynton/Cook, 1983.

Freedman, Aviva. "A Theoretic Context for the Writing Lab." in *Tutoring Writing: A Sourcebook for Writing Labs,* ed. Muriel Harris. Glenview, Illinois: Scott Foresman, 1982.

Graser, Elsa. *Teaching Writing: A Process Approach.* Dubuque, Iowa: Kendall/Hunt, 1983.

Hopkins, "Can Good Composition Teaching Be Done Under Present Conditions?" *English Journal* 1 (1912):

Marshall, James. "Of What Does Skill in Writing Really Consist?" in Newkirk, Thomas, and Lad Tobin. Eds. *Taking Stock: The Writing Process Movement in the '90s.* Portsmouth: Boynton/Cook, 1994.

Neff, Julie. "Learning Disabilities and the Writing Center." in *Intersections: Theory-Practice in the Writing Center,* Edited by Joan A. Mullin and Ray Wallace. Urbana: NCTE, 1994. 81–95.

North, Stephen. "The Idea of a Writing Center." *College English* 46 (1984): 443–447.

Piaget, Jean. *The Language and Thought of the Child.* New York: New American Library, 1974.

Rose, Mike. *Lives on the Boundary.* New York: Free Press, 1989.

Swales, John. *Genre Analysis.* Cambridge: Cambridge University Press, 1990.

Tobin, Lad. "How the Writing Proceess Was Born and Other Conversion Narratives." in Newkirk, Thomas, and Lad Tobin. Eds. *Taking Stock: The Writing Process Movement in the '90s.* Portsmouth: Boynton/Cook, 1994.

Vygotsky, Lev S. *Thought and Language.* trans Eugenia Hanfmann and Gertrude Vakar. Cambridge, Mass.: MIT Press, 1962.

Weiner, Bernard. *Achievement Motivation and Attribution Theory.* New Jersey: General Learning Press, 1974.

Wiksell, Wesley. "The Communications Program at Stephens College." *College English* 9 (1947): 143-145.

Williams, Joseph, and Gregory G. Colom. "The Case for Explicit Teaching: Why What You Don't Know Won't Help You." *Research in the Teaching of English* 27.3 (1993): 252-264.

Winterowd, W. Ross. "Developing a Composition Program." *Reinventing the Rhetorical Tradition.* ed. Aviva Freedman and Ian Pringle. Conway, Arkansas: L&S Books, 1980.

PREPARING FOR TUTORING: REMEMBERING, REFLECTING, ANTICIPATING

You can prepare for an exam by studying the material to be covered. You can prepare to run a marathon by running every day and building up your stamina. In fact, preparation for almost any type of performance—acting, singing, juggling—can be achieved through rigorous practice. But if you have never taught or tutored before, what can you do to prepare yourself for tutoring in a writing center? This chapter discusses issues and raises questions that will enable you to *anticipate* tutoring. You will be asked to reflect on what you already know and believe about writing, to remember your own experience as a student writer, and to anticipate possible interactions with student writers. The process of imagining what is likely to happen during a writing center conference tutoring is a good way to prepare for working in a writing center, so that when you actually begin to tutor, you will be more confident and effective.

Reflecting on Your Own Writing Process

A first and obvious recommendation for anyone who plans to work with writers, whether in a writing center or in a classroom, is to write a great deal yourself and become aware of how you do it. Anyone who teaches writing ought to be a writer— of papers, reports, letters, journals, diaries, notes—engaging in any kind of writing can help you learn about the writing process. The important thing is to write often (possibly every day), observe yourself as you write, and gain insight into your own composing process. How do you generate ideas for a paper? Do you cluster or brainstorm before you write? Do you always know what you plan to say before you sit down to write? Or does your main idea emerge from a haphazardly scribbled, possibly unfocused first draft? Do you sketch an outline for yourself before you write? Or does your organizational structure become apparent to you only after you have been writing? Do you write in stages? Or do you tackle the whole essay in one exhausting marathon session? Do you do all or any of these activities on a computer? These are questions you should ask yourself as a way of anticipating tutoring.

For Writing and Discussion

Spend thirty minutes writing about how you write papers for your classes, using a particular paper you have written to focus your thinking. Some questions you might consider are as follows:

1. How long did you spend writing the paper?

2. Did you spend time thinking about it before you wrote it? When do you think?

3. Did you do any research?

4. Did you use any method for generating text? Clustering? Freewriting? Sketchy notes?

5. Did you write an outline?

6. How many drafts did you write?

7. Do you read aloud when you go over your paper? Do you read to someone else?

8. How do you revise and edit your paper? Do you revise substantially or simply "tinker" with the surface? Do you use a computer?

9. Is the setting important to you when you write? Do you sit in a special chair or at a desk or table, for example?

Writing this paper will help you to think about your own writing process, insight that may give you some good ideas when you tutor. When you finish writing your paper, break into small groups and read your papers aloud to one another, discussing particular ideas that may or may not be applicable for tutoring.

Reflecting on Evaluation

Although many of you have never tutored before, you bring to your new role some fairly definite ideas about writing and teaching, ideas that you absorbed when you were a student or that you hold simply because you are a member of the culture. As a tutor you should become aware of these ideas, so that you can decide how well they correspond to your concept of what tutoring can or ought to be. Some of these ideas you may find quite compatible with your ideal; others you may wish to reject. To gain awareness about some of your positions concerning evaluation, take a few minutes to write a response to the following statements:

Ideas on Evaluation

1. The papers students bring to the writing center should be evaluated primarily for content, not for style and structure.

2. Good spelling is important.

3. Neatness is important.

4. Low grades and poor evaluations usually create incentives for students to work harder.

5. Students who are poor writers are usually unintelligent.

6. It is best to give many more positive than negative evaluations.

7. The worth of a piece of writing depends primarily on how successfully it fulfills the assignment.

8. Students should not be encouraged to grade themselves.

9. Some people can write; other people cannot.

10. It is important to consider alternate grading systems to the generally accepted ones.

Each of the statements on this list can provide a topic for discussion. After indicating the extent to which you agree with each of them, break into small groups and discuss your responses. Are there many differences in how each person responds? Is there a particular response which you think is appropriate or inappropriate for effective tutoring? Do your responses vary according to whether or not you are looking at a first draft?

For example, consider your position on spelling, neatness, and mechanical correctness, the reputed concerns of stereotypical teachers. How do you think you react to papers containing multiple errors? Do you tend to think that writers who make such errors are not intelligent, even if the papers containing these errors are first drafts? Can you or should you overlook these sorts of problems in the interest of other concerns, such as form or content?

Then consider what you believe about motivation and its relationship to grades. Do you work more diligently for a hard grader? Or does the threat of a poor grade freeze you into immobility? What do you think about not grading at all?

Now think about you believe about writing ability. Do you have a secret belief that there are some gifted people who write by inspiration, the romantic myth of our culture? Do you perhaps think that students who can't write properly do not belong in college? Or do you believe that writing is a skill that almost anyone can master if he or she is willing to work hard? Which of these ideas is best suited for working in a writing center?

These are important questions to ask yourself in thinking about tutoring, because even though writing centers are not really in the "evaluation business," and, in fact, make concerted attempts to avoid direct evaluation, tutors may inadvertently give implicit evaluative messages to students that can jeopardize the effectiveness of their tutoring. If you are aware of your position on evaluation, you will be able to exercise some control over the kinds of comments you give to students when you tutor. Directly stated critical comments such as "this paper isn't good because. . ." or "You haven't answered the question. This paper is way off topic" tend to intimidate students without helping them understand what they should do to improve their writing. Tutoring in a writing center means **enabling** students to make their own evaluations and to work with students to develop strategies for improvement.

Reflecting on Collaboration

Writing center pedagogy advocates a **collaborative** relationship between tutor and student—that is, the tutor and the student work together, so that the student gains insight into his or her own writing process while improving the text under discussion. A collaborative relationship means that the tutor does not "take charge" of either the conference or the text, since students learn best when they discover methods and ideas for themselves and are active participants in the learning process.

However, as much as one might believe in the value of collaborative learning, it is not always easy to achieve. John Trimbur points out that tutoring in a writing center setting requires "a balancing act that asks tutors to juggle roles, to shift identity, to know when to act like an expert and when to act like a co-learner" (25). This sort of balance can be difficult to maintain, not only because students often pressure for more directive assistance (students want their grades to improve. They are less concerned with long term writing improvement) but also because most of us, in our own school

I'LL WRITE A CONCLUSION NEXT TIME, **I PROMISE!**

DEALING WITH ASSERTIVENESS

experience, have had little exposure to this sort of learning and have few good models to imitate.

What also makes it difficult to achieve collaboration in the writing center is that our culture does not usually conceive of writing as a collaborative activity, and therefore, collaboration in any form is regarded with a certain amount of suspicion. In a conference presentation several years ago, Karen Hodges discussed the wide diversity in attitude toward collaborative effort among various disciplines, concluding that English Departments, unlike departments in the natural and social sciences, tend to focus heavily on style, and thus, ironically, were least likely to favor collaboration between student and tutor (see Clark 1988). In the humanities, in particular, writing a paper, as opposed to studying for an exam, has historically been viewed as an individual act. Referring to his own participation in study groups as an undergraduate, Trimbur states, "If Western Civilization was seen as a collective problem, permitting a collective response, writing was apparently an individual problem, private and displaced from the informal network of mutual aid" (2). Bruffee, too, points out that "collaboration and community activity is inappropriate and foreign to work in humanistic disciplines, such as English. Humanistic study, we have been led to believe, is a solitary act" (645). Since writing center tutors often come from an English department or humanities background, they are often completely unfamiliar with the idea of collaborative learning.

The other point to reflect on when you think about collaborative writing is to consider the difference between **legitimate** and **illegitimate** collaboration. One point to consider is that true collaboration, in its pure form, can only occur when collaborators are part of the same discourse community and meet as equals. True colleagues regularly communicate by discussing each other's work, assisting one another by suggesting sources, trading drafts, or perhaps suggesting stylistic changes. This type of what could be referred to as "collegial" collaboration is motivated by the desire to offer additional perspectives that can be helpful even to competent writers, and the collaboration may be considered "legitimate" in that there is mutual respect between participants. It assumes that the author, not the collaborator will be ultimately responsible for the evolving text (see Clark 1990). For example, I have a colleague, to whom I might show a draft of a work in progress, and she might indeed make some suggestions for revision. But she would not attempt to completely rewrite my text and the text would ultimately still reflect my ideas, my style, and my purpose.

Illegitimate collaboration, in contrast, occurs when the tutor provides so much input into the student's text that the text reflects as much of the tutor's insights as it does of the student's. The tutor has "taken over" the text to such an extent that it achieves a quality that the student would be incapable of attaining on her own. Aside from the ethics involved from this sort of collaboration, when the tutor assumes too much control over either the conference or the paper, the student doesn't learn very much, although he or she may be happy with the improved grade. But since the tutor has done the work, the student will be in no better position to write the next paper.

Whenever I talk to new tutors about the importance of making sure that students do their own work, I like to illustrate it with the story of an experience I recently had with my vacuum cleaner. Not too long ago, I was faced with the daunting task of changing the bag on a relatively new vacuum cleaner. Although I had mastered the art of changing the bag on my old vacuum cleaner, I had never done so on the new one because my husband had always undertaken that task. On this occasion, however, my husband was out of town, so I decided to tackle the task on my own (had he been in town, I must confess that I probably would not have even attempted to change the bag). But since mechanical tasks are not my strong suit, I had a great deal of difficulty fitting the bag so that it wouldn't blow off as soon as I started the vacuum cleaner. I tried really hard, reading and rereading the directions, trying to get it right. But finally, when I seemed to be making no progress, I did what any liberated woman would do—I called the man next door, who came over and quickly changed the bag for me without any trouble at all, to my great humiliation.

The point of this story is that because the man next door did it for me, I still do not know how to put a new bag on that vacuum cleaner and would encounter the same problem the next time it needed changing. However, had he **shown** me how to do it or directed me while I did it myself, I might then have learned. Therefore, when students come to the writing center, tutors should not completely take over the writing task for them, or else the student will not learn anything that he or she will be able to use at a later time.

To prepare for tutoring, then, I suggest that you reflect on your own attitude toward collaborative effort in writing. Do you ever request assistance from a peer, a friend, or a family member when you write papers for your classes? Have you ever participated in a group project in writing? Do you anticipate being more or less directive in your tutoring? Think in advance about your preconceptions of the tutoring scene. If you envision a situation in which the tutor speaks and the student listens (such a model is easy to imagine), then replace it in your mind with one in which the student is doing more of the talking. Creating a model in your mind is a good way to anticipate tutoring.

Anticipating Tutoring By Remembering How It Feels to be a Student

Many of you were probably composition students at one time in your lives. For some of you, that time may not have been very long ago; for others, it may have been too long ago to remember very clearly. And some of you may prefer to forget.

It is important to remember this time in your life so that you will be able to deal effectively and insightfully with the students you tutor. So to prepare for tutoring, think back on the days when you were the age of your current students. Picture yourself in a composition classroom—get in touch with the sights, the sounds, the smells—and recall some of the papers you wrote at that time. Did you have difficulty with certain topics? Did you sometimes write papers at the last minute? Did you feel sick inside when you received a poor grade on a paper or when your paper was returned to you all marked up? Did you ever talk with an instructor about your writing?

For Writing and Thinking

After thinking about this time in your life, write a short essay in which you recall what it was like for you to be a student writing papers for classes. Be as specific as possible, but don't take a great deal of time to revise. Just write as rapidly as possible. Then break into groups and share what you have written, discussing what you liked and disliked about these experiences. Or, if you do not wish to discuss your own writing at this time, you may prefer to discuss Julie's essay, reproduced below:

Student Paper

Before I came to college, I had always loved to write. In fact, I was so confident about my writing that I usually said outright that I was a "good" writer. In High School, I wrote for the school newspaper, and on my own, I wrote little poems and stories. Writing for me was not a subject I worried a lot about.

Then, in the second year of my Freshman year at college, I took a class in what was supposed to be Creative Writing, which consisted of reading and analyzing short stories and then writing short narratives ourselves. The teacher, one of the "masters' in his field, was absolutely obsessed with symbolism in fiction, and once I was in his class I developed the idea that every short story had to have symbols in it in order for it to be considered any good. This worried me a great deal when I was writing, and I would spend hours trying to think of symbolic codes to insert into my own stories. I hardly thought at all about things like plot or character.

What terrified me particularly, though, was the method the teacher used to analyze and evaluate student papers. Often, he would have the students sit on a chair in front of the room and read their papers aloud to the class (I can still see in my mind the blur of faces and hear the quavering echo of my own voice as I read.). Then, in the interest of academic standards, he would simply rip the paper to shreds, metaphorically, I mean, of course. Often he was nasty or condescending, asking rhetorical questions, actually sneering at us He couldn't believe our ignorance. The rest of the class was too frightened to say very much, so he would always call on someone for a comment, and that person would desperately search around for something—anything—to say.

His written comments were equally destructive to students. Papers were usually returned full of red ink; it seemed at the time that everything I wrote had a circle around it. I recall being particularly surprised and devastated by some of his comments because I had always considered myself a good writer. On one paper I wrote, for example, the professor insisted that I didn't know how to use a comma properly and that I look up the appropriate section in the Harbrace Handbook. Anxious to please, of course I did as he requested, but I never could understand what errors I had made, and was too afraid to ask him.

Curiously enough, I did get something out that class—a great respect of how hard it was to write well, an upgrading of my own standards for good writing, and, of course, an awareness of symbolism. But it was a long time before I was brave enough to sign up for another writing class or before I ever thought of myself as a "good" writer. Actually, I still have many reservations about that.

Questions For Discussion

1. What particular activities and behaviors that you recall from your own experience in writing classes can you apply when you begin to tutor?

2. What particular activities and behaviors from your past were *not effective* in teaching you how to write?

Questions Concerning Julie's Paper

1. Julie seems quite negative about her experiences in the Creative Writing class. What were some of the techniques and experiences she mentions that were not helpful in teaching her to write?

2. Did Julie gain anything positive from that class?

For Discussion

After you have discussed your own essays and perhaps Julie's essay as well, break into groups and formulate a statement of what an ideal tutor should be like. Do you think it will be possible for you to realize your model? Why or why not?

Anticipating Tutoring by Considering How You Work With Others

All kinds of things can happen when you tutor (actually, that's what makes it interesting), and, of course, it is impossible to anticipate every student and every possible situation that might occur. However, you can expect that certain types of situations are likely to happen so that you can prepare yourself for them. Such preparation involves becoming aware of how you are likely to react and thinking about effective strategies.

Dealing With Students From Another Culture

In a writing center, tutors are likely to be working with students from a wide variety of backgrounds, students whose values, and mannerisms are quite different from your own. How will you feel working with these students? Will you be able to transcend cultural stereotypes and prejudices and refrain from judging students before you get to know them?

Moreover, it is sometimes the case that students from other cultures will prejudge you, because they perceive you in terms of a stereotype. As Arkin and Shollar point out:

If students are members of a racial minority, black or Latin, for example, some of them may be tempted to see you as part of the white power structure from which they are excluded, and by whom they are often judged inferior. In doing this, they are stereotyping you, assuming that because some people in the white culture are racists, you too are a racist. If some tutees feel this way, they will naturally be very resistant to working with you; and you, on the other hand, will probably find it difficult to work with these students. Or, you may be a minority tutor assigned some white tutees who think nonwhites inferior. Because these tutees devalue you, they may feel the tutorial is worthless. (128)

One way to prepare yourself for working with people from another culture is to become aware of your own preconceptions and prejudices. In preparation for tutoring, then, take a walk around your high school or college campus and notice people who are of another race or culture. How do you feel about these people? Do you have preconceptions about what strengths and weaknesses they might have?

You might record these observations in a journal and share parts of it with fellow tutors. Then, when you are actually tutoring, you might record your reactions to particular students you meet in the writing center. How do you react to these students? How do you think they react to you?

(✱) YOU CALL THIS A TOPIC SENTENCE?

MANY IDEAS ABOUT TEACHING AND
WRITING ARE CULTURAL IN ORIGIN

Dealing With Assertiveness

Another way of anticipating tutoring is to gain awareness of how you deal with assertiveness, both your own and that of students. In some tutorial situations, you may have to act more assertively than you usually do. How comfortable are you with being assertive? Does it make you anxious to have to confront a student? How do you feel, for example, about the following interchange?

Student: I didn't have time to rewrite my conclusion and I have to hand the paper in to my teacher next period. Can you please rewrite it for me?

Tutor: All right. I don't like to do this. But just this once.

Do you think that the tutor should have been more assertive in his response to the student? How would you have responded to this student's request?

Now read through another example:

Tutor: Have you written a rough draft for the paper?

Student: No, I decided to go to the game and I didn't have time.

Tutor: Well, you keep telling me that you want at least a "B" in the course. But now the paper is due tomorrow and you don't have a draft yet. I guess you really don't care about the grade.

How do you feel about the tutor's response to the student? Do you feel that he was *too* assertive and might possibly anger the student into not coming back? Or can you conceive of a situation in which students might need some kind of confrontation as a motivator?

⊶ For Writing and Discussion: ———— Dealing With Assertiveness

The following situations might arise when you work in a writing center. Consider each one and write a portion of a dialogue in which it is necessary for a tutor to be assertive. Then read your dialogues aloud and discuss them in small groups.

1.   The student is persistently late. She arrives at least fifteen minutes after the time of her appointment.

2. The student has been assigned to come to the writing center by her teacher, but she does not think she needs any help.

3. The student has plagiarized material from the textbook.

4. The student does not think that you know what you are talking about.

Dealing With Assertiveness Through Role Playing

Role playing is an activity in which someone imitates another person's behavior (plays a role) in order to gain awareness, learn a skill, or anticipate problematic situations. Role playing is a helpful activity in preparing for tutoring in that it helps identify problems, generates discussions and feedback, and helps develop self-confidence.

Role Role-playing Exercise

Role-play some of the situations associated with assertiveness that you identified above. In small groups, discuss what you have learned.

Role-playing Other Situations

Here are some other situations that typically occur in a writing center. Role play some of them in small and large groups.

1. The student is completely insecure about his paper.

2. The student blames you for his bad grades.

3. The student is anxious and tries to hide it by continually joking.

4. The student does not think she needs to come to the writing center.

5. The student does not think you are competent.

6. The student has not spent enough time preparing his paper.

7. The teacher's comments on the student paper are extremely unsupportive.

8. The assignment is difficult to figure out.

Coping With Silence

A common situation that you are likely to encounter when you work in a writing center is that of silence—that is, the student is persistently silent, unwilling to respond, no matter what you say or do. You ask a question, and the student does not answer. Uneasy with the heavy silence, you rush in to answer the question yourself. The student merely nods, or worse, sits there stonefaced. Once again, there is silence. You try again. No response. Despite your best efforts, you feel completely ineffectual.

In a situation such as this, when the student does not respond immediately to a comment or a question, Arkin and Shollar recommend counting to ten before rushing in to answer the question yourself. "Give students enough time to gather their thoughts so they can answer your questions (or their own) or comment on the subject matter" (97), they advise. They also recommend allowing time after a student answers a question so that he or she can reflect further before you ask another one. "Rushing in to fill empty space, which new tutors do at times out of anxiety or frustration, will only close down the lines of communication and make tutoring a one way process" (Arkin and Shollar 97). Of course, if the student never responds, you might want to try something else (other than shaking the student by the shoulders) such as assigning a specific writing task. The main point, though, is that you should not feel as if you are a failure if the student chooses not to respond. This happens to everyone.

Coping With Inexperience

Tutors cannot be expected to be experts in every subject or to remember every piece of information they have ever learned, so from time to time, you will find that you do not know the answer to a student's question. The student asks and suddenly your mind becomes blank or confused. If you are new to tutoring, this can be a terrifying experience. However, it is important to keep in mind that not even the most distinguished professors can be expected to know everything. It is perfectly acceptable to show a student that sometimes tutors have to look something up or occasionally ask for help. Say something like, "I'm not too sure about that, and I don't want to mislead you. But let's ask one of the other tutors.

⟶ For Role-playing and Discussion ⎯⎯⎯⎯⎯⎯

With a partner, role play a situation in which the student doesn't respond immediately to the tutor's questions or in which the tutor doesn't know the answer to a question. How does it feel? Will you be able to handle these situations without panicking?

Prepare For Tutoring By Practicing Non-Directive Listening

Carl Rogers, discussing important skills for counselors to develop, states that one of the most important is the ability to listen *with* the speaker, hearing what is said from his or her point of view and thus come to an understanding of what the speaker means. Rogers terms this type of listening "non-directive listening," which can only be conveyed through feedback in which you communicate or reflect exactly what you have heard, so that both you and the student know that what you heard is what he or she meant. A good way to practice non-directive listening is to practice paraphrasing what you hear—putting the student's comments or questions in other words, so that they know that they are being heard. Here is an example:

Student: I just can't relate to this topic.

Tutor: You don't know very much about the topic. This must worry you.

⌖ For Discussion

Respond to the student statements below by paraphrasing them. Then, in small groups, read both sets of comments aloud.

Student: It doesn't matter what I do. I won't get a good grade,

Tutor:

Student: I don't care anything at all about nuclear power. What a boring topic!

Tutor:

Listening For the Feeling

Rogers points out that when you listen with empathy, you should not focus only on the words of the speaker. You should also indicate that you are aware of the feeling behind the statement. For example, if the student says, "I got another 'C' on the paper. I just can't write," you might say, "You must be feeling discouraged."

☛ For Writing and Discussion ─────────────

Write or role play a response to the following student comments:

Student: The teacher hates me.

Tutor:

Student: The topic was too boring for me to work on.

Tutor:

Student: I'll never have to write much anyway. Why worry about it.

Tutor:

─── ⬤

Anticipating Tutoring by Analyzing the Effect Your Responses Are Likely to Have on Students

Sometimes, through chance or intuition, your responses to students are just right. You somehow "sense" the most appropriate thing to say. But sometimes, how you respond to a student can unintentionally generate negative feelings, cutting off, rather than facilitating communication. To prepare for tutoring, then, you can postulate a number of ways tutors can respond to students and imagine what effect they are likely to have.

For example, consider the following situation:

> You are sitting in the writing center waiting for your next student, when Scott, a student with whom you have worked twice before, comes storming in. He throws his books upon a nearby table and walks over to you holding a crumpled paper.
> "You look as if something is wrong," you observe.
> "You're right about that," Scott snaps. "I came to the writing center *two times* last week and I *still* got a "C" on my paper. Coming here has been a total waste of time!"

You can respond to Scott in a number of ways, but the type of response you choose will be likely to generate a corresponding response in Scott. Let us look at some of these responses and the effect they are likely to have.

1.   You can respond to Scott with denial.

"Oh come on, Scott. A grade isn't everything.

Effect: By denying Scott's feelings, you might make him feel belittled, put down. Even when you say it nicely or in a friendly way, your message is clear: what is important to Scott is not that important in reality and not worth getting so upset about. This sort of response does not encourage Scott to continue talking to you. He is likely to walk out, maybe even more angry than he was.

2.   You can respond to Scott by *questioning.*

"Why is it so important to you to get good grades?"

Effect: This response puts Scott in the position of having to defined his feelings, and he may feel put down or misunderstood. He is likely to argue to justify his position.

3.   You can respond to Scott by *sharing your own experience:*

That reminds me of something that once happened to me when I was in college. I worked for days on a paper and still got a "C." Just hang in there. You'll do better on the next paper. Just keep up the good work!"

Effect: This response could be encouraging to Scott but still denies the feelings that the speaker is expressing. It offers "surface optimism," which Scott may or may not believe.

4.   You can respond to Scott by *giving advice:*

What you need to do is get an early start on the next paper. Then maybe you'll be able to write a better paper."

Effect: This response insinuates that Scott's paper wasn't really that good (maybe it wasn't!) or that Scott didn't work hard enough and may well have deserved the "C." If Scott feels that he has already worked as hard as he can on his paper, he may feel that no matter what he does, he'll never get a good grade.

5.   You can respond to Scott by *criticizing or moralizing:*

"Well, if you had worked up a decent draft before you came here, we could have made more progress."

Effect: This response might make you feel better, but it is likely to make Scott feel angry. He will not feel as though his feelings have been understood or accepted and he will probably argue defensively.

6.   You can respond to Scott by *changing the subject:*

"What's the topic for your next paper?"

Effect: With this response, once again, Scott may feel as if he has not really been heard or understood. The focus is taken away from his feelings and their sources.

7. You can make an "I feel" statement.
   "I'm really sorry you didn't get the grade you wanted."
   Effect: This response conveys caring, but takes the focus off Scott and does not encourage him to continue. More importantly, it does not encourage him to use his setback productively and assume greater responsibility for his next paper.

8. You can clarify Scott's feelings by *reflecting what he is saying.*
   "You worked hard on that paper and you're angry that it received a low grade. You must be disappointed."
   Effect: This response allows Scott to feel that he has been heard and understood. Your recognition of his feelings might encourage discussion, rather than self-justification. Scott might even decide to work harder on the next paper.

Obviously, I am arguing in behalf of response #8, in which you reflect Scott's feelings, encourage him to explore the situation, and then, hopefully, decide to work even harder on his next assignment. Of course, there is no guarantee that any response will motivate the desired behavior, though. All you can do is to be aware of which responses are likely to work.

In summary, then, you can anticipate writing by:

1. Being a writer yourself,

2. Reflecting on your own writing process,

3. Reflecting on collaboration and evaluation,

4. Becoming aware of how you respond to others,

5. Anticipating as many situations as possible that might come up when you tutor.

Anticipating tutoring in these ways will help you approach your first real tutorial session with insight and confidence.

⬤ For Discussion: A Problematic Student Paper ———

A student has come into the Writing Center with a paper that has ideas in it which you find offensive. In small groups, discuss how you might work with this student without getting angry. The paper is reproduced on the next page:

Student Paper

The women of today complain about not having the same pay and opportunities as the men. The men of today are complaining that they are being pushed out of the jobs today because all the women have to say is that the employer is discriminating because of sex and that scares them into hiring a women. The fact that women are no longer a minority in numbers ought to open some peoples eyes to the situation at hand. The majority of women today are working there are not many places a person can go where their is not a female employee. There are ore women working today then there ever have been. Granted the majority of jobs that women still have are still the traditional women's job like clerical, cashiers, and teachers. The men of today are better physical workers than women because they are constructed to handle more physical abuse.

Men have always been better than women. The female body is unable to perform to the degree a male can. This is not saying that all males are better than all females at everything. Just that the people who strive to be the best at something it is always a male who is best. The fasts human being is a male. The best sports stars are all male. Not to say that females don't do well it is just that they do not do as well. The males have the respect because it is the warrior that is respected. Through history it is the male who has been the warrior fighting to protect the females.

There has never been a women president or vice-president in the United States. Is this because women haven't tried, no it is because women do not have the respect that a man has. The men have almost always been the leader of big corporations and governments because it is male who is respected around the world. There are some isolated times that women is/was in control, this give hope to the rest of the women who live in a male dominated world. In almost all foreign countries it is the male that is the leader.

Women are not the best people to have working, there is always the chance that one of the women getting pregnant and even if that doesn't happen there is always the time of the month. Even though the male is involved in getting the women pregnant he can still work just as hard for the next nine months. Men wish they had an excuse every month as good as womens. Some women blame there problems on being female, if they are having a bad day they say "I'm just real touchy today I'll be fine in a few days." The female gender is always on an emotional roller coaster. The chemical reactions that happen inside the female body are always changing the emotional state she is in. A person doesn't know if she is going to be kind one moment have something change and be a vicious animal the next. The world needs the stability of men to keep it on an even keel. If women were making all the decisions there would have to be scheduled times for women to vote so that they would be making rational decisions. In 1920 was the first election that women were aloud to vote. Warren Harding was elected because of his good looks and he was one of the worst presidents. Harding was actually responsible for the depression.

The design of the male body is to do lots of hard physical work. The broad shoulders and larger muscles are used for hard work. Most women do not want to do the hard physical work that men have been doing for centuries. Not all the work a man does is physical there are some men who are of the professional nature. These men do not use there muscles for hard physical work. Most people want to have professional jobs to make big money and get away from the menial jobs. The majority of people employed in professional jobs are men. Because of the sheer number of males who hold professional positions it is understandable why the people who are considered best are males. There are some good females who hold professional jobs but they are not outstanding enough to be the best. If the women started at the bottom of the work force doing the hard physical work until they have the respect needed to up there may be better opportunities and pay for women.

Works Cited

Arkin, Marian and Barbara Shollar. *The Tutor Book*. New York: Longman, 1982.

Bruffee, Kenneth. "Collaborative Learning and the Conversation of Mankind." *College English* 46 (1984): 635-652.

Clark, Irene Lurkis. "Collaboration and Ethics in Writing Center Pedagogy." *Writing Center Journal* IX, 1 (Fall/Winter 1988): 3-13.

———"Maintaining Chaos in the Writing Center: A Critical Perspective on Writing Center Dogma." *Writing Center Journal* XI, 1 (Fall/Winter 1990): 81-95.

Hodges, Karen. "The Writing of Dissertations: Collaboration and Ethics." Paper Given at the Conference on College Composition and Communication. Atlanta, March 1987.

Trimbur, John. "Peer Tutoring: A Contradiction in Terms." *The Writing Center Journal* 7.2 (1987): 21-28.

WORKING WITH STUDENTS:
INTERPERSONAL COMMUNICATION

I f one could create an "ideal" writing center conference in which the tutor and the student communicated in a particularly effective and rewarding way, what sort of conference would that be? Is it possible even to imagine the "perfect" conference?

My perspective on a question such as this is that such a conference cannot exist because so much depends on the interaction between a particular student and a particular tutor. There can be no established procedure or model for a "perfect" conference, and even if there were, it would be difficult, if not impossible, to replicate on a regular basis. However, a few ideas concerning student-tutor interactions do pertain to most writing center conferences. These are the following:

1. Students and tutors should work together. The tutor should not monopolize the conference while the student just sits there nodding.

2. Students should come away from the conference having gained an understanding of at least one strategy for improving their texts (or if they have not brought a text, they understand the requirements of the assignment and/or have generated some ideas).

3. Students should come away from the conference having gained some insight into their strengths and weaknesses as writers. They have acquired a better understanding of what facets of the writing process they should work on and a concept of how to approach a subsequent writing task more effectively.

4. Students should come away from the conference feeling comfortable about using the writing center. They are likely to come again.

Admittedly, to reach all of these goals amid the often hurried (and harried) atmosphere in the writing center is not always possible. As you begin working with students in the writing center, though, you might keep them in mind.

What is Helpful For Students?

Although there has been much speculation about what factors contribute most significantly to improvement in student writing ability, two that are generally acknowledged are motivation and practice (not a big surprise). Common sense suggests that a student who really wants to learn how to write and who feels comfortable about trying out ideas and learning from mistakes is more likely to improve than one who is hostile to the whole notion of writing or who worries so much about making a mistake that he or she is unable to write at all. It is, therefore, extremely important for tutors in the writing center to develop a comfortable working relationship with their students, one that encourages students to experiment with their writing and to return to the writing center with multiple drafts.

Suppose, then, that this is your first day of tutoring in the writing center. You approach your first conference with enthusiasm, but also with a bit of anxiety. Although you have read a great deal about composition theory and are a good writer yourself, you wonder what you can do to develop a comfortable and productive working relationship with students. The suggestions in this chapter are designed to help you.

Put the Student at Ease

When students first comes to the writing center, it is important to put them at ease. Fearing ridicule or unfavorable evaluation, many students are embarrassed to show their writing to anyone, particularly someone who seems to be in a position of authority. Some of them may feel that the very fact that they have even come to the writing center indicates that they are "remedial" or poorly qualified in some way. Some of them may have had unpleasant experiences with former teachers. Thus, the first encounter they have with a writing center tutor can do a great deal either to dispel or to reinforce such anxieties. As Rogers has discovered in clinical therapy, "the more a student feels that the environment is safe for personal thinking and feeling, the less tentative become the contributions, the more accelerated the momentum, the profounder the insights and self-satisfaction" (cited in Mandel 626).

So when that first student approaches you with a crumpled paper and a referral form, remember that she is probably a lot more nervous than you are. Introduce yourself, ask the student some friendly questions about classes, the assignment, why she

CHOOSE AN APPROPRIATE SEATING ARRANGEMENT

has come, what needs to be done, what difficulties she has experienced thus far. Above all, indicate by your body language (smiling, offering your hand, looking comfortable and relaxed), as well as by your words, that you are there to help the student, not to judge her, that you approve of working through a paper in multiple drafts and that you recognize that writing is a difficult task, no matter how good a writer one might be. Help the student understand that most writers are not "inspired" and that it is not unusual for even professional writers to work hard to generate acceptable writing.

Here are some suggestions for initiating dialogiue at the beginning a conference that are likely to put the student at ease:

1. *For papers at all stages*

   Greet student in a friendly manner.
   - "Hi. How are you today?"
   - "Is this your first year at——?
   - "Where are you from?"
   - "How can I help you?"
   - "What class is this paper being written for? Do you like the class?"
   - "Can you tell me something about the assignment?"
   - "Is this a topic that you feel comfortable writing about?"
   - "Do you find this topic difficult to write about?"

2. *For prewriting (the student has not yet begun to write and needs to generate ideas)*

   - Where can we locate material for this paper? (from the student's own experience? from an assigned text? from the library?)

- What do you already know about this topic?
- Is this topic controversial?
- To whom does this topic matter?
- What details, images or keywords do you associate with this topic?

3. *For developing a thesis and arranging ideas (the student has a few ideas, perhaps even on paper, but doesn't have a well-formulated thesis)*
   - What is the most important statement you want to make about this topic?
   - What are your reasons for making that statement?
   - How are these ideas you've written down connected to one another?
   - Which of these points are arguments and which are supporting facts or details?

4. *For working with a draft*
   - Can you tell me what this paper is about?
   - Whom do you see as your audience for the paper?
   - Can you read the first two paragraphs aloud and show me your main point?
   - Based on your introduction, what do you imagine that your reader will expect in this paper?
   - Who might disagree with your position? What might this person say?
   - What point do you like best in this paper?

Issues of Authority

In negotiating a productive working relationship with students, it is important to recognize that questions of authority will impact writing center conferences and that it is important to maintain a good balance between tutor involvement in and student authority over the paper. Some students consider their tutor to be an authority on everything pertaining to writing, including ideas and concepts, as well as grammar, word choice and style; such students passively await tutor suggestions and are quite willing to alter their ideas completely. Others resist anything the tutor might offer.

In the following interchange, for example, the tutor completely changes the students' ideas, because, according to the tutor, those ideas are not sufficiently enlightened. This is a situation that is common in the writing center, where tutors are likely to encounter ideas that they would very much like to influence, or even completely change. Keep in mind, though, that the paper belongs to the student. You can gently suggest changes or lead students to propose changes themselves. But the paper should remain the student's own work. In the interchange below, however, the student does not contribute very much to the conference, and the resulting paper is therefore likely to reflect more of the tutor's than of the student's ideas:

Tutor: Hi, how are you today?

Student: Fine.

Tutor: What do you want to work on?

Student: This is an essay about women in the workplace. I want to show that when women work, it has a terrible effect on the family and results in really screwed up kids.

Tutor: Is that really what you want to write about? Don't you think that's a pretty old fashioned idea?

Student: I don't know about that. But I do know that there are all these kids without adequate supervision. That's why our society is so screwed up.

Tutor: I don't think you've thought about the topic enough. The issue of why our society has problems is a lot more complex than that.

Student: Well, I need to write a paper that has something to do with women in the workplace.

Tutor: How about showing that we need better child care so that both men and women can enter the workplace.

Student: Okay. Yeah. That sounds good.

Tutor: Good. Now let's take a look at your paper and see how we can change your thesis statement.

Student: Okay.

In the above dialogue, the tutor has assumed too much dominance over the student's paper, so that the ideas belong to the tutor, not the student. In contrast, in the interchange below, the tutor leads the student toward a refinement of the thesis, but does not assume control over it:

Tutor: Hi, how'ya doin'?

Student: Fine.

Tutor: And what do we have here?

Student: This is assignment three, and it's about advertising and how it appeals to an audience. We got it yesterday.

Tutor: And what direction do you think you might take?

Student: Well, I kinda want to argue that sex sells, but I don't really know what else there is to say, y'know?

Tutor: Do you want to brainstorm? Because I think if we talk about this some more we might discover a more focused argument, a nice working thesis or something. Can you tell me how you think sex sells?

Student: Well, that's just it...I know it's more complicated than that but I'm not sure how.

Tutor: Has sex always been an easy way to reach an audience?

Student: Yeah, basically...I think so, but not in the same way.

Tutor: How so?

Student: Well, I don't think ads use sex the same way they did say twenty or thirty years ago.

Tutor: What do you mean?

Student: I mean, everyone is practicing safe sex now.

Tutor: Why is that?

Student: Because of the AIDS virus.

Tutor: So do you think advertising reflects some sort of change in attitudes towards sex?

Student: Yeah, sex sells differently now that AIDS is such a huge concern. Like in this beer ad here...the couple in the ad, right? They're clearly attracted to each other, and they're having a good time drinking. But at the bottom of the ad, it says "be responsible."

Tutor: And what do you think that refers to?

Student: I guess on one level it means "drink responsibly." But I'm saying it could also mean "practice safe sex" or maybe even "abstain" or something.

Tutor: Well, you're on to something here. You've got a good working thesis, y'know? It's focused and much more argumentative than just "sex sells," right?

Student: Yeah, that's what I was trying to look for.

Tutor: Okay, let's see where we can take this idea. If this beer ad can't rely entirely on sexual appeal in order to sell its product, what other kind of appeal can it use?

Student: Well, "be responsible" is kind of like an ethical appeal.

Tutor: How so?

Student: By asking its audience to behave responsibly, the ad portrays the beer company as ethical.

Tutor: So you think that ads have less appeal now that sex can't sell so blatantly and recklessly?

Student: No, I think nowadays sex can sell more. You'd think that advertisers would either clean up their images or lose a large part of their potential audience since so many people disapprove of promiscuity, but actually you can see that by adding this ethical appeal, the ad can appeal to a share of the audience that might not have otherwise paid attention to the racy images.

Tutor: That's a good point. It's argumentative, too. Like you said, it is easy to just assume that ads are becoming more ethical these days.

Student: Yeah, but really they're just using ethical appeals to draw a larger audience.

C⊶ For Discussion

In pairs, read these two dialogues aloud, noting differences in how the tutor helped the student modify the thesis of the paper.

Authoritarian Attitudes Toward Student Writing Behavior

When you assume the role of tutor, it is easy to fall into an authoritarian, censorious role when students do not put in enough time or effort to their work, leave it until the last minute—in other words—behave like students. It is much more effective, however, for a writing center tutor to be sympathetic and accepting, even though they might find themselves irritated with the student. In the following interchange, for example, Jim, the tutor, indicates to Jane, the student, that he understands that students are sometimes under a great deal of pressure and do not allow enough time for planning a draft, even though such time would be beneficial.

> *Jim (tutor):* Did you have a plan or outline for this paper before you wrote it?
>
> *Jane (Student):* No, I just wrote it. I didn't have much time to work on it.
>
> *Jim:* (smiles and nods): A "night before" job, eh? Sometimes that happens to all of us.

This interchange can be contrasted with the following:

> *Tim (tutor):* Did you have a plan or outline for this paper before you wrote it?
>
> *Jane (Student):* No, I just wrote it. I didn't have much time to work on it.
>
> *Tim:* You should always write an outline before you begin to write. Otherwise your work is going to be disorganized.

This second interchange is not only unnecessarily authoritarian and moralistic, it is also unlikely to produce any change in the student (after all, what can the student do about her lack of outline at this point?). Moreover, it erroneously suggests that outlining is an essential stage in the writing of all students, a notion that many would question.

 **For Discussion** ——————————————————————

In small groups, create a tutor's response to the following interchanges:

Dialogue #1

> *Tutor:* When is this paper due?
>
> *Student:* Tomorrow morning.
>
> *Tutor:* And you haven't started it yet?
>
> *Student:* Yeah, I should have started earlier. But I decided to go to the game.
>
> *Tutor:*

Dialogue #2

Student: I just can't relate to this topic.

Tutor: Have you done any of the background reading?

Student: No. The topic is just too boring.

Tutor:

Dialogue #3

Student: There's no way I can get a good grade on this paper.

Tutor: Why not?

Student: The teacher hates my ideas, so she's going to grade me down no matter how good a paper I write.

Tutor:

Get a Sense of the Student's Writing Process

To work effectively with students in the writing center, you should try to help students develop an effective writing process, not simply to improve a given text. It is therefore a good idea to find out how long the student has been working on the paper, what difficulties he or she may have experienced in writing it, and whether or not these are difficulties that the student has experienced before. Knowing how much time and effort have been put into a draft will help determine what sort of assistance the student might need, since a problematic draft may reflect lack of effort, lack of skill or both. A writer who brings in a disorganized, unfocused draft that was dashed off minutes before the conference may be quite different from a writer that has labored for a week over an equally disorganized, unfocused draft. The drafts may be similar in quality, but the writers are likely to have different abilities, requiring different approaches. To work effectively with students in the writing center, you should try to determine what sort of effort their papers represent.

You can find out how the student wrote the draft simply by asking friendly questions such as "When did you start this paper?" or "Tell me how you went about writing it?" You can also ask the student what he or she wants to work on, what difficulties were encountered, and what attempts were made to solve them. Or you can use a "Writing Process Report" that the student can fill out either before the conference or even while you are looking over a draft (it will give the student something to do instead of simply sitting there watching you read). In asking the student to fill out the form, though, make sure that you emphasize that you are using it simply to gain a greater understanding of what the student might need. Assure the student that you will not use it to assign a grade or make a judgment. Here is a copy of the form:

Writing Process Report

Writing Center conferences are more effective when you and the tutor not only analyze and improve a text but also work to improve your writing process.

Please take a few minutes, then, respond to the following questions about how you wrote your paper.

1. How much time did you spend in prewriting for this essay? How much time in writing and revising it?

   Hours prewriting: _____

   Hours Writing/Revising _____

2. Describe your *prewriting activities*. How did you invent ideas for the paper, select the ones you wanted to use, and plan some tentative structure for your essay?

3. Describe your *revision activities*. What global (i.e. large-scale changes did you make in your plan or in your drafts? How carefully did you check your style and syntax?

4. What *problems* did you encounter in writing this paper? How did you attempt to solve them?

5. What would you like to focus on during this conference?

Find Out When the Paper is Due

The kind of work you decide to do with students in a writing center conference is determined, to some extent, by when the paper is due. If the student comes in well before a paper deadline, you will have a lot of time to develop ideas, generate drafts, and revise. Unfortunately, however, students don't always come to the writing center well in advance. In fact, some of them come in and tell you that the paper is due in an hour! How do you respond when the student tells you this? Here are two interchanges to examine:

Tutor: When is the paper due?

James: Um. In about two hours. Right after lunch.

Tutor: Well, I don't know why you bothered coming in. What do you expect I can do for you when the paper is due in two hours?

In this interchange, the tutor has made it clear that James should have brought his paper in earlier, and of course, the tutor is right. However, the problem with saying so in this manner is that James is likely to become defensive; in fact, he may walk out. So either the conference is going to begin on a note of hostility or else there may be no conference at all. Feeling rebuked by the tutor, James may never return to the writing center (unless he is required to come, in which case, he will come reluctantly); thus, he will miss out on valuable writing center instruction.

To avoid generating a defensive reaction, you might respond to James like this:

Tutor: When is the paper due?

James: Um. In about two hours. Right after lunch.

Tutor: Well, it would have been better if you had come in with the paper earlier. We could have really worked on it then. But I'll be happy to look at it with you and see what sort of things you might work on for the next paper.

In this second interchange, the tutor did not make James feel foolish or angry, so perhaps he might bring his paper in earlier the next time. Another way the tutor could have responded is to ask James if he has the paper on a disk and has easy access to a computer. If James says "yes," James might say, "Well, let's look at the paper together and see what sort of revisions we might be able to make in a short time" (if there are computers in the writing center, they might revise directly on the screen). Even if they can only revise part of the paper, any resulting improvements might encourage James to come in more promptly with his next paper. The other possibility is for the tutor to ask James if he might be able to get an extension on the paper. If

James says "yes," then he and the tutor will be able to begin to work seriously on the paper.

Help Students Assume Responsibility For Their Own Work: Maximizing Student Involvement

For students and tutors to work together productively, it is important that students assume responsibility for their own work right from the beginning. If one views writing as a decision making process, then the goal of writing instruction must be to enable students to judge the appropriateness of the decisions they make as writers, insights that they will be able to apply to subsequent writing tasks. The teaching of a skill such as writing, like the teaching of any skill such as drawing or piano playing, is quite different from presenting a content area such as history or literature, and few would disagree that the goal of writing instruction involves a great deal more than merely teaching students to write in a specific way at a specific time.

However, students often view the writing center simply as a place where they can obtain "help" with a particular paper, and too often, the tutor allows the "quick fix" approach to determine the focus of the conference. Because "traditional educational practices emphasize student passivity and assume that the teacher is the omniscient giver of truth and knowledge" (Hunkins XII), new tutors will often conduct conferences by telling students how to revise their papers, rather than guiding them to discover how to do it for themselves. Of course, its quicker and easier to tell students, rather than to guide them, but tutor dominated conferences, instead of producing autonomous student writers, usually produce students who remain totally dependent upon the teacher or tutor, unlikely ever to assume responsibility for their own writing. This sort of relationship is counterproductive to the goal of writing instruction.

In establishing a working relationship with students, it is therefore advisable for the teacher or tutor to begin their conferences by asking students to choose those areas they wish to emphasize, rather than merely reading their papers and suggesting revisions. For instance, the following two excerpts illustrate two approaches to conferencing, only one of which is geared toward helping students take responsibility for their own work.

Excerpt #1

Sarah: This is an essay my teacher told me to revise. I'm not sure what's wrong with it.

Phillip: Why do you think that something is wrong with it? Can you suggest a few areas to work on, areas that you are not satisfied with?

Excerpt #2

> *Beth:*   I really want to get a good grade in Comp. but I don't know what I'm doing wrong.
>
> *Stan:*   (takes about two minutes to read the paper silently) Hmnn, yes, I can see a few problems that are really interfering with your writing. You have a good vocabulary, that's obvious, but there are some basic problems of structure and style. It'll take some work, though. In other words, we can clear up your problems if you're willing to spend a fair amount of time in the lab.

In the first excerpt, one may note that Phillip did not immediately assume responsibility for the revision and that he indicated right away that the student would have to think about this matter for herself. But in the second interchange, Stan assumed immediate control, instantly diagnosing problems and recommending solutions. Moreover, the solutions offered were depicted as time consuming and tedious, more likely to discourage Beth than to motivate her to revise her work.

Putting students at ease and helping them assume responsibility for their own work can also be facilitated through the seating arrangement you choose for your conferencing session. It is generally known that certain positions tend to acquire symbolic value and to be associated with fixed roles, particularly those that place the tutor in a position of authority, the student in one of submission. Since these roles are often associated with previous unsuccessful encounters with teachers, these roles can be counterproductive to the ultimate goal of tutoring—that is, to have students assume final responsibility for their own writing progress.

To counteract the undesirable effects of fixed role positions, it is best for students and teachers to sit side by side at a table, each holding a pencil. Sitting across from one another reinforces distance, rather than camaraderie, and is also impractical for working together, in that one always has to be reading upside down.

Begin the Conference so as to Maximize Student Involvement

After you put the student at ease and ask some friendly questions to determine what sort of writer the student might be and what sort of effort was involved, you will want to start discussing some aspect of the text (or if there is no text, to generate ideas on the topic), that is, to begin the conference. The way in which you begin conferences and the method you use to gain entrance into the text can have an impact on student involvement, so in addition to asking the student what he or she wishes to work on, here are a few suggestions to maximize student involvement:

1. Ask the student to explain the assignment to you. Then ask them to explain how they attempted to fulfill the assignment. This approach is likely to lead to a discussion of thesis and means of support.

2. If you decide to read the text silently (and some tutors prefer to do this in order to gain a greater understanding of its strengths and weaknesses), have the student write responses to the following questions:

   - The main point (or thesis) of my paper is_____.
   - I have supported this point with the following ideas or examples:_____.

Having the student write responses to these questions (or to other questions) while you read the paper will

- give the student something to do, aside from simply sitting there looking uncomfortable,
- direct the student's attention toward the focus and structure of the text,
- provide a point at which discussion can begin, and
- communicate the impression immediately that the student must get involved in the conference.

While you are reading silently, you can also ask students to fill out the "Writing Process Report" discussed above.

3. You or the student can read part of the paper aloud (some students feel awkward reading aloud, in which case, you can read to the student as he or she comments on the text). Reading aloud can also provide a point of entrance, since problematic sections will become apparent. One helpful strategy is to ask the student to read the introduction aloud and point to the main point or thesis. Another is to have the student point to the section of the text he or she likes best or least.

Be Aware of How Much You Are Talking

Another way to maximize student involvement in the conference is to think about the amount of talking it is desirable for the tutor and the student to do. In any tutoring or teaching situation, there is a tendency for the tutor or teacher to monopolize the conversation; after all, it is the teacher or tutor who has the information to impart and it is he or she who is directing the session. Moreover, often students have difficulty articulating ideas and are unaccustomed to discoursing at length about their work. However, as anyone who has had teaching or tutoring experience knows, when the tutor or teacher gives a mini-lecture during a conference there is a tendency for students to withdraw their attention. Often they fidget in their seats or glance nervously around the room. More significantly, they stop listening to what the tutor is saying and take little responsibility for the success of the conference. Therefore, in order to maximize student attention and responsibility, it is important to generate a substantial amount of student participation.

This issue is worth considering. Assuming one had total control over the conference, how much student participation would be desirable? Presumably, it would not be advantageous for the student to talk all of the time. But what percentage of the conference should be devoted to "teacher talk?" Obviously, the tutor has to do at least some of the talking.

My own feeling on this is that tutors should talk *somewhat* more than students, but not so much as to monopolize the session. The main idea to keep in mind is that learning is most likely to occur when students discover ideas for themselves. If possible, don't simply tell students what to do or simply do it for them, no matter how satisfying or efficient it might be for you to do so.

For example, Alison came to the writing center with the paper concerned with Political Correctness that was included in chapter one. Reread the assignment and the paper, noting the abrasiveness of the tone, the blatancy of the thesis, and the triviality of the examples. Then observe how tutor, Cynthia, attempted to deal with these problems.

Cynthia's conference with Alison:

Cynthia (tutor):	Okay, well, I've read your paper. You seem to feel strongly about the issue of political correctness.
Alison:	I do feel strongly about it. I think it can really prevent people from saying what they think and that is definitely wrong.
Cynthia:	I understand what you are saying. But your examples don't really get to the main issue. And your statement that: "anyone who gets insulted by that can't be very intelligent" is likely to offend your readers, not to convince them of anything. That's not a very diplomatic way of making a point, is it?
Alison:	Oh. I guess not.
Cynthia:	And then you don't really develop your ideas very well. You need to explore some of the complexities of this issue before your essay can be convincing.

Note that Cynthia took a highly active role in the conference, telling Alison what the difficulties were, rather than leading her to discover them for herself. The fact that the tutor monopolized the session can be easily seen from a glance at the format. The tutor sections were discursive; the student sections were brief. Note also that Cynthia was unnecessarily authoritarian in her presentation, discoursing about the problems in the paper and asking a rhetorical question, almost as if she were chastising Alison for not assuming a more judicious tone in her essay. Alison is likely to feel quite intimidated by Cynthia's attitude in this conference.

Now contrast Cynthia's conference with that of Bonnie:

Bonnie's Conference With Alison

Bonnie: Tell me about your paper. What is your main idea or thesis?

Alison: My paper is about how Political Correctness can be harmful to society because it stops people from saying what they think.

Bonnie: Okay. Good. That's what the assignment required. Now can you read me the sentence in the first paragraph where you state that idea?

Alison: (Reads) "Okay, here it is in the second paragraph. "Political Correctness stifles free speech and will ultimately lead to a completely repressive society."

Bonnie: That's a pretty strong statement. Why are you so concerned about this topic.

Alison: It's a serious situation, when people can't say what they think.

Bonnie: Is there a speech code on this campus?

Alison: Yes, there definitely is.

Bonnie: Why do they have a code like this if its going to stifle free speech?

Alison: Well, I suppose it's because some students were making nasty comments about other races. And some students make sexist remarks too.

Bonnie: So the speech codes were aimed at eliminating or at least minimizing racist remarks. Did it work?

Alison: That's the funny thing. It didn't really do much. People just make racist remarks in private—like in secret.

Bonnie: Would it be better if they made the remarks more openly?

Alison: I don't know. But you know, maybe it would. Then people could talk about things out in the open.

Bonnie: So what you are saying is that speech codes don't restrict racist speech. They just bring it underground. You know, that's a good point. Let's write that down.

Alison: (writes) But how about that part about how you can't say "short" anymore. You have to say "vertically challenged." That's the dumbest thing I everheard of.

Bonnie: It does seem pretty silly. Is that what the PC rules were meant for?

Alison: No—they were supposed to prevent people from making racist remarks. But its gotten so that its used in really stupid situations.

Bonnie: You know, that's a really good point too—that the original reason for Political Correctness codes has been lost in trivia.

Alison: Right. That's my point.

Bonnie: Good. Why don't you write that down as well. Can you think of some other examples of how PC has become trivialized?

As you can see in this dialogue, working with students to modify or formulate a thesis is a subtle process, one that involves more careful questioning than simply "telling" students what to do. But such subtlety is crucial in order for students to learn to develop their own ideas. The second interchange thus illustrates the following concepts of writing center tutoring:

1. Unlike Cynthia, Bonnie assumed the role of audience. Because she asked clarifying questions, Alison had to explain what she was attempting to achieve in her paper.

2. Bonnie was supportive of Alison. She praised her for her examples and her concern for the topic.

3. Bonnie did not monopolize the conference. She and Alison took turns talking. She also insured that Alison became an active participant in the conference by having her read aloud and by asking questions.

4. Bonnie led Alison to modify her thesis. She did not merely lecture to her about its limitations.

5. Bonnie suggested specific possibilities for supporting the thesis, suggestions that Alison can understand and is likely to use.

Ask Questions—Don't Provide Answers

Another way you can involve the student actively in the writing center conference is to ask questions designed to stimulate thinking. Questioning can provide students with an opportunity to explore topics and argue points of view. Effective questioning can also give the writing center tutor immediate information about student comprehension and learning. Jacobs and Karliner point out that "the way the student and tutor perceive their roles in a writing conference—either as student and teacher or as two conversants—in large part determines whether the conference results in significant change in the cognitive level of the revision or merely in a patching of the rough draft (489).

In order for the writing center conference to be used to maximum effectiveness, then, tutors must learn to discard their traditional roles as information givers and allow students to become equal participants. This shift in emphasis necessitates their learning to ask "open" questions, those designed to generate a wide range of response, maximizing student involvement, as opposed to "closed" questions, those requiring only one word answers, "yes," "no," or "oh." Try to phrase your questions so as to motivate students to think for themselves and to view the choices they make as their own. They will, then, hopefully, attribute the success of their revision not to the skill of the tutor, but to their own emerging abilities.

Actually, one of my favorite questions is "so what?" or "why does that matter? These questions helps students think about the audience or readers of their papers and of the importance of choosing issues that will move readers to change their minds about a topic or at least think about the topic in a new way. Since no one wants to read a paper that tells them nothing new, the question "so what" can stimulate thinking about the implications of a thesis.

An example of how the question "so what" (said gently and with a smile) can help students think about their topic in a new way is illustrated below in the interchange between Mark, the tutor, and Jason, the student. Jason had come into the writing center with the following assignment:

> There is no question that the electronic media—T.V., radio, movies—have profoundly influenced society in the twentieth century. The media have been seen as factors in everything from the creation of designer jeans to the election of the American president. Because of their influence, the electronic media have generated a great deal of debate regarding their potential for both good and evil.
>
> In a well-written essay, address the following question:
> **Has the influence of the Electronic Media been harmful to society? Why or why not?**

Below is the dialogue between Jason and Mark concerning this assignment.

Mark (tutor): Okay, you claim that a lot of T.V. shows are unrealistic. You say that T.V. promotes racial stereotypes and show all the women as being beautiful. But so what? So what if T.V. is unrealistic?

> *Jason:* Well, it makes people think about other races as nasty. And we all have to live together, you know. If I think about someone from another race as being a criminal, I'm not going to want to be around that person.

In this interchange, Mark's question, "so what," stimulated Jason to think about the connection between stereotypes and societal harm. Considering the implications of his point is likely to lead him to work on establishing that connection in his paper.

Questioning strategies can also be used to reduce ego threat, an aspect of conferencing of particular relevance to anxious writers. In conferring with such students, it is particularly important for tutors to make the atmosphere as comfortable as possible, and one way to do this is to present unfamiliar material in the guise of the familiar. Thus, instead of pointing out the comma splices in the paper of the basic writer, or asking the student if he or she knows what a comma splice is, it is more effective to phrase questions within a familiar context and include necessary definitions in a prefatory statement. For example, one might alert a student to the comma splices in his paper as follows:

> A lot of students have a habit of putting two sentences together by means of a comma, which is incorrect, instead of by a period or a word such as "and" or "but." Can you find examples of such comma splices in your paper?

This sort of question reduces anxiety by providing a definition that the student must know in order to correct the paper, without calling attention to the fact that the student might not be familiar with it.

Directive Versus Non-directive Tutoring: Differing Perspectives

In a *Writing Center Journal* article published a few years ago, titled "A Critique of Pure Tutoring," Linda Shamoon and Deborah Burns question the general acceptance of non-directive tutoring as the standard writing center policy. Although they acknowledge that this instructional scenario has much to recommend it, they question its absolutism, concerned that these precepts constitute an entrenched and pedagogically restrictive "writing center bible." As such, it has dictated inflexible codes of behavior and statements of value that

> seem less the product of research or examined practice and more like articles of faith that serve to validate a tutoring approach which 'feels right,' in fact so right that it is hard for practitioners to accept possible tutoring alternatives as useful or compelling." (135)

In fact, the article suggests, although precepts of non-directive tutoring have attained the force of an ethical or moral code, it is possible that, in many instances, directive tutoring may actually be "a more suitable and effective mode of instruction" (134).

Certainly a non-directive approach can be justified as a method of choice for many students; and as you gain experience in tutoring, you might consider that there are a number of situations in which a directive approach might be more effective. In her advocacy of directive tutoring, Deborah Burns points out that her thesis director, who supervised the writing of her master's thesis using directive intervention, was the person who was most helpful to her in her graduate studies. Yet everything he did violated entrenched writing center policy. "Her director was directive, he substituted his own words for hers, and he stated with disciplinary appropriateness the ideas with which she had been working. Essentially he rewrote them while they watched" (Shamoon and Burns 138).

As a compositionist, Burns puzzled over the effectiveness of her director's interventions. Moreover, Burns observed, he was equally effective with other graduate students; "he took their papers and rewrote them while they watched. They left feeling better able to complete their papers, and they tackled other papers with greater ease and success . . . His practices seem authoritative, intrusive, directive, and product-oriented. Yet these practices created major turning points for a variety of writers" (Shamoon and Burns 138).

⟲ For Writing and Discussion ──────────────

Consider your position in the controversy over directive versus non-directive tutoring. Write a short paper considering where you stand on this issue. Include examples from your own experience.

Establishing a good working relationship between tutors and students has long been a given of all tutorial instruction; however, defining what constitutes such a relationship and specifying behaviors and approaches that best insure that such a relationship will develop have usually been left to intuition. Thinking in advance about the goals of the conference and about how to realize these goals will make it more likely that your conferences will be successful.

Works Cited

Hunkins, Francis. *Involving Students in Questioning*. Allyn and Bacon, Inc.: Boston, 1976.

Jacobs, Suzanne and Adlea B. Karliner. "Helping Student Writers to Think: The Effects of Speech Roles in Individual Conferences on the Quality of Thought in Student Writing." *College English* 38 (January 1977): 489-506.

Mandel, Barrett John. "Teaching Without Judging." *College English* 34 (February 1973): 623-634.

Shamoon, Linda K., and Deborah H. Burns. "A Critique of Pure Tutoring." *The Writing Center Journal* 15.2 (1995): 134-151.

Interpreting Assignments, Developing Ideas

"I don't know what the teacher wants."
"I'm totally confused by this assignment."
"I can't think of anything to write about."

When you work in a writing center, you will often hear students make statements such as these. In fact, one of the most common reasons students come to the writing center is that they are confused by their writing assignments and/or can't come up with workable ideas for their papers. Sometimes, students will recount horror stories of nail chewing, paper-wadding all night vigils, resulting in frustration, rather than in inspiration. They may tell you that they suffer from writing block and are sometimes unable to write anything at all. Or they may manage to write a draft or part of a draft but then discover that it doesn't fulfill the requirements of the assignment or that it says very little, because they are unfamiliar with the genre of writing that the assignment requires. Helping students understand assignments and generate ideas for papers is one of the most important functions a writing center can fulfill.

Working with students on interpreting assignments and generating ideas can be extremely rewarding, but it requires patience and understanding. Confronted with student after anxious student, puzzled, blank of mind, and abandoned of hope, frustrated tutors are often tempted to throw up their hands and exclaim, "They just don't know how to think!" or "They have no imagination!" or, worse, "They're not intelligent enough to think through an assignment." Of course it is important for a writing center tutor not to yield to this temptation, but rather to try to figure out the source of the problem and then work with students on interpreting assignments and developing prewriting strategies. This chapter examines the problems students have fulfilling the requirements of their assignments and presents several techniques you can use to help them.

Why Students Have Difficulty Understanding Assignments

Probably the most common reason that students are confused by a writing assignment is that they don't read it carefully and spend too little time thinking about it. They simply glance at it, perhaps get a sense of the topic to be addressed, and then wait until the last minute to begin writing, without examining it further. Because students don't realize that engaging with an assignment takes time and concentration, an important point to stress is the importance of reading the assignment slowly and beginning to think about it well in advance of when the assignment is due.

However, even when students read their assignments carefully, they sometimes become confused because they are unfamiliar with the terminology used and/or with the genre of the paper they are expected to write, particularly if they come from other cultures. This type of confusion causes them to write papers that talk *around* a topic instead of addressing the assignment directly. Of course, sometimes, the assignments themselves are the source of the problem, many of them so ambiguously and confusingly written that it is unlikely that *anyone* would understand them. (At a conference several years ago, such assignments were referred to as "assignments from hell".)

Problems Students Have With Assignments

Below is a list of problems students typically have in understanding the requirements of their assignments:

1. *Students are often unaware of the necessity of having a thesis.*
   Professors often don't make it clear to students the assignment requires a thesis that is developed throughout the essay. As a result, students simply respond literally to the questions in the assignment prompt without focusing their essays around a central point. For example, when students are asked to "compare and contrast" two articles on a given subject, they simply discuss one article, then the other, without realizing that they are supposed to be deriving a main point or perspective that will structure the essay as a whole. Similarly, if the assignment uses the word "describe," students assume that description is an end in itself, whereas the professor may conceive of description as a mode of presentation used to support a thesis. For example, in a memo to the Director of Residential Life, a description of a room in a residence hall description could serve as support for a thesis that the rooms provided for students are inadequate.

2. *Students often do not understand the role of definition in academic writing.* In working with assignments, students may not understand that definition can be used to provide a context for discussing other facets of the topic. For example, in a prompt which asks students to consider the extent to which television could be considered "harmful" to society, it is necessary for students to establish what they mean by "harmful." In another example, in a prompt which asks students to evaluate whether John Keating (the teacher in the movie "Dead Poets' Society") is a good teacher for the students at Welton School, it is important to establish what they mean by a "good teacher."

3. *Students are often confused by an assignment that asks a lot of questions. Often, they attempt to answer each question separately without forming an overall thesis.*
   Here is an assignment that asks a lot of questions:

   > *In the popular television show Star Trek: Deep Space Nine, what do the writers and producers wish to suggest about society? Do the different races of aliens have analogous groups in our contemporary society? What image does the show provide of law enforcement? Of racial tendencies? Of moral leadership? What ethical message does the show give its viewers?*

4. *Students will often write a bifurcated response to an assignment with a double focus.*
   A question such as "Is the political correctness movement helpful or harmful to a college campus and should the rules regarding political correctness be changed?" is likely to lead to a double answer.

5. *Students often do not know how to narrow an unfocused or vague assignment prompt.*
   A prompt that asks students to "discuss political correctness" on campus is likely to generate description and perhaps many examples, but little analysis.

6. *Students are often confused by assignments that ask students to engage in analysis that they are not equipped to do.*
   For example, although the teacher may have thought deeply about the effects of affirmative action, students would probably have to do some research on this topic in order to have something insightful to say about it.

7.   *Students may be uneasy about responding to an assignment that compels them to present only one side of the issue.*
     For example, consider a question such as :
          Should women be angry about the way they are treated in the workplace? This question does not allow for a diversity of response, since it presupposes that women have received poor treatment.

Helping Students With Assignments

When a student is experiencing difficulty with an assignment, the following sequence of steps can be helpful:

1.   Ask the student to read the assignment aloud.

2.   Ask the student to point to key terms in the assignment that tell what it is that he or she must do in order to write the paper. Circling these terms can be useful.

3.   Ask the student to explain the nature of the writing task that the assignment requires. Explain that most college writing assignments require a thesis or main point and that although they might not know yet what that thesis will be, eventually they will have to formulate one.

4.   Ask the student to identify potential sources of information for the paper. Will the information be based primarily on personal experience or opinion? Should the student locate information from the library or the Internet?

5.   Help the student identify any implicit requirements that may not be directly stated, but which are necessary in order for the assignment to be completed satisfactorily. For example, many college writing assignments require students to define terms, consider questions of degree, or establish a relationship between ideas.

6.   Ask the student to identify a possible audience or audiences for this paper, aside from the teacher who gave the assignment. Explain that although the teacher is, of course, going to read the paper, college essays are written for what is ambiguously termed a "general audience." To help the student understand this concept, have him or her imagine that the paper has been left on a desk in the college library and read by another student. Would this student be able to understand the paper without having access to the assignment? What sort of background information on the topic is this unknown college student likely to have? What sort of in-

formation needs to be included in the paper in order for a general audience to understand it?

A useful strategy for enabling students think about audience is to have them respond to the following questions:

Before the people in my audience have read this paper, they are likely to think _____ about this topic.

After the people in my audience have read this paper, I would like them to think _____ about this topic.

7. Ask the student why this topic **matters.** Why would anyone care about this topic? Is it important to think about it? Are there implications and consequences that should be addressed? Even if these questions do not pertain directly to the assignment, they can often stimulate some interesting discussions.

8. Ask the student to formulate a preliminary thesis or main point for the paper. Stress, however, that it can always be modified, qualified, or changed completely.

Working through these steps will help the student understand the requirements of the assignment. Then you can work on prewriting strategies to develop ideas.

Working With Assignments: A Genre Approach

When students are unsure about how to fulfill the requirements of a college writing assignment, it may be because they are unfamiliar with the genre requirements of college writing. To help students gain this familiarity, the following approaches maybe useful:

1. Help students understand that most college writing assignments require a main point or thesis and that most professors expect a unified essay, even if they haven't indicated their expectations in the assignment prompt. Simply answering each question in the assignment will not generate an acceptable essay.

2. Help students understand the thought processes they are supposed to engage in when they respond to college writing assignments. Have them point to words that indicate strategy (analyze, compare and/or contrast, define, describe, evaluate, explain, summarize) and explain how these words determine the type of essay they plan to write.

3.   Help students understand the role of definition in academic writing. Explain that in academic writing, whenever one makes a value statement (something is "good," "bad" "beneficial," "harmful"), it is important for students to define what they mean.

4.   Explain that an effective thesis for a college writing assignments is one that is likely to have an *impact upon an intended audience*—that is, it ought to change an audience's beliefs about the topic, at least somewhat, perhaps even move the audience toward or against an action or policy.

5.   Explain that a suitable topic for a college writing assignment should be important in some way and should matter to someone. Ask them why the topic is important to think about—why and to whom this topic "matters."

6.   Explain that college writing assignments often expect students to select a complex topic for which there are multiple perspectives and to demonstrate their awareness of this complexity by addressing diverse opinion in their essays. This requirement is especially important if the student is expected to develop a position on a controversial issue for which there are no easy solutions. Here is an example of a topic for which the student must indicate awareness of complexity:

> *If we grant that law enforcement officers must sometimes use force in policing actions, where and how should the line be drawn between acceptable and unacceptable levels of force?*

To write intelligently on this topic, students must demonstrate awareness that this is an extremely complex topic, that on one hand, crime has increased, particularly in large cities, yet, on the other, that excessive police power could result in civil rights abuses. Note that this assignment also requires that students define what they mean by "acceptable" and "unacceptable" as applied to the use of force by police.

7.   Explain that college writing assignments often require students to consider questions of **degree.** Many assignments use phrases such as "to what extent" or "indicate the extent to which," meaning that students must respond in terms of an evaluation or judgment. Here is an example of such an assignment:

> *A myth may be defined as a cultural belief that is largely invisible—unacknowledged or unquestioned—to those*

who accept it. For example, the myth of feminine inferiority made it seem as if women's subordination was part of the natural order, a biologically established, rather than a cultural condition. Because myths and cultural beliefs can destroy the ways in which people perceive the world, they can exert a harmful effect upon how such people think and act.

Writing Task:

Select a contemporary cultural myth that you consider to have a harmful effect upon society. Then in a well-supported essay, address the following writing task:

To what extent is this myth harmful to society? (adapted from U.S.C.'s *Freshman Writing Orientation Notebook, 1991*)

For this assignment, students must indicate that a given cultural myth is harmful to society *to some extent* or *to some degree*. Note that for this assignment, too, the student will have to use definition in order to establish the meaning of the word "harmful" in this context.

For Analysis and Discussion

Examine the following assignment prompts and discuss what makes each one problematic. What sort of difficulties would you expect students to have with these prompts? How would you help students understand what sort of paper they are expected to write?

1. Read "Prejudice" by Peter Rose. Choose one example of prejudice that you have experienced yourself; are very familiar with; or have particularly strong feelings about. Write about its origins, its nature, and how (if it is possible) to eliminate this prejudice?

2. Find three magazine newspaper advertisements that present particular racial stereotypes. How much do the racial stereotypes in advertising influence how people form their own self image?

3. How important are looks in today's society? What are some of the main beauty and acceptability standards of physical appearance today, and how can they be explained and interpreted? Analyze some of the effects

of such standards and pressures on the individual and on society, as well as the political and social meanings they convey.

4.   Read Elizabeth Martinez' essay "A Chicana Looks at 500 Years" and the excerpt from Andrew Carnegie's "The Gospel of Wealth." Write an essay in which you discuss how wealth should be distributed in today's world. How do you think Martinez would answer this question? Compare and contrast your answer to what you think hers would be.

5.   In a cogent, well-argued essay of five to seven pages, consider the influence and effect of advertising in and on our culture. What perceptions or assumptions about American culture do advertisers seem to evidence? And how do these assumptions, as reflected in the commercial media, affect us?

6.   Go to the library and read several different tabloids (e.g. The Star, National Inquirer, or The Globe) focusing on the articles written about famous people. Then write a five page essay in which you argue for or against tabloid journalism. You will want to consider the following questions as well. Do you think this type of journalism is ethical? Do famous people deserve to have no privacy? Is this news? What is news?

 For Analysis and Discussion

Analyze the writing topics below in terms of their requirements. Do they require the student to develop a thesis, define terms, demonstrate awareness of the complexity of an issue, or address the topic in terms of degree? Try to write a response to these topics yourself. Then discuss the requirements of these topics with a group of other tutors.

1.   Writing Assignment
         There is no question that the electronic media— T.V., radio, movies— have profoundly influenced society in the twentieth century. The media have been seen as factors in everything from the creation of designer jeans to the election of the American president. Because of their influence, the electronic media have generated a great deal of debate regarding their potential for both good and evil.

In a well-written essay, address the following question:

Has the influence of the electronic media been harmful to society? Why or why not?

In your response, you should focus on specific ways the media have influenced society. You may wish to consider one or two of the following issues: myths and illusions created by the media, racial and sexual stereotypes, consumerism, social values, political values, the depiction of crime and violence. However, you are not limited to these choices and are encouraged to select your own.

(adapted from U.S.C.'s Freshman Writing Orientation Notebook, 1991)

2.   Writing Assignment

In State of the World, *biologist Thomas Lovejoy, Assistant Secretary for External Affairs of the Smithsonian Institution, is quoted as saying": I am utterly convinced that most of the great environmental struggles will be either won or lost in the 1990's. And that by the next century it will be too late." Scientists, politicians, environmental activists, and concerned citizens have become increasingly alarmed at the rapid deterioration of the environment, and the news media now covers environmental problems on an almost daily basis. Although many solutions are offered, there seems to be little consensus on how to take the steps necessary to prevent environmental disaster.*

In a well-organized essay, address the following question:

How Can Individuals and Societies Effectively Respond to the Environmental Crisis Before It Is Too Late?"

In examining how individuals and societies can respond to the environmental crisis, you will want to focus your analysis by referring to specific environmental issues.

Following is a form you can give to students that will help them understand their writing assignments:

Thinking About Your Assignment: A Worksheet

This worksheet will enable you to learn as much as possible about your assignment, so that you will be able to write your essay with greater insight. Follow each of the steps below, writing your response in the space provided.

1.   Read the assignment aloud to yourself, paying particular attention to the place where the **writing task** is discussed.

2.   List the **key terms** in the assignment that give directions.

_____

List any terms that need to be defined.

_____

3.   Summarize in your own words the type of writing task that the assignment requires. Remember that most college writing assignments require a thesis or main point and that although you may not know yet what that thesis will be, eventually you will have to formulate one.

_____

4.   What type of information does this paper require? Will the information be based primarily on personal experience or opinion? Will you need to find information from the library or the Internet?

_____

5.   Locate any implicit requirements that may not be directly stated, but which are necessary in order for the assignment to be completed satisfactorily.

Does this assignment require you to define terms? If so, which ones?

_____

Does this assignment require you to develop a relationship between ideas? If so, which ideas must be connected?

_____

Does this assignment require you to take a position on a controversial subject? If so, list two opposing views.

_____

_____

Does this assignment require you to consider questions of degree or make a judgment (does it say "to what extent" for example)?

_____

6. Who is the audience for this paper, aside from your teacher? What sort of knowledge about the topic do you assume your audience has?

_____

_____

Respond to the following questions about audience:

Before the people in my audience have read this paper, they are likely to have the following beliefs about this topic:

_____

After the people in my audience have read this paper, I would like them to have the following beliefs about this topic:

_____

7. Why does this topic matter? Why would anyone care about it? Why is it important to think about? Are there implications or consequences that should be addressed?

_____

_____

8. A possible thesis or main point for this paper might be _____

_____

Helping Students Develop Ideas

Even when students understand the purpose of their assignments, they still may experience difficulty in generating ideas; for such students, the non-threatening environment of the writing center provides a comfortable setting for experimenting with possibilities. Some students find that simply coming to the writing center and talking or brainstorming about a topic is sufficient to get them started. For others, more formal strategies may be more effective. Understanding why students have difficulty in generating ideas and helping them learn some strategies to help them is an important part of working in a writing center.

Why Can't Students Think of Ideas for Their Papers?

James Adams in *Conceptual Blockbusting* feels that most of us, but particularly anxiety-ridden students, are prevented from exploring ideas freely because of emotional blocks that inhibit us from doing so. A few of these blocks that are relevant to the problem students have in generating ideas for papers are as follows:

1. *The fear of taking a risk.* Adams points out that since most of us have grown up rewarded when we produce the "right answer" and punished if we make a mistake, that we tend to avoid risk whenever possible. Yet exploring ideas for papers means risk-taking, to some extent. To come up with anything new means considering, at least for a short time, a notion that has not been sanctioned before, a notion that one may later reject as inappropriate in some way. Because students fear the rejection associated with risk taking, they are often unable to entertain new ideas and will reject even a glimmer of creative though which may prove to be unsuitable and subject them to ridicule.

2. *No appetite for chaos.* Since the fear of making a mistake is rooted in insecurity, most of us tend to avoid ambiguity whenever possible, opting for safety over uncertainty, a condition Adams refers to as "having no appetite for chaos." Thus, because they are uncomfortable with the "chaos" which characterizes the stage in the writing process that exists before one generates an idea or focuses a topic, many students reach for order before they have given the topic sufficient exploration. Thus, they find themselves "stuck" with dead end or uninteresting topics.

3. *Preference for judging, rather than generating ideas. This emotional block, according to Adams, also has its root in our preference for safety rather than for risk,* producing in students a tendency to judge an idea too early or indiscriminately. Adams states, "If you are a compulsive idea-judger, you should realize that this is a habit that may exclude ideas from your own mind before they have had time to bear fruit" (47).

4.   *Inability to Incubate.* There is general agreement that the unconscious plays an important role in problem solving, and it is therefore important for students to give their ideas an opportunity to incubate, to wrestle with a problem over several days. Yet students often procrastinate working on their papers until the day before they are due. They then find themselves blocked before they can even get started.

5.   *Lack of motivation.* Students are often asked to write about topics in which they have little interest; their motivation lies only in the grade they hope to receive. Yet, as Adams points out, it is unlikely that students can come up with an interesting idea for a paper, if they aren't motivated, at least somewhat, by the topic itself.

Mike Rose, in *Writer's Block: The Cognitive Dimension*, suggests several related reasons for writer's block:

1.   The rules by which students guide their composing processes are rigid, inappropriately invoked, or incorrect.

2.   Students' assumptions about composing are misleading (such as "really good writing is inspirational and requires little effort.")

3.   Students edit too early in the composing process, thus polishing surface instead of thinking freely.

4.   Students lack appropriate planning and discourse strategies or rely on inflexible or inappropriate strategies.

5.   Students invoke conflicting rules, assumptions, plans, and strategies (for example: "avoid the passive voice," and "keep the 'I' out of reports").

6.   Students evaluate their writing with inappropriate criteria or criteria that are inadequately understood.

For these, and probably for many other reasons, students have a hard time generating topics for their papers and of developing those topics to conclusion. What can writing center tutors do to help students in this problematic area?

Encourage an Atmosphere of Freedom and Experimentation

Since students may be too unsure of themselves to explore the impractical and irrational side of human behavior necessary for creativity, they should be encouraged to experiment with new ideas, entertain possibilities for papers, without fear of ridicule or negative evaluation. It is therefore very important that the environment in a writing center be "hang-loose," as informal as possible without sacrificing seriousness of purpose. Have lots of scrap paper around, lots of pens and pencils. Talk about how many ideas you, yourself, toss out before you settle on one to develop. Empathize about how hard *everyone* finds the generation of new ideas. Encourage using scissors and paste; possibly work in groups to stimulate discussion. Whatever encourages students to explore new ideas and feel comfortable about doing so should be part of the prewriting environment.

Help Students Understand That Discovery of a Main Topic or Subtopic Can Occur at Any Stage of the Writing Process

Many students do not develop their topics adequately because they are under the impression that writing occurs in a series of linear stages: the student thinks about the topic, he prewrites, he writes, he revises, and he edits. However, it is now generally recognized that writing is a *recursive*, rather than a linear process. Although some students work in an orderly fashion from the generation of ideas to the production of sentences, others find new ideas while they are revising previous ones and often move back and forth between phases of the writing process. Flower and Hayes in *A Process Model of Composition* suggest that writing is characterized by "recursiveness" to allow for a "complex intermingling of stages" (46). Mike Rose adheres to the model proposed by Barbara and Fredrick Hayes Roth, which they have labeled "opportunism." They explain this model as follows.

> We assume that people's planning activity is largely *opportunistic*. That is, at each point in the process, the planner's current decisions and observations suggest various opportunities for plan development. The planner's subsequent decisions follow up on selected opportunities. Sometimes, these decision-sequences follow an orderly path and produce a neat top-down expansion. . . . However, some decisions and observations might also suggest less orderly opportunities for plan development (276).

As Mike Rose points out,

> applied to writing, opportunism suggests that the goals, plans, discourse frames, and information that emerge as a writer confronts a task are not always hierarchically sequenced from most general strategy to most specific activity. These goals, plans, frames, etc., can influence each other in a rich variety of ways; for example, while editing a paragraph, a writer may see that material can be organized in a different way or as a writer writes a certain phrase, it could cue other information stored in memory (9).

In the writing center, then, teachers and tutors can help students take advantage of these various opportunities which come along as they write. This means not being afraid to explore new ideas even in a half written draft or exploring directions not previously considered.

Helping Students with Prewriting: Procedures and Strategies

Once students feel comfortable enough to experiment with new ideas and understand that the writing process is recursive, you can help them develop procedures and strategies to generate topics for papers. Below, are some ideas you might find useful in the writing center. Remember, though, that the key words concerning this area are *flexibility* and *variety*. No one strategy is best for all students and all assignments.

Have Students Talk about Their Topics Before They Write

Robert Zoellner, in his article 'Talk-Write: A Behavioral Pedagogy for Composition," states that students will write more clearly and expansively if they approach writing through other behavior (speaking) that has already proven at least reasonably successful. Zoellner bases this "principle of intermodal transfer" on two assumptions:

1. Students are better at talking than writing because they have had more practice.

2. They have the ability to improve their writing because, in trying to do so, they are already using a learned skill, talking.

Until fairly recently, Zoellner's ideas were only theoretical; several years ago, however, George Kennedy's work indicated that Zoellner's recommendations actually work, a validation for using prewriting conferences in the writing center. Kennedy divided a group of basic writers into two groups: the experimental "Speakwrites" and the control "Writeonlys," and both groups watched a film which was used as the stimulus for later exposition. The speakwrites were interviewed individually on the subject of the film and were then asked to write a 30 minutes essay on a general topic generated by the film, using the best techniques for writing they knew. The Writeonlys had no opportunity to discuss the film and were asked only to write the 30 minute essay, similarly being told to use the best techniques they knew. When the essays were graded by independent evaluators, the Speakwrites' essays received significantly higher scores than did the Writeonlys. In general, then, Kennedy's research suggests

ENCOURAGE STUDENTS TO TALK
ABOUT THEIR TOPICS

that writing center tutors can help students generate better ideas for papers by getting them to talk about their topics before they write.

What Should Students Talk About?

Conferences in the writing center devoted to prewriting might focus on several issues related to the topic: student interest in the topic, motivation for writing about it, the perception of the reader, possible-directions in which the paper can go, and, ultimately, the purpose of the paper, leading to the focusing of the thesis.

Suppose, for instance, that a student, Jennifer, has come into the writing center with the following assignment:

> Pick a comic strip. Read back issues covering several weeks. Then write
> a three page typewritten essay in which you analyze the values repre-
> sented by the major character or characters in this strip.

All the student has with her is the comic section of the local newspaper and some very blank white paper. She has a vague idea that she wants to write about the comic strip, *Cathy*, but she hasn't focused her topic or developed a thesis. She also doesn't have a clear understanding of what the assignment entails. She says, "I don't know *what* I'm going to write about." Given this assignment, you might conduct an interchange along the following lines:

Tutor:　I see you are thinking of using the comic strip "Cathy." Why did you choose that one?

Jennifer: Well, it's one of my favorites, and I can really relate to the character.

Tutor: I like it a lot too, But what do you mean, you can "relate" to it?

Jennifer: Well, Cathy is so much like a lot of people I know. I mean, girls in my classes and places like that. I guess she's a lot like me, too, when I come to think about it.

Tutor: In what way?

Student: Well, like she's always on a diet. But she makes a million excuses for breaking it. And then there's the boyfriend problem. She says she wants her freedom and a career. But then she, like, well, falls *apart* anytime she's in a relationship.

Tutor: Sounds like you know a lot about the topic. Anything more you can tell me about Cathy?

Student: Well, she's always being taken advantage of. Her boss, yeah, he's always piling work on her, and she can't seem to say "no."

Tutor: Go on. Anything else?

Student: Yeah. Well, there's her parents, her mother, really. She really doesn't want to be like her mother, but she finds herself doing things her mother would do or worrying what her mother will say. I can really relate to that.

Tutor: All of these things sound very interesting to me. Do you think other people would be interested in a paper about "Cathy?"

Jennifer: Oh, yeah. Like all the girls in my sorority house like to read it. They can relate to it too.

Tutor: Good. So you have a subject and you know something about who would like to read about it, your audience or your readership. Now we have to focus your topic around the writing assignment. Let's reread what you have to do.

(Both reread the assignment)

Well, you have the character. Now let's see about the other word in the assignment that's important to think about.

Jennifer: You mean "analyze the values?" Yeah, I was wondering about that one.

Tutor: Do you know what is meant by values?

Jennifer: Not really.

Tutor: Well, next time it might be a good idea to ask your teacher about all points in the assignment before you begin to think about it. For now, though, let's assume that "values" means what a society considers right or wrong, good or bad.

Jennifer: Right. Okay. I think she said that in class. Like in Cathy's society, being thin and beautiful is so important that food and clothes have made everybody crazy.

Tutor: An obsession, you mean?

Jennifer: Right. And women don't know for sure what they are supposed to do with their lives. Like Cathy wants a career but she's worried that she won't be able to get married and have children like her mother did.

Tutor: Good points there. How about at work?

Jennifer: Well, Cathy wants to be a successful business woman. Be she can't say "no" to men, because she's been brought up to be an obedient little girl. So she always has more work assigned than she wants to do. And she feels, well, like—*used*.

Tutor: It sounds as if you have a terrific women's issues paper here, using "Cathy" as an example of problems young women are facing and the way in which the values in our society affect women.

Jennifer: I'm not sure what you mean.

Tutor: Okay. Let's list all the issues you talked about on a sheet of paper. Then you can find examples in "Cathy" to illustrate what you are talking about.

Jennifer: Like talking about how important it is for a woman to be thin. And how women don't really know what they're supposed to be.

Tutor: Right. You have the idea. And once you've listed these examples and read a few more back issues, then see if you can answer these questions in writing:

(Writes)

1. The purpose of my paper is to prove _____.

2. Before they read my paper, my audience thinks _____ about my topic.

3.   After they read my paper, my audience will think _____
about my topic.

Student: Okay. I'll get back to you in a little while.

In this interchange, the tutor began by asking Jennifer to talk about what she knew about the topic, delineating issues that could be used in the paper. She then helped the student define the writing assignment, explored a possible direction for the paper, then gave her time to think about the purpose and focus she might want to develop. Hopefully, Jennifer will think some more about this topic so that she will be able to answer the questions with useful information.

The tutor in this interchange not only generated discussion on the topic; she also helped the student understand the writing assignment more clearly. This is a very useful approach for a prewriting conference, as very frequently students do not understand what is meant by some of the terms in the assignment and never get around to asking the classroom instructor for clarifications. As was discussed earlier in this chapter, terms such as "develop a thesis" or "analyze the values" are often misinterpreted by students, so they merely describe a topic in a general sense, recount the plot or scheme of a movie, television show, novel, or comic strip, without making any point at all. Even when the student has already written a draft, it is helpful to go back to the assignment and have the student underline all the key words—the words which are crucial to fulfilling the assignment. You can then find out if the student really understands the requirements or has explored the topic adequately. You can also help students discover whether or not they fully understand an assignment by having then fill in the form at the end of this chapter.

To reiterate the point of this section, then, a helpful way for writing center tutors to help students generate ideas for their papers is to engage then in purposeful conversation about the topic. Mack and Skjei, in *Overcoming Writing Blocks* similarly suggests that defining "in writing, as precisely as possible just what you're there to accomplish" will sharpen thinking and reduce anxiety, marking the writing task "seem less intimidating" (79).

Encourage Student to Do *Something* Before They Attempt to Write

Often students are unable to write because they have given no thought to the topic they are assigned. They hastily read the assignment, forget about it for a few days, and then, the night before it is due, sit down and chew their pencil. Yet few if any professional writers attempt to write in this way. Janet Emig, in 1964, collected data from both professional and academic writers, which revealed that although there was great diversity and individuality in planning practices, ranging from the elaborated outline to informal conversations with friends, all writers indicated that they engaged in "some form of planning prior to the production of planned discourse" (67). It makes sense, then, that students, too, could profit from learning a variety of flexible learning strategies, to which they can turn when faced with the ghastly white paper. The writing center tutor should instruct students on how to use some of these techniques and then allow students time to practice them.

What Kind of Prewriting Techniques Should a Writing Center Tutor Use?

To generate thinking about what sort of prewriting techniques you should present to students in the writing center, consider how you, yourself, write papers for your classes. Do you jot down notes on scraps of paper? Do you do extensive research in the library? Do you use an outline? Do you work on a computer?

A number of useful prewriting strategies exist today and I will explain a few of them. But you as writing center tutor should decide which ones work best for you in dealing with students. No one technique is equally useful for everyone.

Intuitive Versus Intellectual Approaches to Prewriting

Sabina Johnson divides prewriting strategies into the "intuitive" and the "intellectual." Intuitive approaches seek to generate ideas by "forcing the writer to dredge up from his unconscious the impressions stored there of the material" (235). Unstructured and seemingly haphazard, intuitive approaches require the writer to move from the material into the self, depending upon the interplay between the spontaneous utterances of the writer and the unconscious from which they emerge. Several "intuitive" approaches to prewriting include brainstorming, freewriting, and journal keeping.

Intellectual approaches, in contrast, depend on "a format set of questions which the writer applies to her material much as she might hold up a prism to a beam of light so as to analyze it or break it down into components, from the study of which she may form an idea about the whole and its parts" (Johnson 235). Intellectual approaches require the writer to move from the self into the material. Intellectual approaches may also be referred to as *heuristics*, a heuristic being a technique for discovering ideas or finding solutions to problems. In my discussion of various heuristics, however, I will follow Ross Winterowd in referring to them as "discovery procedures," for, indeed, that is what they are.

Intuitive Approaches

Brainstorming and Clustering

A discovery procedure that is largely unstructured, brainstorming encourages the writer to write down anything that comes to mind about the topic, no matter how peculiar the ideas might be. Brainstorming can be done either with pencil and paper or on a computer, if a student is comfortable using it. After the student brainstorms a topic, the writing center instructor can go over the list, looking for patterns and directions for developing the paper. There are also several ways in which brainstorming can be used in a more structured way. After the student lists as many possibilities as possible, have him or her make lists of opposites and alternatives. For example, in the paper concerned with the cartoon strip, "Cathy," the student may have written "Cathy and her relationships with men." Thinking in terms of opposites the student could then write "Cathy and her relationships with women" leading to exploration of the topic "Cathy's different faces."

Brainstorming can also be done in conjunction with *clustering*, a procedure in which key ideas are circled, which then suggest other ideas to make up the cluster. For

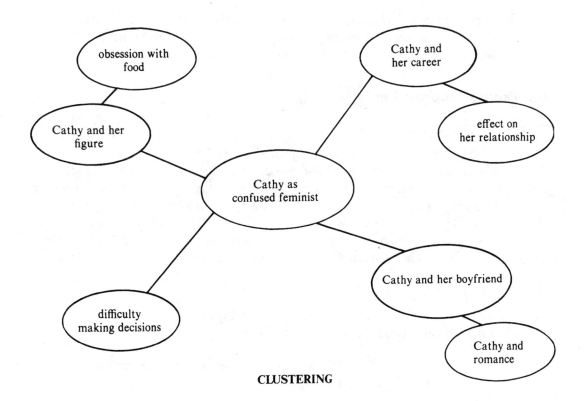

CLUSTERING

instance, in the paper concerned with "Cathy," a key idea might be "Cathy as confused feminist." Several related ideas might be "Cathy and her career," "Cathy and her boyfriend," or "Cathy and her figure." Once these key ideas are written down, then several related ideas could be generated, such as "Cathy and romance," which might be considered a subcluster of "Cathy and her boyfriend." (See page 85.)

Freewriting

A technique advocated by Peter Elbow and Ken Macrorie, freewriting allows students to get their thoughts onto the page without worrying about appropriateness or correctness. It is a means of exploring an idea, sometimes enabling student to move in directions they never would have though of. Peter Elbow explains freewriting as follows:

> The idea is simply to write for ten minutes. . . . Don't stop for anything. Go quickly without rushing. Never stop to look back, to cross something out, to wonder how to spell something, to wonder what word or thought to use, to think about what you are doing. If you can't think of a word or a spelling, just use a squiggle or else write, "I can't think of it." The easiest thing is just to put down whatever is in your mind." (3)

The important point to remember about freewriting is that the student must write fast enough to use his own language, without worrying about being judged. Freewriting, like brainstorming, can also be done easily on a computer.

Intellectual Approaches

The Journalistic Questions

One of the most well-known discovery procedures is the journalistic series of questions "Who? What? Where? When? Why? and How?" Each of these questions should be answered as completely as possible, in order to generate a maximum of possibilities for writing. For instance, on the assignment based on "Cathy," it is not enough simply to answer the question "Who" with the one-word response, "Cathy." Instead, it is more effective to talk about the various personalities Cathy has, depending on who she is with—romantic self with a boyfriend, liberated self with her mother, anxiety ridden self with her friends.

The Pentad

Similar to the journalistic questions, Kenneth Burke's "Pentad" asks students to explore topics through the following five categories:

Act: What was done? (Cathy couldn't stick to her diet and ate everything in the refrigerator)

Agent: Who did it? (Cathy—who longs to be slim and glamorous, yet who also wants to be taken seriously as a career person.)

Agency: By what means or with what was it done? (with loads of food—sweets, cookies, ice cream—all associated with nourishment.)

Scene: Where and when was it done? (In the kitchen, after a fight with her boyfriend)

Purpose: Why was it done? (as an expression of disgust with her own weakness and with the whole obsession.)

The Pentad is useful for analyzing actions that occur in literature, a play, a movie, short story or novel, or comic strip. This discovery procedure can also yield twenty ratios, by considering any one term from the standpoints of all the others. For instance, you might consider Agent (in our example, Cathy) from the standpoint of the other four terms?

agent-scene: What does the scene reveal about Cathy?

agent-agency: What does the comic strip format reveal about Cathy?

agent-act: What does the situation depicted in the strip reveal about Cathy?

agent-purpose: What do Cathy's motives reveal about her? What is the cartoonist trying to say?

Answering Discovery Questions. Blum, Brinkman, Hoffman and Peck suggest that students ask themselves a series of "discovery questions" to generate material for papers. The questions they suggest are as follows:

- What can you *describe* about your topic?
- What *changes* have occurred in it?
- Can you relate an *incident* about it?
- What do you *remember* about it?
- What are its *parts, sections,* or *elements*?
- Can you give *instructions* for making or doing it?
- How do you *respond* or *feel* about it?
- Why is it *valuable* or *important*?
- What *causes* it?
- What *results* from it?
- Can you clarify it by comparing it to something?
- Are you *for* or *against* it? Why?

They then suggest that the student scan the responses to these to determine which ideas might be developed into a paper.

In helping students who come to the writing center with generating material for their papers, then, the instructor should:

● Encourage an atmosphere of freedom and experimentation,
● Help students understand that discovery of a main topic, topic or subtopic can occur at any stage of the writing process,
● Have students talk about their topics before they write,
● Encourage students to do *something* before they write (fill out a sheet, brainstorm, freewrite, use a discovery procedure, answer exploration questions. Create a "Points to Make" list?

Students will be grateful and will develop ideas they can really use.

Some Additional Techniques For Helping Students Develop Ideas

Two additional strategies for helping students develop ideas for their writing assignments are the "Points to Make List" and "Exploration Questions." In our writing center, we keep these forms on all the tables so that they are easily available.

The Points-To-Make List

Created by Jack Blum at the University of Southern California.

Overview

Brainstorming is usually just the first step in generating an interesting and well-thought out essay, with ideas that go beyond the superficial. Before you begin to draft an essay, you should spend some time sorting and narrowing down your ideas in a **points-to-make list.** Although different writers do this in individual ways, most good writers will take time to write down, examine, and revise their ideas in an informal list that is not as rigid as an outline. It is also an important tool to help develop an effective rough plan and thesis statement.

Procedure

1. *Create a preliminary list*
   Review your brainstorming notes and readings. It might be useful to do this with a highlighter or different-colored pen so that you can clearly

mark the ideas that you think might be effective in your essay. At this stage, don't worry if you're interested in a number of different (and possibly unrelated) ideas. In fact, be as inclusive as you can. Just develop a primary list of points (ideas and/or opinions you have about this topic) and evidence (facts, examples, and quotes) that you like for your essay. Then in the space provided below, list out those points (try to fill out at least 10-12 spaces).

_____	_____
_____	_____
_____	_____
_____	_____
_____	_____

Reminder The above list will probably include many different kinds of ideas, some broad, some narrow, some opinions, some explanations. Don't be concerned about this variety of ideas, and don't try to jump to a thesis statement too soon. Sometimes you need to work with ideas for a while before you finally arrive at what you "really want to say." Especially be aware of the trap that many students fall into—A MERE LIST OF POINTS IS *NOT* A THESIS STATEMENT.

2.   *Examine, narrow and reorder your list.*

Exploration Questions

(Useful for Developing Ideas for an Argumentative Essay)

1. Is there a controversy associated with this topic? If so, briefly outline the nature of the controversy.

   _____

   _____

2. Were you brought up to have an opinion on this controversy? What opinion did your family and community have on this topic?

   _____

   _____

3. How did your school experiences influence your conception of the topic? Did your teachers and classmates feel the same way about it as did your family? Were there any points of disagreement?

   _____

   _____

4. Can you think of at least two people who hold differing views about this topic? If so, describe these people and summarize what you believe were their points of view.

   _____

   _____

5. Has your opinion changed about this topic in any way? Why or why not?

   _____

   _____

6. Do you think that this topic is important for people to think about? Why or why not?

   _____

   _____

For Further Exploration

A student has come into the writing center with the assignment listed below. He says that he is not sure what the assignment requires and feels that he is stuck. Using a technique for interpreting assignments and generating ideas discussed in this chapter, write a dialogue between yourself and the student to help him get started.

Writing Assignment

In State of the World, *biologist Thomas Lovejoy, Assistant Secretary for External Affairs of the Smithsonian Institution, is quoted as saying: "I am utterly convinced that most of the great environmental struggles will be either won or lost in the 1990's. And that by the next century it will be too late." Scientists, politicians, environmental activists, and concerned citizens have become increasingly alarmed at the rapid deterioration of the environment, and the news media now covers environmental problems on an almost daily basis. Although many solutions are offered, there seems to be little consensus on how to take the steps necessary to prevent environmental disaster.*

In a well-organized essay, address the following question:

How Can Individuals and Societies Effectively Respond to the Environmental Crisis Before It is "Too Late."

In examining how individuals and societies can respond to the environmental crisis, you will want to focus your analysis by referring to specific environmental issues.

Works Cited

Adams, James. *Conceptual Blockbusting,* second edition. New York: W.W. Norton and Company, 1979.

Belanoff, Pat, Peter Elbow, and Sheryl Fontain. *Nothing Begins With "N": New Investigations of Free Writing.* Carbondale, Illinois: Southern Illinois Press, 1991.

Blum, Jack, Carolyn Brinkman, Elizabeth Hoffman, and David Peck. *A Guide to the Whole Writing Process.* Boston: Houghton Mifflin, 1984.

Elbow, Peter. *Writing Without Teachers.* New York: Oxford University Press, 1973.

Emig, Janet. "The Composing Process: Review of the Literature." *Contemporary Rhetoric: A Conceptual Background With Readings.* Ed. W. Ross Winterowd. New York: Harcourt Brace Javanovich, 1975.

Hayes-Roth, Barbara and Frederick Hayes-Roth. "A Cognitive Model of Planning." *Cognitive Science.* 3 (1979):275–310.

Flower, Linda and John R. Hayes. *A Process Model of Composition.* Technical Report No. 1, Document Design Project. Carnegie Mellon University, 1979.

Johnson, Sabina Thorne. "The Ant and the Grasshopper: Some Reflections on Prewriting." *College English* 43 (March 1981): 232–242.

Kennedy, George E. "The Nature and Quality of Compensatory Oral Expression and its Effect on Writing in Students of College Composition." *Report to the National Institute of Education.* Washington State University, 1983.

LeFevre. Karen Burke. *Invention as a Social Act.* Carbonale, Illinois: Southern Illinois University Press, 1987.

Mack, Karin and Skejei, Eric. *Overcoming Writing Blocks.* Los Angeles: J.B. Tarcher, 1979.

Rose, Mike. *Writer's Block: The Cognitive Dimension.* Carbondate and Edwardsville: Southern Illinois University Press, 1984.

Young, Richard. "Invention: A Topographical Survey. In *Teaching Composition: Ten Bibliographical Essays.* Ed. Gary Tate. Fort Worth: Texas Christian University Press, 1976.

Zoeller, Robert, "Talk-Write: A Behavioral Pedagogy For Composition." *College English 30* (January 1969):2678–320.

5

PURPOSE, THESIS, AUDIENCE

long time ago, when I was in elementary school, all the young women in the eighth grade were required to take a sewing class in order to make their own graduation dresses. So every Tuesday and Thursday afternoons, a bunch of very silly and generally incompetent young girls would sit in Mrs. Prestopino's sewing room, diligently working on our creations. Of course, some of us were better seamstresses than were others, and so, the rate at which we worked and the kinds of problems we had varied considerably among us.

Mrs. Prestopino was able to cope with the differences in her students, though, because she was a wise woman with some extremely sound pedagogical principles. Rather than requiring every girl to work on the same task at the same rate, she sensibly allowed full scope for individual differences. Serenely, Mrs. Prestopino would sit at her big sewing table at the front of the room, seemingly undisturbed by girlish chattering or the whirr of the sewing machines. When any girl had a problem or needed instruction in the next stage of dressmaking, Mrs. Prestopino would then summon the girl to her table and give her the necessary help.

Possessing neither skill in, nor patience for sewing, I was a frequent visitor to Mrs. Prestopino's large table, and I know that she always adhered to the following principles of instruction:

1. She was always encouraging, managing to find something to praise and noting improvement, even in the most unattractive garments.

2. Her assignment of a particular task was based on a well-informed, practical understanding of how dresses are made.

3. She did not overwhelm her students with complex instructions. Rather, she focused on only a few tasks at a time, sometimes on only one.

These principles can be applied to writing center tutoring in the following ways:

1. Tutors should encourage students with words of praise and note improvement whenever possible;

2. Discussion should focus on global areas of a text, in particular, the concepts of **purpose, thesis** and **audience,** before addressing surface problems;

3. Interchanges between tutors and students should concentrate on only a few aspects of a text at a time. Neither tutors nor students should expect that the text will be "perfect" after only one or two visits to the writing center.

Certainly, the dress I was attempting to make needed a great deal of work and was far from perfect (actually, I must confess that despite Mrs. Prestopino's wisdom, it *never* looked particularly good). But each time I approached her table, Mrs. Prestopino praised the work I had done and then helped me learn something new; because I was not skilled, she often assigned only one task at a time. She did not begin at the top of the dress and work her way down, noting problems as she came upon them. Instead, she worked with one central problem, mentioning others only after I was ready to master them.

Good writing center tutors, then, like Mrs. Prestopino, are skilled diagnosticians who are aware of all the areas needing work in a student paper. But they work with the student on a few or maybe on only one part of the text at a time, focusing on others only when the student is ready. As the well-known teacher, theorist, and writer,

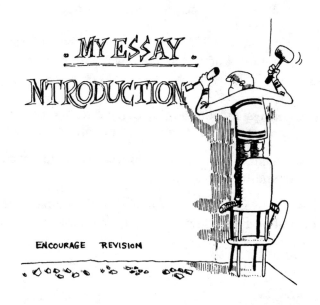

Donald Murray, points out, effective writing teachers are like skilled physicians in their ability to focus on important problems before attending to minor ones:

> When an accident victim is carried into the hospital emergency ward, the doctor does not start treating the patient at the top and slowly work down without a sense of priority, spending a great deal of time on the black eye before he gets to the punctured lung. Yet that is what the English teacher too often does. (19)

Murray emphasizes that the writing teacher (and this refers equally well to the writing center tutor) "should be able to spot the most critical problem in each student's writing to give that student a prescription which will be effective for him" (19). In fact, Murray points out,

> If you look at a paper covered in red . . .you will usually find that twelve or fifteen of the problems are really symptoms of one problem. A student, for example, who has not given order to his views, who is illogical in his structure, will run into all sorts of problems in syntax. Confused and complex syntax usually is an attempt to fit information in where it doesn't belong . . .The good diagnostician will know he did not have a problem in grammar, although he was writing ungrammatically; he had a problem in thinking because he was not thinking logically. (19)

What the writing center tutor must keep in mind, then, is that it is neither possible nor desirable to discuss every aspect of a student paper in only one conference session. Although student papers often contain a bewildering array of problems and errors, constraints of time and attention make it necessary for a writing center tutor to select only one or two areas for discussion during a conference and then to choose a sequence for further instruction. It is important, therefore, for writing center tutors to be aware of this necessity and to base their decisions on a carefully considered and informed concept of what constitutes good composition instruction. This chapter discusses several approaches for working with student drafts, focusing on **purpose, thesis, and audience.**

Getting Involved with the Text

If a student's paper is not too long, many tutors like to read it through completely to gain a sense of its strengths and weaknesses. Some like to read it aloud or hear it read aloud. Others prefer to read it silently. I find reading aloud extremely helpful as it gives me an oral, as well as a written, sense of the text, and when students listen to their papers being read aloud, they notice areas that need additional work that they did not detect when they were reading it silently. The same is true when students read aloud. However, some students feel very uncomfortable about reading aloud, and you should not insist that they do so.

If you choose to read the text silently, it is a good idea to give the student something purposeful to do, so that he or she will not just sit there looking around the room. One suggestion is to have the student write down what he or she perceives as the main point of the paper and then list ideas that support it, a strategy that can serve as a springboard for discussion. Another suggestion is to have students fill out the "Student Focus Worksheet" presented at the end of this chapter.

No matter how you choose to get involved with the text, though, be sure to begin the conference by praising *something* in the paper. A friendly, supportive remark can do a great deal toward putting students at ease and giving them a sense of confidence. If you can't think of anything in the text itself to praise, you might express enthusiasm for the topic or indicate appreciation for the student's hard work.

Becoming Involved with an Unfamiliar Text: Points of Contact

Although it would be helpful for you to read the student's draft in advance of the conference, what happens frequently in a writing center is that students will simply "drop in" and ask you for advice on a draft, even though you haven't read it yet and know little about the assignment or the topic. It is therefore important for you to find a way to become **involved** with the text fairly quickly, that is, to locate **points of contact** with it that will enable you to talk about it.

Beginning the Conversation

Some students come to the writing center with a clear idea about what they would like to discuss. So before reading any part of a draft, you should begin the conversation by asking the following questions:

1. What would you like to work on today?

2. Was this draft difficult to write? Why or why not?

3. What part of this draft are you least satisfied with?

4. Is there any section that you particularly want to concentrate on?

Often the student's responses to these questions will be sufficient for beginning a conversation, thereby serving as the point of contact.

Getting Involved with the Text Without Reading It Completely

Discussing the student's concerns is an excellent way to begin a conference. But suppose that the student simply takes out a draft out of her backpack and hands it to you, expecting you to know where to begin. Writing center conferences are usually short (most last only a half hour), and there will probably not be enough time for you to read the paper through from beginning to end. How, then, can you begin discussion about a paper that you haven't read? Fortunately, it is not necessary to read an entire draft in order to get involved with it. In fact, you can sometimes focus on a draft more efficiently if you *don't* spend a lot of time reading it. Instead, ask a few questions about the assignment and then read a few paragraphs—two paragraphs at the beginning and one at the end of a draft will probably enable you to learn enough about the paper to begin discussing it. Then approach your discussion of the paper by focusing on purpose, thesis, and audience. Several strategies for doing so are summarized below:

Approaching a Draft Through Purpose, Thesis, and Audience: Points of Contact

1. *The Purpose and the Assignment*
    If the student has a copy of the assignment, have him or her read it aloud to you and explain its purpose. Often, when a student reexamines the assignment, he or she will discern immediately where the draft needs additional focus or clarification.

2. *The Purpose and the Thesis*
    Have the student read aloud the first two paragraphs and point to the thesis sentence or sentences that express the purpose of the essay. Discuss the extent to which the thesis might need additional clarification, emphasis, or focus.

3. *The Purpose, the Thesis, and the Topic*
    Frequently, a vague or missing thesis is due to a poor choice of topic. Ask the student if the goals of the assignment require a controversial topic. If so, ask the student to explain the controversy and articulate at least two viewpoints. Have both sides been addressed in the draft? Another issue to address in the context of the topic is the extent to which the issue being discussed is important. Ask the student why this topic matters. Who will be affected? What are some potential consequences?

4. *The Purpose, the Thesis and the Audience*
    Ask students if he or she can envision a potential audience for this paper. Who is this paper being written for? What sort of impact does the student

wish to have on this audience and how can this impact be achieved through the text? Has the opposing point of view been acknowledged? Is it necessary to do so?

To focus the discussion on audience, have students answer the following questions:

> Before my audience reads this paper, they think _____ about the topic.
>
> After my audience reads this paper, I want them to think _____ about this paper.

Have students read aloud the introduction and discuss what sort of impact this introduction is likely to have on a potential audience. Will the audience be interested in reading further? Has the student appealed to the audience's values and concerns? Is there anything in the introduction that might cause the audience to resist, rather than acknowledge, the writer's main point?

5. *The Purpose, the Thesis, the Audience, and the Support*
   Have the student explain how the essay is structured and underline each of the main points. Look at each main point and ask the student what relationship that point has to the thesis. Is that relationship logical and clear? Are transitions needed? Are there sections of the paper where links to the thesis should be more explicit? Are their unnecessary repetitions? Has sufficient attention been given to alternative points of view?

6. *The Purpose, the Thesis, the Audience and the Use of Examples*
   Ask students to note the underlined main points and locate examples used to illustrate those points. Are these examples typical? Do they serve their purpose? Are they interesting? Are additional examples needed?

7. *The Purpose, the Thesis, the Audience, and the Writer's Tone*
   Ask the student to read aloud the section of the paper that most strongly expresses the main point. What effect is that section likely to have on the intended audience? Does the writer appear to be someone who is credible, someone whose ideas are worth considering? Are these ideas stated with conviction? Are they so strongly stated that the audience might resist or even become offended? What sort of tone characterizes this essay? Does the tone contribute to or detract from the credibility of the writer?

For Analysis and Discussion

Read Daniel's paper on the topic of Euthanasia. Then in small groups, discuss how you would use purpose, thesis, and audience as points of contact to begin a writing center conference with Daniel. How would you use the writing center conference to help Daniel begin to revise?

Daniel's Paper: Euthanasia

The constitution states that every man has "the right to life, liberty, and the pursuit of happiness." Euthanasia is the right to a happy death. One that is as free of pain as possible. Yet many states are opposed to it. This is an idea that many Americans support.

According to the Los Angeles Times, on Thursday, March 7, 1996, the federal appeals court declared that the terminally ill have a constitutional right to a dignified and humane death by determining that Washington's ban on doctor assisted suicide is unconstitutional . (1) The discussion on physician assisted suicide has been argued relentlessly between many groups. Religious organizations are one such group. They claim that this type of suicide is a violation of the law of God.

Euthanasia has been supported since the 1930's in the United States ("Choices in Dying" 1). In 1975, nationwide attention to the subject of euthanasia was seen in the case of Karen Anne Quinlan (Weinstein A16). The New Jersey Supreme Court ruled that Quinlan could be disconnected from a mechanical respirator, which kept her alive. Up until March 13, 1996, physician assisted suicide was legal only in two places in the world: the state of Oregon (1994) and the Northern territories of Australia ("Choices" 1). With the court's decision, doctors in nine states will be able to prescribe lethal drugs to terminally ill patients.

The main opposition to the legalization of physician assisted suicide is the Roman Catholic Church and other church organizations. Such religious groups firmly believe that euthanasia defies the law of God. They believe that euthanasia should not be legal because it allows the killing of another human being. Though their statements are generally true, they do not realize that some people would rather die than be put through the torture of needles and machines.

Another group opposed to the legalization for euthanasia are those who believe that it will steer society in a negative direction. They feel that with euthanasia legalized, further laws permitting voluntary death will follow. Judge Robert Beezer states, "After voluntary euthanasia, it is a short step to a 'best interests' analysis for terminally ill patients who have not expressed their constitutionally sanctioned desire to be dispatched from this world" (A16). Beezer says that society will become more death oriented. Although his arguments seem valid, his reasoning seems faulty. Society must remember that the constitution protects euthanasia and that the extreme situations which Beezer speaks of are not protected, death should be the choice of the patient, not the doctor.

My grandfather is one such person who refused medical assistance to prolong his life and his death was the result of his denial. Prior to his death he had many chances to prolong his life, such as dialysis and hospitalization. He made a choice by refusing all of the medical assistance. His theory is that God decides when one should die. He led a very happy life all the way till the end and if he would have decided to sustain it, it would have been his choice. My grandfather was very fortunate because he was able to die in the presence of his family without doctors and nurses hovering over him with medical equipment. Many people do not get this benefit because doctors are required by law to do as much as possible to "save" their patient. A patient should have a say in what their doctors are to do with them since it is their body.

The one group of people who will benefit from the legalization of euthanasia are the terminally ill. This account has been acknowledged by some church organizations as well. patients with illnesses such as AIDS and Cancer would have the option to terminate their lives instead of having to go through the pain and suffering required to extend their lives. Because doctors are required, by law, to sustain a person's life by any means; many people do not have a say in these situations. However, some people have found ways around this.

Living wills, which were first established in the state of California in 1978 and are now legal in all fifty states give people the right to have doctors connect or disconnect life supporting machines when the procedure merely delays an inevitable death ("Choice in Dying" 1). The main difference between a living will and euthanasia is that euthanasia usually involves a conscious patient wanting to die, while a living will does not. Because doctor assisted suicide is not yet legal in most states, the residents of these states must use the living will as an alternative. The only problem is that it does not help patients with terminal diseases, such as AIDS and Cancer, because they are not yet in the state where they rely on life supporting machines. Their right to the pursuit of happiness is delayed in this situation (2).

Doctors in nine states now possess the power to prescribe lethal substances to terminally ill patients. The patients of these doctors are now able to pursue happiness through a painless death without delay. Since there is still a strong opposition to euthanasia, patients in the remaining forty-one states will have to seek other alternatives. Their right to choose will be very limited. Thus, there will be a population of suffering citizens—citizens who are protected under the Constitution of the United States of America, which is supposed to guarantee life, liberty, and the pursuit of happiness.

Works Cited

Humphrey, Derek. [dhumphry@efn.org]. "Euthanasia Research Guidance Organization." [http://www.rights.org/~deathnet/ergo.html]

Weinstein, Henry, and Larry B. Stammer. "Assisted Deaths Ruled Legal." Los Angeles Times. Thursday, March 7, 1996. A1, A16.

[web@choices.org]. "Choice in Dying.." [http://www.echonyx.com/~choice/issues.html]. 1995.

[rights@islandnet.com]/ "DeathNet." [http://www.rights.org/~deathnet/opentest2.html]. February 25, 1996.

Working With Daniel's Paper in the Writing Center

There are several approaches a tutor might take with Daniel's paper; indeed, there is no one "right" way to work with a student on a paper. However, there are several ways to begin a conference that are *unlikely* to be effective. Here is an example of what <u>not</u> to do in a writing center conference:

Tutor: Why don't you read the first paragraph aloud to me.

Daniel: *(reads paper aloud)* I think I have a sentence fragment in the first paragraph.

Tutor: Very good. Do you know how to fix it?

Daniel: Should I link that sentence to the one before it ?

Tutor: Right. And you should also look at how you cited your source in the secondparagraph. The page reference should go before, not after, the period.

Daniel: Oh, okay. I think I did that somewhere else too.

In the above interchange, the writing center tutor and Daniel simply read the paper through, the tutor pointing out errors as they occurred; instead of formulating an approach to the text as a whole, the writing center tutor focused on relatively minor problems with Daniel's sentence structure and method of citation. Moreover, in this interchange, the tutor gave Daniel the false impression that he should pay attention to surface detail before he has focused his thesis. Such a sequence is likely to prevent Daniel from reshaping his paper because he will be inhibited by this disproportionate concentration on surface detail.

Unfortunately, an almost fanatic concern with surface correctness has character-ized composition teaching for a long time, a concern that you might recognize from your own school background and that still persists despite considerable research that demonstrates the ineffectiveness of such an approach. As Erika Lindemann points out, "for generations, most English teachers have given first priority to correct usage. . .All writers disagree with this emphasis. Language should be used correctly, but the final careful editing cannot take place until the writer has discovered, by writing, what he has to say and how he wants to say it" (105).

Many students, too, conceive of revision solely in terms of changing the "words." Nancy Sommers' study of revision strategies of student writers and experienced adult writers suggest that "students understand the revision process as a rewording activity . . .The students place a symbolic importance on their selection and rejection of words as the determiners of success or failure for their compositions. When revising, they primarily ask themselves: Can I find a better word or phrase?" (381). Sommers points out that although the students did not see revision as an activity for the development or modification of ideas, that the adult writers conceived of revising as "finding the form and shaper of their argument" (384). After a concern for form, the experienced writers indicated a second objective—a concern for their readership. They did not deal with external facets of their papers until their paper was in relatively final form.

In general, then, it is best not to work on surface difficulties in a student paper be-fore helping the student focus a topic, develop a thesis, and construct an organiza-tional scheme. Help students understand that writing is primarily concerned with communicating an idea to an audience and that often writers do not really clarify their ideas until they have rewritten the paper many times, adding deleting substitut-ing, and rearranging. Urge students to save the proofreading and editing until a later time.

I should point out, though, that there may be a few instances when you would choose to begin with a relatively minor writing difficult, even if the paper under con-sideration also needed more substantial revision. Sometimes a student is referred to the writing center by an instructor who is planning to deal with structural revision in the classroom and who, therefore, has assigned a specific surface skill for the student to learn on his or her own. Or perhaps you may choose to begin working with a par-ticular student on a surface area of writing simply because it is a more manageable task for the student to complete, one that will provide the student with an immediate feeling of achievement. Many students come to a writing center having experienced a great deal of frustration associated with writing. For such students, it might be psy-chologically advantageous to be assigned to work on an easily learned skill, such as comma placement, rather than be confronted with the more difficult and time con-suming undertaking of focusing a thesis or restructuring the paper as a whole.

Generally, however, it is better to begin with the global issues of writing and to save surface editing for a later time. As Murray points out, a writing teacher (or a writing center tutor) "is not trying to identify and correct every fault in a paper; he is not trying to cover every point in a conference. He is trying to find one central problem on each paper and prescribe a treatment" (20).

Working with Daniel's Paper through Purpose, Thesis, and Audience:

Rather than focusing on sentence level error, an effective strategy for beginning a conference would be to ask Daniel why he has written this paper—that is, what is his main purpose and whom he is trying to convince. At first, students may quip that they are writing the paper to pass a course or to please a teacher. However, this is an important question for you to ask and for students to ask themselves whenever they write, as it focuses attention on creating a paper that has a main point, a paper that matters. Here are some questions you could use to help Daniel think about the purpose of and audience for of his paper:

1. What important point does your paper make? Can you point to a sentence or section in the paper where that point is established?

2. Can you complete these sentences? (Daniel could work on these sentences while the tutor is reading the paper.)

    ● The purpose of my paper is to prove (show, establish) _____.
    ● Before my readers read my paper, they think _____ about the topic.
    ● After my readers read my paper, they will think _____ about the topic.

3. To whom is this paper being addressed?

4. Why is your paper important?

Here is an example of a conference in which tutor Bill challenges Daniel to think about the purpose and point of his paper.

Bill: Well, you certainly have a lot of information in this paper. You mention some really important points.

Jason: You mean its perfect just as it is?

Bill: Well, I think we need to clarify your focus a little. Euthanasia is a big topic, and I'm not absolutely sure that I understand exactly what you mean when you talk about Euthanasia in this paper. Are you referring to a patient's right to go to a doctor, someone like Doctor Jack Kevorkian, for instance, and swallow a lethal dose of something in order to die? Or are you talking about doctors' not keeping terminally ill patients alive on life support?

Daniel: Oh, you mean doctor assisted suicide—, that's been in the news a lot and a lot of people are worried about it. I think I'm in favor of that—I mean, if someone is suffering and knows there's no hope—well, why not?

Bill: Is that what you want to focus on in your paper?

Daniel: I think so.

Bill: Okay. Then can you show me the place in your paper where you state that as your main idea.

Daniel: *(looks over the paper)* Oh, I see what you mean. I talk a lot about doctors not prolonging life by artificial means. But I don't talk at all about patients taking a really active role in their own deaths. Do you think I should change the paper to include that?

Bill: You can. But what's really important is for you to think about defining what you mean by Euthanasia a little more specifically. So make a note of that so you'll remember this conversation when you begin revising.

Daniel: Okay. Actually, I think I'll stick to the topic of doctor' not keeping terminally ill patients alive by artificial means.

Bill: That's okay. Just make sure that you make it clear to your reader how you are defining Euthanasia. Also, I'd like to be sure that I really understand your purpose in this paper. Can you explain to me exactly what your position is?

Jason: I'm in favor of it, of course. I mean, you have all these terminally ill people who are really suffering, people with no hope. Its cruel to keep them alive when they have no hope and have only a miserable life ahead of them. Couldn't you tell that from the paper?

Bill: I did have that impression. But let's make sure that your position would be clear to anyone who reads it. Can you show me where you make that point explicitly? Is it in the first couple of paragraphs, for example?

Daniel: (looks through the paper). Yeah, I see your point. My first two paragraphs talk about opinions on the subject. But I have no main statement. Yeah—I should make that clear (writes a note to himself). But here, —the paragraph about my grandfather and the one that comes after it are pretty explicit. But I guess its not that clear in the paragraphs before that.

Bill: That's right. And, by the way, I really like that paragraph about your grandfather. But its true that although you have a lot of interesting information in the beginning of the paper, I wasn't sure what your position was until I got almost to the middle. Sometimes, that's a good strategy.

Daniel: Not for this class. The professor said that I should have a thesis statement somewhere in the first two paragraphs. I can't believe I left that out.

Bill: Well, its good to show both sides of an issue. It shows that you understand how complex the subject is.

Daniel: Should I just come right out an state my point, then? Would that be better?

Bill: That would be one approach, and we can work on that. But before you decide how to revise this paper, let me ask you another question. To whom is this paper addressed? In other words, what kind of audience are you imagining would be interested in or influenced by this paper?

Daniel: Well, I'm not sure what you mean.

Bill: Well, supposing you were writing for an audience who felt exactly about this subject the way you do. How would that change your approach to the topic.

Daniel: Exactly as I do? I guess if my audience felt exactly as I do, then there would be no point in writing the paper, except that I have to for this course.

Bill: That's right. So in order for your paper to have a purpose, to make it matter, you should imagine an audience who doesn't agree with your ideas, at least not at first. Your purpose, then, is to convince your audience that your ideas are worth considering.

Daniel: Okay. I see your point. So I imagine a group of people who are really opposed to Euthanasia. They think that people should be kept alive as long as possible. Even by artificial means, if necessary. Or, if I go with the Kevorkian stuff, then I imagine a group who thinks Kevorkian is a murderer.

Bill: That's right. So—if you imagine an audience like that, how will you convince them to listen to you?

Daniel: It won't be easy. But I guess I could talk about my grandfather and how his life was under his own control.

Bill: That's a great idea! Now lets work on a statement that makes your position more explicit and shows that you are addressing your paper with a particular audience in mind.

The Interrelationship of Thesis, Purpose, and Audience

In the above interchange, Bill helped Daniel rethink his paper in terms of thesis, purpose, and audience. In framing his questions, Bill actually assumed the role of the audience when he said that he didn't quite understand Daniel's position. Playing the part of the audience can help students realize that what they may have intended to say may not actually be written in their early drafts, a problem experienced by all writers at one time or another. As was discussed earlier, beginning writers, in particular, often produce "writer-based prose," characterized by gaps in logic or sketchily presented events. Consider, for example, the following paragraph:

> Sometimes my angry feelings explode inside of me. Last night, for instance, I rushed out of the house, jumped into my car, and raced up this hill near my house. I tore the paper out of my notebook and ripped it into a thousand pieces. I felt a lot better after that. But later on, when I had to have my car towed down the hill, I wondered if it had been worth it.

In this excerpt, there are several missing pieces of information. Why was the student so angry? What did the paper have to do with it (had it been given a failing grade?) Why did the car have to be towed? It seems as if the student wrote this draft under the impression that the audience was thoroughly familiar with the situation.

Writing center tutors can help students become aware of when they have written "writer-based prose." Comments such as "Wait. I didn't understand that section," or "What do you mean by that?" help students realize which sections of a text might require additional clarification or discussion. As James Moffet says in *Teaching the Universe of Discourse*, "writing mistakes are not made in ignorance of common sense requirements; they are made for other reasons that advice cannot prevent. Usually, the student thinks he has made a logical transition in a narrative point, which means . . . he is deceived by his own egocentricity. What he needs is not rules but awareness" (202).

Approaching a writing center conference by focusing on audience is also useful when a student paper expresses an offensive or unexamined viewpoint. Sometimes students don't realize that their views may be biased or sexist; they are completely un-aware that their papers could be offensive to their readers. In such cases, I suggest that tutors not become personally involved with the position expressed and not get angry (even if it is tempting to do so). Instead, work with the student to imagine how the text is likely to affect its audience. Remind the student that the aim of a text is to convince an audience of a position or at least to move an audience to change its mind about a topic; therefore, an outrageous or unsupported view is not likely to be successful.

Approaching Instruction Through Narrowing and Focusing the Topic

A common problem students bring to the writing center is that of overly broad, unfocused topics, and a useful way to spend a writing center conference is to work on narrowing and focusing. First, let's define these terms. What is the difference between "narrowing" and "focusing?"

Richard Coe maintains that *narrowing* limits a writer to a part of the original topic. "It is equivalent to what a photographer does by zooming in with a zoom lens (or switching to a long lens). The name of the photograph becomes smaller, the outer boundaries of the topic are reduced" (272). Thus, when one focuses a topic, the broad subject "world peace" might become "Peace in the Philippines," or "The Literacy Crisis" might become "The Literacy Crisis in Los Angeles." Usually, the narrowing of a topic is determined by a real division in the subject matter.

Focusing , according to Coe, limits a writer to a particular aspect of the original topic. This restriction is determined largely by how the writer looks at the topic, equivalent to what a photographer does by adjusting focal length. "The frame of the picture or outer boundaries of the writing topic remain the same, but distinct aspects come into sharp focus and receive emphasis" (273). Thus, "Peace in the Philippines" might become "What are the Obstacles to Peace in the Philippines?" "The Literacy Crisis in Los Angeles" might become "What are the Causes of the Literacy Crisis in Los Angeles?"

Fostering Further Development: Returning to Idea Generation

Finding a new focus for a paper often means selecting one aspect of a draft and working with prewriting techniques in order to develop it. In their early drafts, many students list a number of ideas without developing them fully—the "laundry list approach." This approach means that no topic can be discussed adequately—the student mentions something and then moves on to something else. To focus and develop his paper, Daniel might use exploration or audience awareness questions to develop material that would have a greater impact on his presumed readers.

Being Flexible About Revisions

Although writing center tutors ask questions to stimulate revisions of early drafts, it is important to remain flexible about possible directions a student might take. Students are quite resentful of any tutor that attempts to push the paper in a particular direction (note that Bill, above, did not specify a particular approach to the topic of Euthanasia). It is also important to keep in mind that students often hate to eliminate anything they have written, even if it doesn't connect well with a new direction they may take in a revision. They recall how much work it was for them to write those sections and often feel that everything they have written should be included—*nothing* should be wasted, even if it is slightly off topic. Thus, decisions to eliminate anything should always be made by students. Usually, once students see that they have generated additional material and that they are able to probe a topic more deeply because of this additional focus, they will be more inclined to detach themselves from pieces of their writing and perhaps save them for another paper.

When working with texts in the writing center, then, the following principles apply:

1. The focus of a writing center conference should be chosen deliberately. Paper diagnosis and work on revision should not be done haphazardly.

2. The focus of a writing center conference should be based on an informed view of the writing process.

3. In general, global areas of discourse should be discussed before surface problems.

4. During a writing center conference, it is best to discuss one or two concepts at a time. Don't overwhelm the student by trying to cover everything in one conference.

Conference Format Worksheet
Planning the Focus and Sequence of Instruction

1. To improve this paper, the writer should concentrate on the following areas:

    1. _____
    2. _____
    3. _____
    4. _____

2. Which area will you concentrate on during the first conference?

3. Assuming you can get the student to return for additional conferences, what sequence of instruction will you develop? (What will you work on first, what second, etc.).

    _____

    _____

    _____

    _____

    _____

    _____

Works Cited

Coe, Richard. "If Not to Narrow, Then How to Focus: Two Techniques for Focusing." *College Composition and Communication* 32 (October 1981): 272–278.

Flower, Linda. *Problem-Solving Strategies For Writers.* New York: Harcourt Brace Jovanovich, 1981.

Lindemann, Erika. *A Rhetoric For Writing Teachers.* New York: Oxford University Press, 1982.

Moffett, James. *Teaching the Universe of Discourse.* New York: Houghton Mifflin, 1968.

Murray, Donald. *A Writer Teaches Writing.* Boston: Houghton Mifflin, 1968.

Sommers, Nancy. "Revision Strategies of Student Writers and Experienced Adult Writers." *College Composition and Communication* 31 (December 1980): 378–389.

HELPING STUDENTS REVISE: GLOBAL AND SURFACE LEVEL REVISION

Addressing purpose, thesis and audience can serve as useful focal points for initiating discussion about a student text during a writing center conference. Ultimately, however, the student will need to revise the essay both in terms of organization and structure and at the sentence level. This chapter presents various strategies you can use to help students revise their paper.

What is Revision?

A widespread misconception about writing is that revising a paper means simply correcting punctuation and spelling—in other words, to make the surface "clean" and error free. However, although ultimately one wants a clean and polished paper, correcting the surface before reexamining the thesis and the structure is like polishing fifty pieces of wood before deciding which pieces are going to be used to build a table. In working with students on revising, help them to construct a solid table before polishing the wood.

Revising the Thesis

Often in a first draft, students tend to write down a lot of information about the topic, without using that information in support of a thesis or a main idea. Or else their thesis attempts to cover too broad a field, resulting in a superficial, sometimes disjointed paper. To begin revision of a first draft, ask students to read the thesis sentence aloud. Does the thesis indicate a potential controversy about the topic? Is it too broad or narrow? Is it a thesis that the student will be able to support?

For Discussion and Writing

A student has come into the writing center with a draft of an essay that was written in response to the following writing prompt:

Is there a need for a Men's Movement?

Read the paper and discuss in small groups how you would focus a conference with this student. Then write a brief hypothetical dialogue between yourself and the writer of this paper in which you discuss ways that the paper could be revised.

Draft #1 The Men's Movement

Since the formation of the women's movement, a great many changes have been demanded of men; among other things, they have been asked to be more sensitive to women's needs and more understanding and supportive of women. As a result, a variety of men's movements have developed, designed either to help men change or to defend the often criticized male. One such movement, of which Robert Bly is considered the leader, supports many of these changes but argues that modern man is not happy and must undergo greater transformations.

In 1990, Robert Bly write a book titled *Iron John,* which has become known as the manifesto of the men's movement that he leads (Bly 307). The story of Iron John involves a boy and his golden ball. While the boy is joyfully playing with the ball, he accidentally allows it to roll into the cage of Iron John, "a large man covered with hair from head to foot" who was found at the bottom of a pond. Throughout his life, the boy makes several attempts to get the ball back but is told by Iron John that he can only have it if he releases him from his cage. In order to set Iron John free, the boy has to steal the key to the cage from underneath his mother's pillow. The scenario of the boy and this bright beautiful ball represents the youthful innocence, inner harmony, and happiness which Bly believes all men lose early in life. *Iron John* is symbolic of the "Wild Man" that must be released for us to get back our "golden ball."

For Discussion

Draft #2 is a revision of Draft #1. In small groups, discuss the differences between the two drafts.

⎘ Draft #2 The Men's Movement

Since the formation of the women's movement, a great many changes have been demanded of men; among other things, they have been asked to be more sensitive to women's needs and more understanding and supportive of women. As a result, a variety of men's movements have developed, designed either to help men change or to enable men to reassert their rights. One such movement, of which Robert Bly is considered the leader argues that because of the women's movement, which has had an emasculating effect on men, modern men are not happy and must seek to reestablish their lost masculinity. However, although Bly is raising points worth considering, a men's movement such as he defines in Iron John cannot be considered necessary in American culture because men still hold a great deal of power. Moreover, a movement such as that advocated by Bly would adversely affect men's attitudes toward women leading to increased hostility between the sexes.

The "manifesto" of Bly's concept of a men's movement appears in Bly's book, *Iron John,* published in 1990. The story involves a boy who accidentally allows his favorite plaything, a golden ball, to roll into the cage of Iron John, "a large man covered with hair from head to foot" living at the bottom of a pond. As Bly recounts the story, the boy makes several attempts throughout his life to get the ball back but is told by Iron John that he can reclaim the ball only by releasing Iron John from his cage. Moreover, in order to do so, the boy must steal the key to the cage which is hidden underneath his mother's pillow. According to Bly, the scenario of the boy and this bright beautiful ball may be considered a metaphor for the condition of modern man, the golden ball representing the youthful innocence, inner harmony, and happiness which Bly believes all men lose early in life and which, he feels, can be reclaimed only by a men's movement. *Iron John* is symbolic of the "Wild Man" that must be released for us to get back our "golden ball."

Going Beyond the Five Paragraph Essay

Adapted from a handout created by John Edlund at California State University, Los Angeles.

Many high school students have learned a type of organization called the "five-paragraph essay." The pattern works like this:

1. *Introduction:* Thesis and three reasons

2. *Body Paragraph One:* Discuss reason number one.

3.   *Body Paragraph Two:* Discuss reason number two.

4.   *Body Paragraph Two:* Discuss reason number three.

5.   *Conclusion:* Summarize

Although the five paragraph essay format does provide a basic organizational structure, there are many potential problems. To list a few:

- students often follow this format without thinking about it, thus letting the form generate the content. They put more emphasis on how to organize the content than on what they want to say. Nor do they consider the purpose of the piece of writing or the readers' needs.
- The format encourages too much repetition. Often the same three phrases are repeated in the introduction, the body paragraphs, and the conclusion. The reader gets bored.
- Such an essay is usually too short to require a summary at the end. The summary repeats ideas that the reader has just read about and hasn't had time to forget.

In the writing center, you will met students who have been taught the five-paragraph essay as absolute rule, and it is important to help them understand that there is no rule that says that a college essay, or any other kind of essay, must have five paragraphs and five paragraphs only. Paragraph divisions perform two functions: 1) they help the reader understand the text by organizing it into groups of ideas that work together, and 2) they help the eye return to the proper place in the text after looking away for a brief moment. A text without enough breaks is difficult to read because you keep losing your place.

If a student comes into the writing center with a five paragraph essay, work with the student on developing and expanding ideas that will require additional paragraphs. Explain to the student that five paragraphs are not required of college essays, that most newspaper editorials, magazine articles, scholarly articles, and most examples of writing do not have five paragraphs and encourage the student to break out of this mold. Most students experience relief when they are given this additional freedom, but some will feel anxious because they have lost what they have perceived as an anchor.

Helping Students Develop Organizational Strategies

Whether or not a student paper has five or one hundred paragraphs, faulty organization is a common problem, both on an overall conceptual level and/or within individual paragraphs. A paper, as a whole, may be considered "disorganized" when its main points are not grouped thematically, are not strongly linked to the main idea or thesis of the paper, or are not presented in a logical sequence. In some instances, though, the paper may be globally well structured, but individual paragraphs may need reorganization. These paragraphs will be characterized by sentences that are not grouped according to the ideas they express or may jump from one idea to another without adequate connection. Sometimes, of course, a paper may be disorganized in both ways.

Helping Students Perceive Faulty Organization

When a student brings in a disorganized paper, there is a great temptation to simply seize it, point out that it is disorganized, and then reorganize it yourself. Creating structural order is a particularly satisfying task—perhaps it fulfills the same needs as reorganizing a desk or a closet. In the interest of helping students become better writers, though, resist this temptation—instead, help students *learn to recognize* that their papers are disorganized and then help them develop strategies they can use to revise.

Students May Recognize Faulty Organization Themselves

Sometimes, when students bring their papers to the writing center and begin to reread them, they, themselves, will recognize the need for reorganization, without the tutor having to say or do anything. When this occurs, it is usually because sufficient time has elapsed since the paper was written, so that students are able to view it from a more distant perspective and will thus be able to notice problems more easily than when they are immersed in the actual writing process. It is generally known that when writers put their writing aside for a while, in fact for even a short amount of time, that they are better able to perceive what needs revision. This principle also pertains to helping students recognize faulty organization, and it means that by simply providing the opportunity for students to look over their texts, you will be helping them perceive faulty organization, without your having to do anything further.

Faulty Organization Sometimes Means Faulty Thinking

Another point to keep in mind about faulty organization is that it is often not the primary problem with the paper—rather it may be a *symptom* of inadequate reflection— the paper is poorly organized because the student has not really clarified what it is that he or she is trying to say. It may contain a few ideas, developed with sketchy examples, but is characterized by an overall incoherence that may be viewed initially as an organizational problem. In addressing what may seem to be organizational problems in the writing center, then, it is a good idea begin by talking to the student about the goals of the paper in relation to audience and about what the paper is supposed to accomplish. What often happens is that once the student's ideas are clarified and after the draft is revised, the organizational problems disappear by themselves.

For example, Suzanne came to the Writing Center with the following paper concerned with an educational reform. The assignment and the paper are reproduced below:

> *Assignment:*
> *Write an essay in which you argue for a significant reform within the educational system that you have known as a student. Support your case with evidence and arguments drawn from your own experience.*

Suzanne's Draft: Exams: Who Needs Them?

The purpose of education is to gather information that will add to the existing knowledge in our minds. A method has been developed by many teachers in which they believe will help the student provide evidence of what they have learned. Their method is giving exams. Wed have all been faced with the pressures that proceed an upcoming exam. As a result, many students are confronted with doubts of why they have to take an exam. They also consider the question of whether or not it is fair.

We all try to avoid any kind of pressure that may overcome us. In many ways, we usually seem to get defeated by it. The knowledge of having to take an upcoming accumulative exam can exert a great amount of pressure. Having many other worries and activities to think about and to take care of, a handicap results. Many students have other pressures on them as well, many other courses to think about instead of just one. Also, some students are away from home for the first time and have to face that pressure as well. Just getting laundry done is sometimes a big pressure, especially for someone who has never done it before. So with many other engagements, time becomes limited and the hours of studying lessened. The countless minutes pass endlessly as one tries to recall all the information learned from the beginning of the year. Many are familiar with this process. It is the process of cramming. As a result, many students stay up until they think they've studied enough only to encounter that their minds have blanked out before the test because of lack of sleep and too much input of information all at once. This ineffective method makes many students feel that they are being forced to study. Many students then become reluctant to study and therefore rebel by finding no other alternative but to cheat.

To my understanding, exams, in many cases are unfair. It exerts pressure on students, creates tension between other activities and wastes time. I believe that exams are unfair because the effort put into studying throughout the year doesn't always reflect how well a person did on the exam. It may seem that a full year of hard work is wasted as a student "bombs" the exam because of unavoidable circumstances that disrupts one's ability to study or concentrate.

As one faces the trauma of exam taking, one begins to doubt the necessity of it. I don't find it a necessity to study endlessly for an exam only to find that what I have studied is not found on the test. Many times, the questions pertain to trivial details of the study and therefore result in a lower grade. It is useless to try to let so much information enter all at once only to discover that it has been forgotten within the following week. Taking an exam is unnecessary in that it is not effective in showing all that one has accomplished throughout the year, in just one test.

Others find that taking tests are necessary for a student to ingrain the knowledge into their heads. On the contrary, I believe that it is a means of easily forgetting what has been learned due to the cramming process that many students practice. Some also believe that it is a helpful way of gathering knowledge and making sense of it all. It would be more difficult, though, to make sense out of something when one is under pressure. In my opinion, exams do not determine how much knowledge a person has accumulated.

I would only agree with exam taking if the contents were focused on broad, not trivial details. I think that schools should only use the exam method only with daily or weekly quizzes. The grades on these quizzes would indicate a student's progress throughout the year. This would result in a grade rightly earned without one exam grade completely dominating. In this process, the amount of students cramming would lessen. Also, the less information there is to study, the easier it is to remember. Working on one small portion at a time would create a less pressurized method of learning.

Suzanne came to the writing center because she felt that her paper was "disorganized." However, when the tutor read the draft, he realized that what she perceived as "disorganization" was really a lack of sustained reflection about the subject. Before she could "reorganize" her paper, Suzanne needed to do some additional thinking about her thesis and the main points she was using to support it. Here is the conference Todd, a tutor in the writing center, had with Suzanne:

> *Todd:* Okay, you have a lot of good ideas in this draft, things we can work with. But before we start, tell me what was the assignment again?
>
> *Suzanne:* (Looking over the assignment sheet) I'm supposed to talk about a reform in the educational system and support it with my own experience.

Todd: Right. Okay. Now— can you summarize the reform you are arguing for.

Suzanne: Its here in my title. I think exams should be eliminated.

Todd: Okay. And can you summarize your reasons?

Suzanne: Well, its like I say here. They cause a lot of pressure. And people cram for them so they don't learn anything.

Todd: So you think all exams should be eliminated.

Suzanne: Definitely. I mean, I hardly got any sleep during finals week. I was so nervous. And I ate a lot of junk food too.

Todd: I can relate to that. But think about this idea for a minute. You say that all exams should be eliminated, and your paper doesn't distinguish between different kinds of exams or different situations. But— how about—okay—When you go to a doctor, does he or she have a medical degree?

Suzanne: Of course. I wouldn't go to some quack who didn't have a degree.

Todd: And what does that degree mean? I mean, how do you get a medical degree?

Suzanne: Well, I don't know exactly, but I guess it means that the doctor took courses and passed his medical boards—stuff like that.

Todd: Passed his boards? Is that some kind of an exam?

Suzanne: Oh boy. Yeah, some kind of exam, I suppose. But, wait a minute-I think the exams doctors have to take have more to do with what they learn in their classes. Or maybe they have more to do with what they will be doing when they become doctors. You know, like practical stuff.

Todd: You mean that their exams are better connected to subject matter and to their work.

Suzanne: That's right. Oh, and maybe they have more of them, so that not everything is connected to that one final exam. Its wrong to put everything on one test. Its too much pressure. I hardly got any sleep during finals week—I really looked awful.

Todd: Wait—so its final exams, big exams, that you think need reform?

Suzanne: Well, its like I say in my paper. Final exams cause pressure—so much pressure that people start to cram and then they don't learn anything and lose a lot of sleep. I was exhausted, I can tell you. And I don't think I learned anything either. I forgot it all right afterwards.

Todd: So the pressure interferes with learning?

Suzanne: That's right. People get crazy and just memorize for the test. Also, they don't learn anything because they forget what they studied as soon as the test is over.

Todd: Okay. Lets think about getting some of these ideas down on paper. Can you write down your main thesis?

Suzanne: (Writes) "The system of having one main final exam at the end of a course should be changed."

Todd: Great! Now, can you list at least two reasons for your opinion?

Suzanne: (Writes) "1. Final exams cause too much pressure." Hmnn, I don't know if I can think of anything else.

Todd: Sure you can. What did you say about learning just now?

Suzanne: Oh. Right. (Writes) "2. Final exams don't help students learn."

Todd: Terrific! Now lets look over your paper again and see how it fits these ideas.

Suzanne: Do you mean I have to write the whole paper over again?

Todd: No. Let's take this pink marker and mark every sentence that has to do with the idea of pressure. Then lets use the blue marker to mark sentences that have to do with learning. You see, when you mark the text this way, you can often find a lot of good ideas you can use. Now let's talk about grouping these ideas and also about some ideas you might have for reforming the exam system. That might be another section.

In this interchange, Todd did not immediately focus on organization because it was apparent that Suzanne needed to think more deeply about her thesis. However, once she had a few ideas, he used the system of marking sentences to locate those that could be grouped together. This is a strategy that is useful for detecting conceptual as well as sentence level disorganization.

Suzanne's Revision/Exams: Who Needs Them?

The purpose of education is to gather information that will add to the existing knowledge in our minds. A method has been developed by many teachers in which they believe will help the student provide evidence of what they have learned. Their method is giving exams. Wed have all been faced with the pressures that proceed an upcoming exam. As a result, many students are confronted with doubts of why they have to take an exam. They also consider the question of whether or not it is fair.

We all try to avoid any kind of pressure that may overcome us. In many ways, we usually seem to get defeated by it. The knowledge of having to take an up-coming accumulative exam can exert a great amount of pressure. Having many other worries and activities to think about and to take care of, a handicap results. Many students have other pressures on them as well, many other courses to think about instead of just one. Also, some students are away from home for the first time and have to face that pressure as well. Just getting laundry done is sometimes a big pressure, especially for someone who has never done it before. So with many other engagements, time becomes limited and the hours of studying lessened. The countless minutes pass endlessly as one tries to recall all the information learned from the beginning of the year. Many are familiar with this process. It is the process of cramming. As a result, many students stay up until they think they've studied enough only to encounter that their minds have blanked out before the test be-cause of lack of sleep and too much input of information all at once. This ineffective method makes many students feel that they are being forced to study. Many stu-dents then become reluctant to study and therefore rebel by finding no other alter-native but to cheat.

To my understanding, exams, in many cases are unfair. It exerts pressure on students, creates tension between other activities and wastes time. I believe that exams are unfair because the effort put into studying throughout the year doesn't al-ways reflect how well a person did on the exam. It may seem that a full year of hard work is wasted as a student "bombs" the exam because of unavoidable circumstances that disrupts one's ability to study or concentrate.

As one faces the trauma of exam taking, one begins to doubt the necessity of it. I don't find it a necessity to study endlessly for an exam only to find that what I have studied is not found on the test. Many times, the questions pertain to trivial details of the study and therefore result in a lower grade. It is useless to try to let so much in-formation enter all at once only to discover that it has been forgotten within the fol-lowing week. Taking an exam is unnecessary in that it is not effective in showing all that one has accomplished throughout the year, in just one test.

Others find that taking tests are necessary for a student to ingrain the knowl-edge into their heads. On the contrary, I believe that it is a means of easily forgetting what has been learned due to the cramming process that many students practice. Some also believe that it is a helpful way of gathering knowledge and making sense of it all. It would be more difficult, though, to make sense out of something when one is under pressure. In my opinion, exams do not determine how much knowledge a per-son has accumulated.

I would only agree with exam taking if the contents were focused on broad, not trivial details. I think that schools should only use the exam method only with daily or weekly quizzes. The grades on these quizzes would indicate a student's progress throughout the year. This would result in a grade rightly earned without one exam grade completely dominating. In this process, the amount of students cramming would lessen. Also, the less information there is to study, the easier it is to remember. Working on one small portion at a time would create a less pressurized method of learning.

Detecting Faulty Organization Through Outlining and Tree Diagrams

Outlining is often regarded as a technique to use before one writes a draft; however, many students find it useful to outline afterwards, as a means of detecting faulty organization or inadequate development. After talking with Todd, Suzanne might find it useful to construct an outline of her ideas before she begins to rewrite her paper, in that the outline would illuminate in bare bones form what has been created and what needs additional work. For example, if Suzanne had outlined her paper, the outline might have looked like this:

I.   Exams cause a lot of pressure and make students question their fairness.

II. Exams cause pressure

    A.   Students like to avoid pressure.

    B.   Students have other engagements.

    C.   Students become reluctant to study and may cheat.

III. Exams are unfair.

    A.   Students sometimes bomb exams.

    B.   Exams test trivial knowledge.

IV. Cramming doesn't lead to learning.

V.   Exams should be based on broad knowledge, not trivial details.

The process of outlining highlights that Suzanne had not developed the concept of "unfairness" in the third paragraph, nor the section about how cramming interferes with learning. Outlining each paragraph might have enabled Suzanne to think more clearly about her ideas, to develop them more fully, and to refine her thesis. Of course, it is also possible that if she had written an outline *before* she began to write, it might have helped her focus her ideas more clearly. However, although outlining is often recommended, not all students find it useful, particularly when they attempt to outline before they know what they want to say. In the Writing Center, though, you might have students outline at least a part of their papers in order to help them detect faulty organization and poor thesis development.

Tree diagramming is another way to create an outline. A tree diagram of Suzanne's essay would look like this:

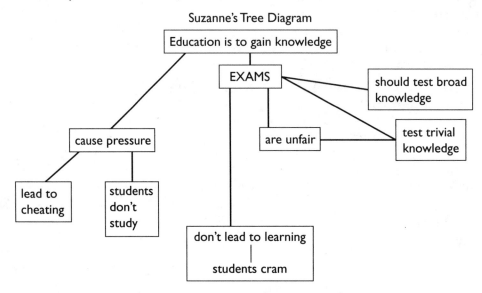

Whichever method you choose to use, keep in mind that the purpose of any form of outline constructed *after* a draft has been written is to focus student attention on its ideas and structure. The particular form of the outline itself is secondary to that goal.

Other Methods of Detecting Faulty Organization

Students can also learn to detect faulty organization by focusing on how each paragraph relates to the overall thesis. You might ask students the question, "What is this paragraph about?" and "How does it relate to your thesis?" For example, if Suzanne had asked herself these questions in reference to paragraph #5, she might have discovered that the paragraph was more concerned with the problems of cramming than with the exam system. Other questions which are useful to ask are:

- What is the function of this paragraph?
- Does it develop the ideas in the previous paragraph?
- Does it contradict the ideas in the previous paragraph?
- Is it an example? Is it a definition?
- Does it introduce a new topic?

An Organizational Scheme Should be Chosen Deliberately

Another way to help students develop a better sense of how to organize their papers is to ask them *why* they have chosen a particular organizational pattern. Often, they will discover that they haven't *chosen* the pattern at all—the paper reflects the order in which the student happened to have thought of ideas. Urge students, then, to reconsider the order of their ideas, and emphasize that an organizational scheme should be determined consciously. Point out that the order of ideas should be *graded* in some way. For example, if a student were writing about vacation possibilities in Bermuda, those possibilities might be presented in terms of how expensive they are (from inexpensive to expensive), how interesting they are (from ordinary to exotic), how time consuming they are (from short to long), and other ways as well. In Suzanne's paper, the argument that final exams don't facilitate learning is probably of greater importance than the argument that they cause pressure (after all, should *anything* that causes pressure be eliminated?) or the fact that they result in cramming. Since educational practices are usually justified in terms of their effect on learning, this argument might appropriately be presented first and given additional emphasis.

Reorganization Can Create the Need For Additional Material

Work on organizational problems may reveal the need for additional subject matter, which may require more brainstorming, clustering or use of prewriting strategies. If this should happen when you work with students in the Writing Center, you should stress that this is not unusual, that the writing process is recursive, and that good writers often think of new ideas when they revise. In the example cited above, Suzanne discovered that she really had not addressed an educational reform in sufficient detail, that to propose the elimination of final exams was too simplistic, and that she needed to think about some alternatives. Of course, generating additional material means more work, and for this reason, students will sometimes resist doing it. As a tutor you can help students overcome resistance by encouraging them to aim for the best possible draft, even if it means more thinking and writing. To some extent, helping students become better writers means helping them aim for a higher standard in their work.

Tightening Organization Through Transitions

You can help students develop a tight organizational structure and an overall more coherent text by teaching them to use transitions in their writing. Transitions serve as signposts or cues to readers, pointing backwards and forwards within the text and serving to connect ideas. Below is a list of common transitions that may be useful for your students:

- Transitions that explain or introduce ideas: for example, for instance, thus, in particular
- Transitions that compare: similarly, in the same way
- Transitions that contrast: however, in contrast to, on the other hand, on the contrary
- Transitions that show cause and effect: thus, consequently, as a result, therefore

Transitions can also enhance sentence level coherence, a topic that is addressed at the end of this chapter.

Using a Function Outline

A *function outline* consists of brief statements about how each paragraph functions within an essay in terms of its relationship either to the thesis or to one of its supporting points; its purpose is to focus student attention on thesis development and coherence and to initiate revision. Function outlines may be written either on a separate sheet of paper, such as a Function Outline Worksheet, or in the margins of the text itself. It can be used both for preparing students for their writing center visits, in which case students will prepare them before they come to the writing center, and for initiating revision at the beginning of a writing center conference. The following steps can be used to help students write a function outline in the Writing Center:

1. Ask the student to show you a copy of the assignment and to explain the assignment to you.

2. Have the student number the paragraphs in the essay.

3. Have the student highlight or underline the thesis statement and indicate what he or she feels are the main supporting points.

4. Have the student highlight what he or she feels is the main point of each paragraph.

5. Go through the essay, paragraph by paragraph, asking the student how each paragraph functions to support the main point of the essay. Does it develop a main supporting point? Does it provide background material? Is it an example? Does it present a counter argument? Ask the student to point to specific words or cueing devices in the paragraph that refer back

to the thesis and remind the reader of the main point to be developed. If cueing devices do not appear, work with the student to add necessary material.

6. Ask the student if there are places in the paragraph that seem to head in another, perhaps related or even different, direction. If so, ask if these sections can be refocused or whether the thesis, itself, should be modified to accommodate a potential new direction.

7. Having worked through the entire essay, ask the student what areas of the paper need modification or elaboration. Does he or she feels that the thesis statement should be modified in any way? If so, what new cueing and support would be needed?

Function Outline Worksheet

A Function Outline consists of brief statements about how each paragraph functions within an essay in terms of its relationship either to the thesis or to one of its supporting points; the purpose of writing a Function Outline is to focus attention on thesis development and coherence and to initiate revision. Function outlines may be written either in the margins of the essay itself or on a separate sheet of paper, such as the Function Outline Worksheet below:

Steps For Writing a Function Outline

1. Number all the paragraphs in your essay.

2. Highlight or underline the thesis statement. Write the thesis statement below.

Thesis Statement

_____

_____

3. Skim the essay, highlighting the main supporting points. Briefly summarize these points below.

First Main Point _____

_____

Second Main Point _____

_____

Third Main Point _____

_____

Fourth Main Point _____

_____

Fifth Main Point _____

_____

4. Go through the essay, paragraph by paragraph, noting how each one functions to support the main point of the essay. As you read, think about the following questions: Does the paragraph develop a main supporting point? Does it provide background material? Is it an example? Does it present a counter argument? Locate specific words or cueing devices in the paragraph that refer back to the thesis and remind the reader of the main point to be developed. If cueing devices do not appear, think about what material you might want to add.

    Other questions to consider: Are there places in the paragraph that seem to head in another, perhaps related, direction. If so, can these sections can be refocused or do you wish to modify the thesis to accommodate a potential new direction?

    In the space below, indicate the function of each paragraph in your essay.

Paragraph #1 _____

_____

Paragraph #2 _____

_____

Paragraph #3 _____

_____

Paragraph #4 _____

_____

Paragraph #5 _____

_____

Paragraph #6 _____

_____

Paragraph #7 _____

_____

Paragraph #8 _____

_____

Paragraph #9 _____

_____

Paragraph #10 _____

_____

5.   Having worked through the entire essay, note which areas of the paper need modification or elaboration. Do you feel that the thesis statement should be modified in any way? If so, what new cueing and support would be needed?

Working With Introductions and Conclusions

Introductions

Students probably spend more time laboring over their introductions than they do on other parts of their papers; in fact, many students become so bogged down in the introduction that they never write the rest of the paper. One reason for this is that students are especially concerned about their introductions, since readers often use them subconsciously to formulate their opinion of the rest of the essay. Another reason is that students are often taught that the introduction must attract the reader's attention, and, therefore, they spend a lot of time trying to think of eye-catching strategies instead of presenting ideas in a straightforward manner. But I think that the most common reason that students have difficulties with introductions is that they attempt to write them before they have a clear sense of what they want to say and are thus struggling to introduce a topic before they have formulated a clear approach to it. My recommendation for such students is that they *not* begin with the introduction, and, instead, save it until the rest of the paper has been written. Once students have a better sense of what the paper is about, they often find that the introduction is not so difficult.

However, even when students know what they want to say, good introductions are sometimes difficult to write, and students may bring in introductions that are vague, do not clarify the thesis, fail to define necessary terms, or ramble off in directions beyond the scope of the paper. Of course, except for the necessity of containing a thesis statement (and even here, there may be exceptions) there is no one *right* way to write an introduction. As in all writing, the effectiveness of an introduction is determined by topic, purpose, and audience—however, if students need help in writing an introduction, they might find the following possibilities useful:

Strategies For Writing an Introduction

1. Present a commonly held view and then contrast it with the writer's view.
   Commonly held belief
   > *However* (or other word indicating contrast)
   > The writer's view

2. Provide background and then present the purpose.
   Background
   Purpose Statement

3. Begin with several examples.
   Example
   Example
   Example
   Generalization

4.   Begin with an illustrative anecdote.
        Anecdote
        Thesis statement derived from anecdote

5.   Move from the general to the specific.
        General Statement
        Narrower Statement
        Specific Statement
        Thesis

These approaches are all pretty straightforward and do not include the zippy slogan or catchy descriptions that students have been taught are essential to a good introduction. In fact, so thoroughly have students been taught that their introductions must attract the reader's attention, that they sometimes write introductions that have nothing to do with the content of the paper! My feeling is that if students are able to incorporate a catchy introduction, they should do so, but if not, a straightforward one will be quite acceptable. Often, when students stop worrying about being witty or cute, they are able to write introductions more easily.

Conclusions

Conclusions are not usually as problematic as introductions, but still can cause students some difficulty. Sometimes students will write conclusions which fail to conclude, leaving the reader without a sense that the essay is complete. Other times, the student will introduce an irrelevant or unnecessary detail, usually because he or she is having difficulty in thinking of what to say. If students are having difficulty with conclusions, you might suggest the following:

1.   Refer to what was said in the introduction, either the context that was set, the historical background that was discussed, or questions that were raised.

2.   Affirm why the topic is important.

3.   Summarize the main points (but be careful of being redundant).

Global Revision: A Check Sheet

In working with students on global revision, the following questions are useful to ask:

1.   Are there thesis problems? Is the thesis too broad or too narrow?

2. Has the context or the background of the paper been adequately described or summarized so that even a reader who knows nothing about the assignment would be able to understand the purpose of the paper?

3. Has the audience been taken into consideration? Has the paper been written with a particular audience in mind? Does the paper address the concerns of that audience?

4. Are reasons given for the position? Do the reasons directly refer back tot he thesis? Are those reasons supported with examples?

5. Is there a personal voice? Writing becomes interesting when the reader can sense a writer behind the prose. Do the style and examples reflect a real person writing? Is the tone appropriate to the task?

6. Is there an acknowledgment of the opposing viewpoint? If not, the reader may get the feeling that the writer either hasn't thought of the opposing viewpoint or is unable to deal with it.

7. Is there a need for additional facts or information?

Working with Sentence Level Problems

Help Students Evaluate Their Sentences

Once students have worked on thesis development and organizational structure, they can start paying attention to the patterns of their sentences. Are their sentences varied? Do they connect smoothly together? Or do some sentences "sound" awkward, choppy, or difficult to understand?

Awareness of sentence level effectiveness and stylistic grace can be fostered through reading aloud—either the student reads aloud to you or you read their papers aloud to them. Reading aloud can help the student notice when the sentences are choppy and should be combined or when the prose is so wordy that one is breathless at the end of every sentence. As William Strong points out, many "professional writers . . . seem to spend considerable time hearing the way sentences fit together to make up the 'melody' of their writing" (xv).

Reading aloud focuses students' attention on sentence-level difficulties that actually appear in their papers, not on problems which happen to be included in an exercise book. Pay attention to the kinds of sentences students are actually writing. Then notice what kinds of sentences they are *not* writing as well. As Lindemann states:

> Instead of analyzing sentences in a textbook, students need to discover what kinds of sentences their own writing contains. Instead of drilling students on various sentence shapes, we need to show them how to create those shapes and how to handle the punctuation problems unfamiliar constructions create. Instead of discussing sentence patterns students already know how to write, we need to individualize instruction so that students are practicing sentence types they may be avoiding for fear of making mistakes in punctuation or subject-verb agreement. The goal of our teaching should be to enlarge the student's repertoire of sentence options and rhetorical choices (105).

Assign exercises, then, when the paper suggests to you that the student will benefit from them. Then, once you have assigned the work, go through a few examples with the student and show her how they apply to her writing. Don't simply isolate the student in a cubicle with an exercise book and then forget about her.

Sentence Combining

If students are writing short, choppy sentences, they can benefit tremendously from work in sentence combining. Sentence combining derives from generative-transformational theory, which suggests that all writers transform sentences intuitively by adding to, deleting from, or rearranging kernel sentences. Sentence combining utilizes this principle.

Sentence combining exercises usually present lists of sentences, many of which are organized into clusters, each of which represents a part of one longer sentence. Students are asked to combine the clusters into one sentence and to experiment with different ways of combining them. For example, in William Strong's book *Sentence Combining: A Composing Book*, the student is presented with the following two clustered sentences:

1.1   It was Friday night.

1.2   He was feeling good.

2.1   He had worked hard.

2.2   He had gotten a raise.

The student is asked to combine these four clusters into the following:

It was Friday night, and he was feeling good.

Because he had worked hard, he had gotten a raise.

Or else the student could combine all of them, as follows:

It was Friday night, and he was feeling good, because he had worked hard and gotten a raise.

Strong advocates that students should learn to understand that "good" sentences are not necessarily "long" ones, but rather those which are appropriate to the context of the paragraph. Strong also advises student to "listen" to sentences by whispering them loud and to experiment with new sentence patterns by writing them in a notebook.

In the writing center, you can work with students on sentence combining exercises (see the list of books you can use at the end of this chapter) and then go back to the student's own writing to see where the new knowledge can be applied. Sentence combining is not effective unless students begin to combine sentences they are actually using and to incorporate new sentence patterns into their own writing.

Making Sentences More Readable

Although many students write short, choppy sentences, others write sentences which are wordy, inflated, unclear, tangled and too complex, making their papers very difficult to process. However, simply telling an awkward or overly wordy writer to "be clear and direct" is not particularly useful. Students must be *shown* how to write clearly, and then, perhaps, they will develop an intuitive feel for graceful, clearly written prose. A good way to show them is to make them aware of a few principles of *readability*.

Teaching Readability in the Writing Center

Joseph Williams notes a very useful principle of readability which is quite easy to teach and which is very effective in helping students write clear, direct sentences. He suggests that the subject of each clause or sentence should be the *doer* or performer of each action and that the verb of each sentence should express the crucial action. For example, you might ask students which of the following two sentences is easier to understand after a rapid first reading:

1. The runner's fatigue prevented his qualification for the Olympic trials because he finished poorly in the local meet.

2. The fatigued runner did not qualify for the Olympic trials because he finished poorly in the local meet.

Most students will agree that the second sentence is easier to process than the first one. Then ask students "why" they suppose this is so, a question that will focus their attention on the components of the two sentences. At first, students will probably venture that one sentence is longer than the other, but if they count the words in each, they will realize that both have approximately the same number of words. At this point, you can point out that the number of words in a sentence usually has nothing to do with clarity, rather that clarity is achieved by the way in which the sentence is constructed—that is, in the way each word, phrase, and clause expresses who is, or is not, doing what to whom.

You can then point out that the second sentence uses the subject of each clause to show *who acts*, who is the doer or performer of each action, and that it uses the verbs of each clause to express the action. The actor or doer, then, of a readable sentence is usually in the subject position. The action is usually in the verb.

Subject	Verb
runner	did not qualify
he	finished

A few more examples will help clarify this:

In the following sentence, the subject is *not* the performer. The sentence is not written in a direct style:

> A reapplication for her driver's license was necessary after her traffic ticket was given to her.

It can be corrected as follows:

> She needed to reapply for her driver's license after she got a traffic ticket.

In the less readable sentence, the performer is *she*, but the subject of the sentence is *reapplication*. In the more readable sentence, *she* fills the subject position and the action, *reapply*, fills the position of the verb.

Here is another set of examples:

Subject not the performer:	The decision of individual grades will be made by the teacher after all the papers are completed by the students.
Corrected:	The teacher will decide individual grades after the students complete all their papers.

Once students understand this principle of readability, they should go back to their papers and rewrite some of their own sentences in a more direct style. They can also work on another principle of readability which is that vigorous sentences express action in a verb, rather than in a noun. For instance, in the following hard-to-process sentence, all of the major actions are expressed in nouns which derive from verbs (nominalizations):

> Upon completion of the orientation session, the one-month training of the salesmen with the sales managers will begin.

One can change this sentence into a more vigorous one as follows:

> When they complete the orientation session, the salesmen will train with the sales mangers for one month.

Changing the noun *completion* to the verb *complete*, and the noun *training* to the action verb *train*, makes this sentence more readable. Two other principles of readability which students can learn easily are as follows:

Avoid the negative.

Eliminate unnecessary emphatics and empty expressions.

Thus, the sentence "Not many students did not buy the yearbook," is more difficult to understand than "Many students bought a yearbook." State things positively whenever possible. In another example, the sentence, "For the most part, Majestic is a fast horse; the fact is, however, that for all intents and purposes any horse can beat him on a muddy track." is less readable than:

> Majestic is a fast horse; however, any horse can beat him on a muddy track."

The second sentence has been pruned of the empty "filler" expression, "for the most part," "the fact is," and "for all intents and purposes."

To sum up, students can easily learn these four principles of readability:

1. The "doer" of the sentence should be in the subject position. The action of the sentence should be in the verb.

2. In general, it is best to express action in a verb.

3. Avoid the negative.

4. Prune sentences of empty expressions.

Other principles of readability are contained in the list at the end of the chapter.

Teach Students to Make Connections

Transitions can strengthen the overall coherence of a paper and can also contribute to a smoother style. Transitions are achieved by a number of connecting devices: grammatical signals, such as conjunctions; punctuation signals, such as colons; or verbal cues, such as pronouns. For example, you might have the student read the paragraph below and notice the many connecting devices which have been used to tie the paragraph together.

1) Our family camping trip required a great deal of advance preparation. 2) Once we decided where we wanted to go, we had to arrange for campsite reservations, since during the summer, campgrounds fill up very quickly. 3) Then we had to assemble a great deal of equipment: a tent, a stove, sleeping bags, ground pads, a light, cooking utensils, and an ice chest. 4) Some of these we already had, but others we had to buy, rent, or borrow. 5) Finally, we had to plan our meals in advance, as we were not going to be near stores for most of the trip. 6) It was a lot of work. 7) But our camping trip was really successful because we had taken the time to prepare.

Some of the transitional devices you may note are as follows:

Punctuation:	the use of the colon in sentence #3 cues the reader that a list will follow.
Pronouns:	The use of "we" in sentences 2, 3, 4, and 5 and the use of "our" in sentence #6 refers back to "our" family.
Summary nouns:	The collective noun, "equipment" refers to "tent, sleeping bags, and ground pads," etc.
Rewording of the same idea:	"To prepare" in the last sentence refers back to "advance preparation."
Parallel structure:	The grammatical parallel construction in sentence #4—"Some of these we had, but others we had to buy, rent, or borrow," emphasizes the parallel connection of the idea.

Grammar and Punctuation

No question in composition studies has generated as much controversy as that concerning whether or not the teaching of formal grammar helps improve student writing. Whenever the "literacy crisis" is mentioned, someone is bound to suggest the teaching of grammar and numerous textbooks are published each year which include several sections of grammar based exercises. Yet several studies also suggest that "the teaching of formal grammar has a negligible, or because it usually displaces some instruction and practice in composition, even a harmful effect on improvement in writing" (Braddock et al 37–38).

A useful discussion of the controversy concerning grammar may be found in Patrick Hartwell's article in *College English*, "Grammar, Grammars, and Teaching of Grammar" (1984). Hartwell maintains that "seventy-five years of experimental research has for all practical purposes told us nothing. The two sides are unable to agree on how to interpret such research" (106). Yet tutors in the writing center who wish to help students with sentence level errors often wish that grammar could provide the needed assistance; moreover, students are often referred to the writing center with specific instructions to "work on grammar." Students, themselves, are often under the impression that learning grammar will help them learn to write.

Finding a Pattern of Error

Working with students on a one-to-one basis in the writing center can help you locate those areas in the student's own writing which may respond easily to limited instruction in grammar. Perhaps the students never learned that a comma usually follows introductory phrases or clauses as in the sentence.

"As I was going to St. Ives, I met a man with seven wives."

A simple explanation and a few examples can help students understand this concept. However, in looking for a pattern of error, it is important to distinguish between genuine errors and those due simply to carelessness. Having students read sentences aloud can help you determine this. Often when students read their writing aloud, they will correct a variety of spelling, grammar and punctuation errors, often without noticing that what they read departs from what they wrote.

If you do find an area where a limited grammatical explanation might help eliminate error, be careful that your explanations do not cause more confusion than enlightenment. Most students do not have a working knowledge of grammar; thus any grammatical terms you use must be accompanied by very specific examples of what you mean. For instance, suppose a student has written a sentence such as the following:

Singing in the shower, my foot slipped.

In helping the student understand this error, do not say "the problem here is that you have a 'dangling participle, since many students do not understand the word "participle." Instead, explain that the word "singing" must refer to a specific person in the sentence. The student will then be able to recognize that since no person is referred to in the sentence and since, obviously, it could not be the "foot" which was singing, that the sentence needs to be revised. A few examples of this sort and some practice revising sentences with similar difficulties will help students understand this sort of error.

Limited Grammar Instruction

Students are frequently referred to the writing center because they write sentence fragments, run-on sentences, or have errors in subject-verb agreement; moreover, these errors are often those which most disturb readers. For helping students recognize these types of errors, it can be helpful for students to acquire a limited knowledge of such "grammatical" terms as "subject," "verb," "dependent and independent clause." At the end of this chapter is an exercise sheet derived from Muriel Harris and de Beaugrande that can aid students in working with sentences. Teaching students a few grammatical terms can also help you explain punctuation errors.

Editing and Proofreading

Once the thesis is focused, the structure is set, the paragraphs are connected, and the sentences are varied, readable, and graceful, finally, it is time to edit the paper for error and proofread for spelling and typographical mistakes. This is the time for you to discern a pattern of error that the student can learn to correct. This is the time to instruct the student on recognition of a sentence fragment or a run-on, to test for the agreement of his subjects and verbs, to know where to place his commas. Numerous instructional materials exist on these relatively easy to teach skills, and computerized style and spelling checkers can also be extremely useful.

You can also help the student develop proofreading skills. Reading aloud to a friend or to oneself is an excellent way to detect careless error. Or you might recommend that students read their papers into a tape recorder, listen back to it without the paper in front of them, then listen again, marking errors and making corrections. Another suggestion is to have students covers all lines with an index card or book and go over each line, one at a time. Isolating lines can focus attention on surface detail and surface error, which may be lost in context when the paper is viewed as a whole. Or, another idea is to have students read their papers backwards. It's important, though, that students understand that they cannot rip the paper out of the typewriter or printer and then hand it in. Even the most experienced writer and the most careful typist has to proofread before submitting a paper.

You might have students work through the following questions when they edit their papers.

1. Are most of the sentences subject-verb-object sentences? Or are they wordy, passive constructions which use "there is" and "there are."

2. Can any sentences be combined?

3. Do the sentences move easily from one to another?

4.   Are there errors in punctuation? Spelling? Usage?

5.   Have I proofread for careless error?

Imitation

Although the goal of writing center instruction is to help students do their own work as much as possible, it is often helpful to actually show students a writing technique and have them imitate what you do. In the past, imitation was a preferred and respected teaching method; through imitation, it was thought that learners could expand previous ineffective methods into something more effective which ultimately became their own. Sometimes, then, it might be useful for a tutor to show a student how to develop examples, correct an awkward sentence, maybe rephrase something. Other suggestions might include showing students how to look for examples in a literary text or using the process of association to expand or redirect a thesis. Numerous writing techniques we have developed for ourselves can be acquired by students through the process of imitation.

Teach the Student What Works for You

All of you were or are students; all of you have written papers; many of you will continue to write throughout your lives. Because you write, you have developed strategies which work for you, and these are the strategies you should recommend to your students in the writing center. Tell your students if you use scissors and paste to restructure your papers or about typing papers triple space so that you can revise easily. Maybe you work with a word processor or you xerox many copies of your early drafts so that you can easily manipulate the structure. Talk about what works for you, and your students may find your suggestions very helpful. A writing center conference should be a place where students learn the tools of the trade, techniques they can continue to use at other times. The strategies suggested in this chapter are only a beginning. You, as writing center teacher, will develop many more.

Working with Sentences*

If you are working with a student who is having trouble with Sentence Fragments, Run-On-Sentences, or Subject Verb Agreement, this information can help the student identify these errors.

---

*This exercise is derived from the work of Muriel Harris, *Teaching One-To-One: The Writing Conference* (Illinois: NCTE, 1986) and Robert de Beaugrande, "Forward to the Basics: Getting Down to Grammar," *College Composition and Communication* 35 (1984): 358–67.

1. Finding the Subject and the Predicate.

All sentences have two parts, the naming part, called the **subject,** and the part which tells something about the subject, called the **predicate.**

Examine the following sentences:

> The rabbit jumped across the field.
> The actress flung her script out of the window.

To find the predicate: Make up a who/what question about the sentence. Eg. *What* jumped across the field? *Who* flung her script out of the window? The **predicate** is all the words in the who/what question which was in the original sentence.

> predicate = jumped across the field.
> predicate = flung her script out of the window.

The subject is the rest of the sentence.

> subject = The rabbit
> subject = The actress

Practice: Find the subject and the predicate in the following sentences by asking a who/what question:

1. Mothers can usually figure out when a child is lying.

2. Dogs and cats are extremely popular pets in the United States.

3. Mary gulped down her sandwich and ran out of the room.

4. The room was full of furniture of all shapes and sizes.

2. Finding Independent and Dependent Clauses

Independent Clauses

An **independent clause** has a subject and a predicate and can stand alone as a complete sentence.

To find out whether a sentence is an independent clause, make up a yes/no question about the sentence, that is, a question which sensibly could be answered with yes or no. Eg.

> The rabbit jumped across the field.
> Did the rabbit jump across the field?

> The actress flung her script across the room.
> Did the actress fling her script across the room?

Only the independent clauses can sensibly be rephrased as yes/no questions?

Dependent Clauses and Fragments

Only an independent clause can stand alone as a sentence. Some word groups are "dependent clauses." They have a subject and a predicate, but cannot stand alone because they need to be part of another sentence. Eg.

Because she was insulted.

A word group such as this is a **dependent clause**. If it is used as if it were a sentence, it is called a **fragment**. Writing fragments instead of sentences can cause your writing to be graded down. To see whether or not a sentence is a fragment, make up a yes/no question. Eg.

Did because she was insulted? (This makes no sense) The word group "because she was insulted" is not a sentence, but a fragment. It would go well with the first sentence, "The actress flung her script across the room." Thus, "The actress flung her script across the room because she was insulted."

Detecting Run-on Sentences or Comma Splices

Run-on sentences are two independent clauses fused together. Eg.
He hit the ball in the air the catcher made a grab for it.

A comma splice consists of two independent clauses linked by a comma. Eg.

He hit the ball in the air, the catcher made a grab for it.

To detect whether or not you have a run-on sentence or a comma splice, ask a yes/no question about the sentence. In a run-on sentence or coma splice you will get two questions instead of one. Eg.

Did he hit the ball? Did the catcher make a grab for it?

Run-on sentences and comma splices are other errors which can lower grades. Practice in these techniques can help students work with their sentences.

Sentence Combining: *A Short List of Resources*

Christensen, Francis and Bonniejean Christensen. *A New Rhetoric.* New York: Harper and Row, 1976.

Daiker Donald, Andrew Kerek and Max Morenberg, eds. *Sentence Combining and the Teaching of Writing.* Conway, Arkansas: L and S Books, 1979.

————. *The Writer's Options: College Sentence Combining.* New York: Harper and Row, 1979.

O'Hare, Frank. *Sentence Combining: Improving Student Writing Without Formal Grammar Instruction.* NCTE, 1973.

———. *Sentencecraft.* Columbus Ohio: Girn and Company, 1974.

Strong, William. *Sentence Combining.* New York: Random House, 1973.

———. *Sentence Combining and Paragraph Building.* New York: Random House, 1981.

Some Additional Ideas on Readability

Earlier in this section, I suggested four principles of readability which students can learn easily. However, numerous other factors have been cited as contributing to the "readability" of a text, among them:

1. Sentence length,

2. word length,

3. the number of prepositions in the text,

4. the number of different arguments in the text,

5. the inferences required to connect a text base,

6. the number of long term memory searches and reorganizations that are necessary to construct the text.

There are also about fifty readability "formulas"; however, what must be understood about these formulas is that they have preditive value only. If long words and sentences *caused* comprehension difficulty, then shortening them would remove the difficulty, a procedure which does not often work. For example, it is said that an abstract complex discussion is accomplished by many conjunctions, yet the conjunctions do not *cause* the difficulty—they are merely an index of it. Formulas are obviously limited. They cannot be discriminate between scrambled and well-ordered words or scrambled sentences or paragraphs.

However, although surface level factors do not by themselves determine the readability of a text, there are certain stylistic features we can help students become aware of so that they can make their writing more readable. Below are twelve techniques developed by Margaret McLaren which students can use to improve the "readability" of their papers:

1. Do not attempt to sound "important" when you write. Try to be natural. Most of us talk more naturally than we write. So if we can write accurately and concisely but at the same time recapture the relaxed informality—not of course the sentence structure—we use when speaking, we can communicate

with our readers more effectively. For instance, we'd never say:

> We regret to inform clients that the policy of this institute is to disallow applications for credit except in inordinately exceptional circumstances.

We're much more likely to say instead:

> Sorry, we don't allow credit except in very special circumstances.

Why not write that too, perhaps changing the "don't" to "do not" if we need to follow the conventions of formal writing?

2. Use the natural subject-verb-object work order of English as directly as you can. Natural speech patterns make the subject to the sentence the agent or doer of the action.

We tend to say:

> Mr. Smith kept his appointment

more readily than:

> His appointment was kept by Mr. Smith.

Passives do have a place when writers want to be hesitant or are reluctant to accept responsibility for an action. The sentence

> His appointment was kept by Mr. Smith.

may be necessary if we want to focus attention on the appointment rather than on Mr. Smith, but it lacks the punch of the active version. Try to state who is the doer (or agent) in the subject of the sentence. Try to state what is being done in the verb.

3. Use verbs rather than nouns.

Instead of saying:

> Our first requirement is the identification of the probable nature of the engine failure.

we'd do better to write:

> We need to find out why the engine will not work.

4.   Prefer the concrete to the abstract.

  Instead of saying:

  The new ownership has followed the policy of purchasing mini-computer type equipment.

  we can simply say:

  The new owners have bought a mini-computer.

5.   Use simple words, if they mean the same as their longer equivalents, but be sure to use words appropriate to your readers. If you are writing for zoologists, "balaena australis" might be the best term; if you are writing for almost anyone else, "whale" most certainly would be better.

6.   Prune "fluff words" wherever you can. When we're talking we use quite a number of words which carry little meaning but give us time to think. Early written drafts are likely to contain several empty words like "case" and "factor" and "situation" which simply weight down the sentences. They may also contain wordy prepositional phrases like "subsequent to" and "in the vicinity of" which can well be cut.

7.   Look closely at words commonly found in pairs, such as these:

past memories	each individual
true facts	personal opinion
specified in detail	completely finish

Often the idea can be more forcefully conveyed by one word.

8.   Be sparing with impersonal constructions beginning with "it" or "there," and with verbs which do no more than link parts of sentences. In particular try to replace the word "is" which Richard Lanham (*Revising Prose*) calls the "weakest verb in the language."

The sentence:

  There are sixteen people in the room who think. . . .

can become:

  The sixteen people in the room think. . . .

9.   Prefer the affirmative to the negative.

> Not many candidates have not succeeded in this course.

is more dynamic worded this way:

> Few candidates failed this course.

10.   Spurn cliches. Imagery can spark up any kind of writing so long as it is fresh; wilted, it only makes writing look uncared for and takes up potentially useful space.

11.   Vary your vocabulary, sentence structure and paragraph length wherever you can. If your sentences tend to be two or three lines long each, play around with them so that some are half a line long and others much longer. At key places use short sentences.

12.   Achieve semantic closure as early as possible. The more a reader must keep in mind before achieving semantic closure, the more difficult the reading will be.

A sentence such as the following is difficult to process:

> Grandview school children, who were dismissed from school yesterday when a chemical explosion occurred in the surrounding area causing several thousand dollars worth of damage to plant and animal life, among them Mrs. Colingsworth's dog, Rover, not to mention her prize orchard, were allowed to return to school today.

Readability: A Short List of Resources

Kintsch, W. and Vipond, D. "Reading Comprehension and Readability in Educational Practice and Psychological Theory," in *Perspectives on Memory Research*, ed. Lars-Goran Nilsson. Hillsdale, New Jersey: Lawrence Erlbaum Associates, 1979.

Klare, G. R. "Assessing Readability." *Reading Research Quarterly* (1974/5), 10, 62–102.

Lanham, R. *Revising Prose*. New York: Charles Scribner's Sons, 1979.

McLaren, Margaret. "Another Approach to Readability," *Journal of Business Communication* 19, 2 (Spring 1982): 51–58.

Williams, Joseph. *Style: Ten Lessons in Clarity and Grace*. Glencoe, Illinois: Scott Foresmann, 1981.

Additional Works Discussing the Role of Grammar on Writing Instruction

Hunter, Susan and Ray Wallace, eds. *The Place of Grammar in Writing Instruction.* Portsmouth: Boyton/Cook, 1995.

Noguchi, Rei. *Grammar and the Teaching of Writing.* Urbana: NCTE, 1991.

Weaver, Constance. *Teaching Grammar in Context.* Portsmouth: Boynton/Cook, 1996.

In diagnosing problems with a text and proposing revision strategies, though, be careful not to overwhelm the student with too many suggestions at one time. To quickly reel off what may need additional work can be confusing and intimidating for students, and some may then not attempt to do anything. So if you wish a student to learn some organizational strategies so that the next paper will be better organized, you should not then also focus on sentence level errors, such as sentence fragments or comma placement. You might aim for a policy of "one strategy per session." Or you might ask yourself the question " What does the student now know how to do that he or she could not do before?" Asking this question will serve as a check against using the conference merely for "quick-fix" rewrites, from which the student might emerge with a revised draft, but without having acquired additional writing ability. The point to remember is that a writing conference should be used not only to point out to students where their work needs revision, but also to help students learn effective ways to revise. Don't simply discuss what ought to be done; suggest ways to do it, and, when possible, *show* students how to do it, so they can then do it themselves.

Work Cited

Bartholmae, David. "The Study of Error." *College Composition and Communication* 31 (1980): 253–269.

Braddock, Richard, Richard Lloyd Jones, and Lowell Schoer. *Research in Written Composition.* Urbana, Illinois: National Council of Teachers of English, 1963.

Hartwell, Patrick. "Grammar, Grammar, and the Teaching of Grammar." *College English* 47 (1985): 105–27.

Lindemann. *A Rhetoric for Writing Teachers.* New York: Oxford University Press, 1982.

Strong, William. *Sentence Combining:* A Composing Book. New York: Random House, 1973.

Williams, Joseph. Style: *Ten Lessons in Clarity and Grace.* Glencoe, Illinois: Scott Foresman, 1981.

Dealing with Learning Disabilities in the Writing Center

Julie Neff-Lippman
University of Puget Sound

Tall, slender and blond, Alex strides into the Writing Center in white tennis shorts and T-shirt, smiles and says, "I think I have a 1 o'clock appointment for someone to look at my politics paper." Putting his Calculus book and Egyptian art book on the desk, he pulls a disk and a hard copy of the paper from his backpack as he sits down in the chair reserved for the writer. "My politics professor says that he won't accept this paper as is; I've spell checked it three times, and I still can't see what's wrong with it," Alex says.

Alex looks like any other sophomore at the University—confident, active, intelligent. Except there is one difference between Alex and other sophomores: Alex was diagnosed when he was 8 with a serious learning disability in reading and written language, classic dyslexia. While Alex has trouble with written language, he has no trouble with spatial tasks. He's a physics and studio art major and plans on going to architectural school when he graduates from college. He plays varsity tennis and has few social problems except occasionally feeling "stupid" when he can't spell or transcribe a word correctly.

Alex's dyslexia was diagnosed in fourth grade, and he has found ways to cope with it. In middle school, he received help with spelling and transcription while he was enrolled in a gifted program. When he took the SATs, he received extra time and scored 500 verbal and 750 math. Since he's been on campus, he's received regular help from the learning disabilities specialist, but he prefers working on his papers in the Writing Center. Alex understands his disability and has taken steps to receive the help he needs.

But Alex still has problems. His politics professor has told him he doesn't believe in learning disabilities. "You're a bright young man," he said to Alex. "You could correct those errors if you just became more vigilant. Hang up that tennis racquet and put some effort into learning to spell." His English professor told him that his disability was simply a "crutch for the privileged."

Ten minutes late, Mari trudges into the Writing Center, looking as if she is carrying the weight of an elephant on her ample shoulders. Before her backpack hits the floor, she has taken a seat and is talking. She leans over the chair, and touches the tutor's arm as she continues to talk: "I started this paper, but I only have a page and a half and it's supposed to be at least four. Hot out. It shouldn't be so hot in October. I just can't study in this heat. Did I tell you my car broke down last week? It's no wonder I can't write this paper. I was so worried last week I couldn't start it and now it's due day after tomorrow." Words tumble out of her mouth. Mari leans closer to the tutor as the tutor pulls back in her chair.

Mari has a spatial learning disability. Her disability affects her visual perception and her ability to interact socially. (Neff 85) She speaks inappropriately and at inappropriate times, she has a poor sense of timing and can't measure social spaces. Getting organized is one of her biggest problems along with developing an appropriate structure for her writing. Although she occasionally misspells words, she doesn't have the severe problems with spelling that Alex does. Organization and development are her biggest problems with writing, but she also has trouble seeing the spatial features of sentences; for instance, punctuation.

Once Mari focuses and gets herself organized, she is capable of producing college-level work, though not without a struggle. She was diagnosed with the spatial disability after her senior year in high school, so she hasn't had much experience dealing with her learning problems or developing compensatory strategies. A misfit throughout high school, she also has numerous social problems that she's working on with a counselor and with the learning disabilities specialist. Mari essentially has no friends in her own peer group. She spends time with the resident assistant in her dorm, the girl who passes out towels at the pool, and the receptionist in the counseling office. Occasionally stopping by just to say "hi," she enjoys the writing center because the tutors there are friendly, positive, and encouraging. Her professors ignore her as much as they can, complaining that her constant talking takes up too much class time and office time. One biology professor told her, after she had knocked over a whole row of test tubes, that people like her "shouldn't be in college." Another had limited her to just two questions per class meeting.

Because in many ways students with learning disabilities challenge writing center beliefs about how much help students should receive, students like Mari and Alex raise significant practical, legal, and moral questions for all of us who work in writing centers.

- How much help should we provide?
- How do we work with someone who is socially inappropriate?
- How can we help someone who is so disorganized?
- Should we edit the student's paper?
- How do we deal with faculty who have little knowledge or understanding about disabilities?
- Are you sure we're not just wasting our time with students who shouldn't be here anyway?
- How do we know if a student has a learning disability?
- How much time should we devote to students with learning disabilities?

Understanding Learning Disabilities

Because of misinformation in the popular press about students, many people do not understand learning disabilities. Before you begin working with learning disabled students, it is important for you to be aware of some of the mistaken beliefs people have about learning disabled people.

Checking Your Attitudes About Learning Disabilities

To check your own attitudes about learning disabilities, decide how much you agree or disagree with each of the following statements. Put a 5 beside it if you strongly agree; a 4 if you generally agree; a 3 if you are neutral; a two if you disagree; and a 1 if you strongly disagree. When you've finished, share your answers with others in the group.

1. Learning disabled students belong in special education, not in college programs.

2. Learning disabled students are less intelligent than other students.

3. Learning disabilities don't really exist. They are just a socially constructed condition to help disadvantaged students.

4. Most students will out-grow their learning disability.

5. Learning disabilities are difficult to diagnose and the diagnosis must be done by someone trained in the field.

6. Learning disabilities only affect one or two aspects of a student's life.

7. Students with learning disabilities may get into college, but they don't graduate.

8. Medication can cure a learning disability.

9. Faculty may decide whether or not to grant a student accommodations.

10. Learning disabled students simply don't go to the best schools.

11. Learning disabled students are looking for excuses.

12. Students with learning disabilities shouldn't get too much help in college because eventually they'll have to make it on their own.

When you've finished reading the chapter, come back to this list to see if your answers have changed.

What Is a Learning Disability?

Learning disabilities grow out of some kind of brain dysfunction that manifests itself in the discrepancy between potential and performance on a series of standardized tests (Stockdale and Poussin). Although there is still some disagreement about the precise definition of learning disabilities, a working definition provided by the *National Joint Committee on Learning Disabilities,* in 1988 is as follows:

> Learning disabilities is a general term that refers to a heterogeneous group of disorders manifested by significant difficulties in the acquisition and use of listening, speaking, reading, writing, reasoning, or mathematical abilities. These discoders are intrinsic to the individual, presumed to be due to central nervous systm dysfunction, and occur throughout the life cycle. Although learning disabilities may occur with other disabling conditions (for example, sensory impairment or emotional disturbance) or with extrinsic influences (such as cultural difference, insufficient or inappropriate instruction), they are not the result of those conditions or influences.

Learning problems that grow out of a physical condition, visual or hearing impairment, retardation, emotional problems, or a disadvantaged home or school situation are not considered learning disabilities.

Some learning disabilities can be traced to particular brain injuries; for example, the person with receptive language processing problems had normal brain function until he suffered a brain injury in a car accident. Others are born with a brain dysfunction such as Turner's Syndrome, which has physiological cause.

In 1985 studying brains of cadavers, Albert Gallaberta discovered significant differences between the brains of people with dyslexia and those without. (222) More recently, researchers using positron emission tomography (PET) observed differences in the functioning of normal brains and brains with language or spatial processing problems. Researchers have also used magnetic resonance imaging (MRI) to study differences in brain structure, which may help explain learning disabilities. (Gaddes & Edgell 5)

While there are many different kinds of learning disabilities, there are three characteristics that student with disabilities in written language share:

1. The individual demonstrates average to superior ability in areas not affected by the disability.

2. Each has a significant discrepancy between apparent ability and actual performance due to a processing deficit.

3. The deficit is not caused by lack of effort or substandard schooling or cultural differences. (West)

How Do We Know Who Has a Learning Disability?

Using a series of nationally normed standardized tests like the Woodcock-Johnson Tests of Achievement, learning disability specialists can determine if a person is learning disabled. The Woodcock test assesses the individual's performance and measures it against his or her potential. Giving the tests and analyzing the results takes specialized training in the area of learning disabilities, testing, and /or assessment. As in most things, expertise in one area does not mean expertise in another: most doctors, special education teachers, and psychologists are not qualified to give and evaluate these tests unless they have special training to do so.

Most faculty and most of us who work in writing centers are not qualified to determine who has a learning disability and who does not. Yet students with disabilities have serious implications for writing centers. How do we know who qualifies for what services? And how can we protect the students' right to confidentiality? Appropriate documentation is essential. Many students believe they have a learning disability ("My uncle's a doctor and he thinks so." "My third grade teacher told me I am.") But what legally qualifies as a learning disability varies from state to state and has changed over time. (Neff 82)

Writing Centers need to work with the learning disabilities coordinator or the 504 officer on campus. To deny a student with a learning disability this appropriate help violates his or her civil rights. To provide a student who only thinks he has a disability with accommodations will hurt the credibility of the writing center with faculty and will provide the student who does not have a learning disability with an inappropriate crutch.

Writing centers need to have a working relationship with the college's coordinator of disabilities or the Affirmative Action officer. With the students' permission, the writing center director can provide the tutors with a list of legally qualified individuals and what they qualify for as it relates to writing.

Asking students if they have a disability, or taking their word for it or the word of a faculty member is a dangerous practice—the kind of practice that can put the school in danger of a lawsuit, can compromise the students' right to learn, and can hurt the reputation of the writing center.

Who Can Have a Learning Disability?

Students with learning disabilities like Mari and Alex have been enrolling in colleges over the past few decades. As the diagnosis of disabilities improves and as students with learning disabilities increasingly see college, rather than a trade, as an option, more and more students with learning disabilities are choosing college.

Although there is some evidence that there is a genetic basis for learning disabilities (Levine 399–404), learning disabilities do not afflict any particular group of people. Caucasians are as likely to be learning disabled as are Blacks or Hispanics. Men are somewhat more likely to have learning disabilities than women, but the gender gap is not large. (Galaburda 199) Old people as well as young have this disability. Typically people who have a learning disability are not "stupid" or "slow"; they have normal to above normal intelligence with a problem or problems in certain areas. In fact, it is possible for someone to be gifted and learning disabled at the same time—Thomas Jefferson, Albert Einstein, and Thomas Edison (Lovitt). People with learning disabilities choose all kinds of colleges from community and vocational colleges to prestigious four year institutions. They also choose all kinds of careers—medicine, law, architecture, publishing, and academics.

Do Learning Disabilities Really Exist?

Although there have been books like Gerald Coles' *The Learning Mystique,* 1987, that attempt to debunk the idea of learning disabilities, more recent brain research (Gaddes, Edgell 5) has shown that there is a physiological basis for a learning disability. You may also encounter faculty or other university personnel who will say that they don't believe in learning disabilities. Of course, they are entitled to their beliefs; however, they are not entitled to discriminate against people with learning disabilities any more than they are entitled to discriminate against people because of their race, religion, or sexual orientation. The Americans with Disabilities Act (ADA) of 1992 and the Rehabilitation Act of 1973 guarantees students with disabilities the right to equal access to university programs and activities. "Colleges and universities must give individuals with disabilities equal opportunity and equal access to employment opportunities, programs, services and activities in the most integrated setting possible.

Institutions must refrain from separating or segregating indiviuals with disabilities from others." (DiScala 5) Learning disabled students may seek services from a learning disabilities specialist, but they are also entitled to visit the writing center. Many students with disabilities prefer the writing center because they use it along with students who do not have a disability.

It is to everyone's benefit to work out appropriate and "reasonable" accommodation for any student with a disability in the classroom or in the writing center. Failure to do so could mean a law suit or a time-consuming investigation by the Office of Civil Rights.

Working With Alex

In some ways you might treat Alex as you would any other student—finding out about the assignment, when it is due, and who the audience is—looking first at the higher order concerns (thesis/focus, organization, development, and voice/tone) and then moving on to the sentence-level problems. In many ways, writing center practices are perfect for students with learning disabilities.

In Alex's case, the errors are so numerous that it is difficult to check for higher order concerns. In addition, Alex's professor has asked for the paper by this afternoon. Because Alex is dyslexic, he is entitled under "reasonable accommodations" to a full edit, meaning that he might have someone just "fix" the paper, but in the long-run the "fix" is not going to help Alex become a better writer. It's much better to involve Alex in the process. Involving Alex also means that you will not be changing the ideas as Alex and the tutor sit at the computer together to work on Alex's paper.

The Assignment

> *Take the position of the guardian ad litem and argue for either allepathic or homeopathic medical treatment for Tim Z. The paper should be no longer than 3 pages.*

 ### Alex's Paper/*The Allopathic Decision*

The recomendtion of the guardian regard the minor, Tim Z , is that he undergo allopathic treaent for the confined diagnosis of acute lymphoblastic leukemia. Surpport for this determination exists in the fact that the only documented scientific evidence resides on the side of allpathic medicine. Since the goal of the guardian ad litem is to ensure the best interest of the child, survival of the minor is the main consideration. Therefore, allopathic medicine is the only solution.

Evidence supportig this concusion exit in the fats. Though allopthic treatment coexist of a regimen of x-rays and internous drugs, nine percent of patent into remission. After this point, a complete recovery often results upon a survival of three years. those who reach the three year mark, e-five percent survive an additional year f (Anton, Strauss, Stone). Transfered, this means alpathic medicine a tantmount to a provn success.

Side-lines of allopathic treat, which are individual subjecti, and may nt occur, include sterility, stuntd growth, and earning disorders. Success in treatig the later exist with x-rays and intravenous drugs (Anton, Strauss, Stone). Regardl of the side-affects of allopathic medine, to suffer side-affects the minor must be alive.

No scientific base to support homeopathic treatment. In fact, regarding the basis for this method, Andrew Weil states, "homeopaths do not know" (37). Additionally, the place effect plays such a large role that it skrews the percep of the results. This affect, which is the success use of inverted solutions, has nothing to do with homeo and everything to do with the manifestation of "a person's beliefs and hopes . . . combined with their suggested ability (Carroll, 2). No data except to support successful homeopathic treatment of this cancer, therefore the side-effects of treatment parallel the no treatment decision.

The eletion of no medcal treatment provide two possible consquences, the first posibility is that with in four to six months the minor will die.. During this time, he will suffer enlarged orgasms which are likely to dysfunction, anemia, increased bleeding, fever, and susceptibility to infection (Anton, Strauss, Stone). The second is that the child will achieve spontaneous readmission. However, this is not highly probably, and is not a freezable alternative.

Without allopathic treatment Tim Z will suffer the painful affects of this killer dis-ease, however with allopathic treatment, there are possible results. The first is the remision will not occur, and the minor will suffer. The second is that the treatment will be reflective, but the mirror will go into spontaneous readmission. These results are identical to the homeopathic or not treatment situations. In the end, the third and greater probabity is that, with allpathic treatment, the minor will enter remission, his suffer will end, and he will live.

The Writing Conferences

Fortunately, Alex brought the paper on disk. Having a tutor correct a hard copy would be of little use to Alex because when he copied the changes into the text on the computer, he would likely make the same mistakes again and some new ones too. Therefore, sitting at the computer with Alex is the best solution; besides, anyone would need Alex to help interpret the paper. The tutor should be at the keyboard with Alex sitting beside her, so that he can be a full participant in the process. This kind of collaboration lets Alex maintain control of the text.

To begin, the tutor skims the paper to get a sense of it. Although the argument is difficult to follow, she realizes that both sentence structure and word choice aren't those of a basic writer. Next she reads the title aloud: The Allopathic. The tutor pauses giving Alex a chance to make changes.

Alex: Oh, that should be Allopathic Decision.

The tutor makes the change. Even more than most students, students with learning disabilities need positive feedback and encouragement. So often they're labeled as "dumb" or "lazy" because of spelling mistakes and other surface errors.

Tutor: Sounds like an interesting paper from the title. It must have been hard to take a stand when you had to include so much in so little space.

Alex: Yes, I spent hours doing the searches for information and then I had to eliminate a lot of it.

Tutor reads the first line of the paper out loud. "The recommendation of the guardian regard the minor."
At this point, the tutor pauses allowing Alex time to think about changes.

Alex: "Oh that should be 'guardian ad litem regarding.'"

The tutor types in the missing word and corrects the spelling; then she reads the corrected version.

Alex: "The rest of that sentence should be 'Tim Z is that he undergo allopathis (traditional) treatment for the confirmed diagnosis of acute lymphoblastic leukemia.'"

As Alex says the sentence the tutor makes the corrections repeating Alex's words to make sure the sentences say exactly what he wants them to say.
Because Alex is already developing a tone that says "How could I be so dumb as to write that," the tutor reassures Alex as she goes on.

Tutor: This next section sounds great.

Paragraph two has plenty of errors. The tutor continues to read aloud and type while Alex makes the corrections. The tutor's attitude to these changes is "no big deal." The collaboration continues as Alex and tutor take turns reading and correcting. Interestingly, Alex can always hear the wrong word even when he can't see it, and he knows the words even though he had trouble getting them down on paper. The combination of the tutor's voice and the written text helps Alex find his own errors. The tutor doesn't want to appropriate Alex's paper, so she continues with the give-and-take nature of the conference.

The process is slow, but Alex is entitled by law to a full edit of his papers. This editing may feel unfair to you or to other students who want the tutor's time, in the same way some feel handicapped parking places are unfair. But these accommodations, along with handicapped parking spaces, are just a few ways new laws have made things more fair for people who have disabilities.

Working with Alex is a pleasure and tutors look forward to appointments with him. Hard-working, personable, and most appreciative of the help, he usually brings his papers to the writing center rather than to disability services because he likes the atmosphere and the attitude of the tutors. He is learning strategies for dealing with his written work at the same time he is making the product acceptable to his professor.

As the tutor clicks on the printer icon, Alex says, "Thanks so much for the help. I couldn't have done this without you. And without the edits, Taranovski wouldn't accept the paper."

Working with Mari

Mari presents a whole different set of problems, not the least of which is her social inappropriateness. Her visual spatial and motor spatial disability means she has trouble with numerous spatial tasks—finding her classrooms, managing time, and organizing papers.

Before the writing conference actually begins, it is reasonable for the tutor to set perimeters regarding Mari's behavior. Mari is late for her appointment and like other students she risks losing it if she is late. It is appropriate for the tutor to repeat the rules about late arrivals to Mari. Because Mari has violated social conventions of touching and distance, the tutor needs to correct Mari's behavior verbally. Mari cannot read facial expressions and may ignore other social markers. The tutor will need to ask Mari not to touch her and may need to tell her to sit back in the chair. If Mari forgets, the tutor should mention it again. Similarly the tutor will need to control the conversation by saying to Mari that it is now Mari's turn to listen and the tutor's turn to talk. Being this explicit with most people might seem rude, but it will help a person with spatial learning disabilities learn to manage his or her personal space.

Typical Behaviors

While Mari does not exhibit rigidity or manipulative behavior, she does exhibit many of the typical behaviors of students with learning disabilities, especially those who have not had sufficient time to deal with their learning problems and adopt appropriate compensatory strategies. Note that Alex does not, at this time, exhibit any of these behaviors.

1. Anxiety over beginning a paper

2. Negative self talk which detracts from focusing on the topic

3. Difficulty with time (late for appointments or confused about which day)

4. Difficulty attending to task

5. Multiple excuses for the poor quality of work

6. Anger concerning the number of corrections needed

7. Difficulty accepting the parameters of an assignment

8. Rigid behavior

9. Manipulative behavior

10. Inappropriate social interaction concerning, space, time, and speech volume.

Starting the Appointment

With so many problems, where does a tutor begin with Mari? First the tutor needs to take control of the situation and establish appropriate social boundaries. It is possible to be firm yet pleasant and friendly.

Tutor: Hi Mari. It's good to see you. You're lucky. Two more minutes and you would have lost your appointment."

Mari: I know; I know. I'm always late and always behind.

Tutor: Well, you're here now and that's good. Why don't you sit back a bit, like this two shoe lengths. It makes me nervous to sit too close to someone.

Mari needs this kind of instruction, and because the tutor put it in a positive way and smiled encouragingly, Mari does not take offense.

Tutor: "So Mari, what are you working on today? You always have interesting topics. What's the assignment?"

Mari: "I have to write a 4–6 page paper for my Introduction to Music class."

Tutor: "What's the topic?"

Mari: "It's suppose to compare and contrast two musicians or composers from the same era."

Tutor: "Who did you pick?"

Mari: "It's not long enough and I know I have some spelling problems I've said everything I have to say. I'm never good at papers. I don't know what to do!"

Tutor: "But who did you pick?"

Mari: Well, I wanted to do Miles Davis. I've always like some of his small groups and his sidemen like Julian "Cannonball" Adderly on the alto sax and Paul Chambers on bass. I really love jazz; I don't know why. Here's the paper.

Tutor: "What was the assignment?"

The Assignment

Compare and contrast two composers or performers who lived and worked during the same time period. The paper must be at least three pages, typed and double spaced.

Mari's Paper

Charlie Parker got into the jazz scene at a relativly young age, incontrast with John Coltrane, who did not become poplar untill a later age. Parker is best known as a major formulaic improviser, as one can discover upon listening to different takes of same tunes that he recorded, an example of this would be "Embrace able You," in which Parkers melodic line is completely different between takes. Pretty much the entirety of Parkers carer was spent in the Bop era. His virtuosic playing and distinctive biting sound set him apart from the other prominent saxophone player's in his day. His ability to compose and improvise on pieces with a different chord for each melody note was exceptional. Parker also demonstrated his exceptional improvisational skills in the way that he led his recording sessions. He would often come into the studio with his compositions sketched sparsely on scraps of paper. He would explain the general outlines of his pieces to his band members, and the recording would begin with tiiile, if any rehearsal. Although he was plagued with drup and alcolol addiction throughout his adult life, parker managed to contribue a great deal to the development of Bop jazz playjing efore his lifestyle led to his untimely death in 1955.

While Mari is worried about length and spelling problems, it is easy to see that the paper has more significant problems. Mari does not understand that the paper needs an introduction and paragraph development, and she did not notice that she had completely omitted the discussion of Coltrane. Mari thought she was holding an intricate necklace that was too short; instead she had only a handful of attractive beads that did not resemble a necklace. Similarly, Mari had the information to write the paper, but she did not know she had it. The tutor had to help her "know" she had the information. (Neff 84) The problem with length grows out of lack of development and organization. She is not aware of the pattern needed to take a reader to a conclusion and she can't see the elaboration necessary to create the pattern of space (Stockdale). In very specific ways, the tutor will need to help Mari see how the paper needs to be transformed to make it acceptable to the professor.

> *Tutor:* Wait a minute. You said you "wanted" to do Miles Davis?
>
> *Mari:*   Oh. I decided to contrast Charlie Parker and John Coltrane.

The tutor knows that Mari is likely to follow a variety of tangents with equal energy, so she has decided not to ask about the change and instead accept the second topic.

Helping Mari

In many ways the writing conference begins much as any writing conference begins with the tutor finding out about the assignment, the due date and what the student's concerns are for the paper. However, with the student who has a learning disability, the tutor will need to be much more specific about the changes and will need to guide the student with the disability through the process, often providing the student with oral instructions and a written record of the changes. The tutor will need to find some concrete ways to talk about the organization, the thesis, and the development of this paper.

> *Tutor:* "Mari, while I read will you jot down 2 reasons why you like John Coltrane and 2 reasons you like Charlie Parker."

The tutor writes 'Coltrane' on the paper and writes a number 1 and a number 2 below it, doing the same for 'Parker.' It is important for the tutor to give Mari as much structure as possible.
Mari writes

Coltrane 1. experimentations with free jazz 2. perfectionism

Parker 1. improvisational skills 2. Spontaneous recordings.

> *Tutor:* Mari, this is not a bad start. You're being too hard on yourself. Clearly you know a lot about the jazz of Charlie Parker; I bet you know even more than you're telling me in this paper.

The tutor notices that Mari has given oral clues that suggest she does know more than the paper indicates.

> *Mari:* That's really all I know and I need 3 more pages, 750 more words.

> *Tutor:* Tell me why you like Charlie Parker? What did you jot down?

This question opened the flood gates for Mari. She not only told about why she liked him but also about her favorite songs, his genius, and how his personal problems were both a blessing and a curse for his music. Meantime, the tutor was taking notes, getting down on paper what Mari was saying.

> *Tutor:* Wow. I'm impressed. You know a lot. So tell me about Coltrane. Why do you like him?

Again the details along with the generalizations, conclusions, and connections poured from Mari as the tutor jotted notes as fast as she could. When Mari finished, she leaned back in her chair.

> *Tutor:* Look at how much material you have for this paper. You're going to have plenty to say, maybe you'll have to cut. (The tutor held out the papers that contained the notes for Mari to see.) Are you ready to talk about organization?

Organizing Mari

The tutor handed Mari a pen and took a pencil and asked Mari to see if she could make connections between ideas noted on the paper. The tutor demonstrated, but Mari soon took over the task. Mari may not be good at organizing but she was great at making connections, sometimes seeing those the tutor had missed. Soon all of the notes referring to life style were circled in pen as Mari saw the connections, marked them and then added more information. The tutor then gave Mari a red pen and suggested she mark all of the references to saxophone style. She then moved to a green pen to mark improvisational ability musical preferences. Once again, with modeling and direction, Mari was able to complete the task. The colors gave a tentative order to the chaos on the page.

Tutor: OK Mari, what could you say about Coltrane and Parker?

Mari: "Well, what I really want to say is 'Both Coltrane and Parker were virtuosic saxophone players, who played in the same era, but while Parker was known for his formulaic licks, Coltrane was noted for his 'sheets of sound.'"

Tutor: You know Mari, that sounds like a thesis.

The tutor pointed to the particular pieces of evidence that Mari had developed and color coded, explaining how they would be sections of the paper. With Mari directing and the tutor questioning, the tutor wrote out a tentative outline.

When the tutor asked her about the placement of the thesis, Mari realized it should appear in the introduction, but she didn't know where. The tutor explained how it should be placed at the end of the introduction where the reader would easily find it. She also explained how some of the other information Mari had about Coltrane and Parker could be placed in the introduction as a way to place the paper in context. They also discussed how some of the information might not fit in the essay at all because it did not develop the thesis. Most importantly, the tutor gave Mari all of the directions orally and put all of them in writing. They also went back to the original essay to examine what Mari would include and what needed to be explained to her audience. Without the tutor to help construct it for her, Mari had no sense of audience.

Finally the tutor asked Mari if she'd like to hold pieces of the essay in her hand. Using torn chunks of paper with key words written on them in colored ink, the advisor showed Mari how the whole paper might go together, pointing out that each section of the paper might be several paragraphs. Being able to touch the parts of the paper helped Mari understand how the paper would come together on the page.

The writing conference was over, but the tutor encouraged Mari to work at the computers in the Writing Center where she could ask a question or get support if she needed it. The advisor also asked Mari if she would like another appointment in a day or so to go over the paper again, this time looking for paragraph development and issues of spelling and punctuation.

Both Mari and Alex demonstrate many of the problems typical for students with learning disabilities.

Typical Problems

1. Poor organization
2. No thesis statement
3. Tense problems

4. Missing or incorrect inflectional endings

5. Missing or incorrect basic service words

6. Fragments or run on sentences

7. Multiple and inconsistent spelling errors

8. Pronoun reference errors

9. Chronic difficulty thinking of the "right" word

10. Lack of context for the paper (West)

Learning disabled students will come to the writing center with a variety of special needs. In every case, it is important that we provide the help they are entitled to in a positive way, treating them as the intelligent people they are and encouraging them to be responsible, independent learners.

Works Cited

Cole, Gerald. *The Learning Mystique.* New York: Pantheon Books, 1987.

DiScala, Jeanette. "Providing Disability Accommodations and Equal Opportunity." URMIA *Journal.* September 1995. 4–9.

Gaddes, William H. and Edgall, Dorothy. *Learning and Brain Function,* 3rd ed. New York: Springer-Verlag. 1994.

Galaburda, Albert M. *Dyslexia and Development.* Cambridge, Mass.: Harvard University Press, 1993.

Galaburda, Albert M. "Developmental Dyslexia: Four Consecutive Patients with Cortical Anomolies." *The Annals of Neurology.* Vol. 18. No. 2, Aug. 1985. 222–233.

Levine, Melvin D., MD. *Developmental Variation and Learning Disorders.* Toronto: Educators Publishing Service, Inc.

Lipp, Janice. "Turning Problems into Opportunities." *Another Door to Learning* newsletter, 1991. 1–3.

Lovitt, Thomas. *Introduction to Learning Disabilities.* Needham Heights, Mass.: Allyn and Bacon.

Neff, Julie. "Learning Disabilities and the Writing Center." *Intersections.* Urbana, IL: NCTE, 1994.

Silver, Larry B. *The Misunderstood Child.* New York: McGraw-Hill Book Company, 1984.

Stockdale, Carol. Interview. September, 1997.

Stockdale, Carol, and Possin, Carol. *Categories of Attention and Learning Disabilities.* Tacoma, Wash: ARK Foundation Press, 1997.

Stockdale, Carol, and Possin, Carol. *Spatial Relations and Learning.* Tacoma, Wash.: ARK Foundation Press, 1997.

West, Ivey. *Students with Disabilities* brochure. Tacoma, Wash.: University of Puget Sound. 1997.

West, Ivey. Writing Center Handout. Tacoma, Wash.: University of Puget Sound, 1994.

Woodcock, Richard and M. Bonner Johnson. Woodcock-Johnson Tests of Achievement. Allen, TX: Teaching Resources.

Working with Computers in the Writing Center

"I don't know how I ever managed without it."
"It's completely changed my life!"
"Everybody should have one."

Anyone reading these comments out of context might assume that they referred to some miraculous new drug, household cleanser, or cosmetic. The fact that these or equally laudatory remarks were made by writers about their computers, however, is a testament to the prominence of computers in the field of writing. Most writers, once they overcome some initial hesitation, find computers not only extremely helpful, but an absolute necessity, and composition programs are now incorporating computers into their curriculum; frequently, these computers are located in or near the writing center. As a result, those who work in writing centers should understand what computers can and cannot do. This chapter does not attempt to cover the growing field of computers and writing. However, it does suggest some basic concepts for working with computers in the writing center as a means of helping you understand your role as tutor in a computerized writing lab.

Computers Cannot Replace Tutors

When computers began to be used in the teaching of composition, some teachers and tutors regarded them with suspicion verging on terror. Some had a generalized fear of machines of any sort; others were concerned that computer assisted instruction and computerized response to student writing would ultimately put teachers and tutors out of business. However, now that computers have been part of the academic scene for many years, it has become apparent that although word processing programs are extremely useful, and although database and spread sheet programs can count, sort, reorganize, and do all sorts of complicated mathematical computations, computers cannot deal adequately with an endeavor as complex as teaching students to write and think. Computers can ask students questions, but they cannot evaluate student response; computers can provide feedback about sentence structure and style in a text, but such feedback is helpful only when students know how to interpret and apply it. Word processors can provide useful assistance in invention, revision, and editing, but they cannot, by themselves, teach students how to perform these activities effectively, nor has anyone demonstrated that word processors enhance writing ability. Despite increased enthusiasm for the computer over the past several years, and despite considerable interest in "artificial intelligence," the computer still cannot respond satisfactorily to "meaning" in a text, and meaning is what writing and writing centers are really about.

If you are working in a writing center that uses computers, then, you need not worry that you are going to be replaced by a machine, no matter how the machine is improved. Computers are wonderfully useful tools for writing (I would be lost without mine and wonder how I ever managed without it), but they cannot, by themselves, enable students to learn to write. However, as a tutor, you can utilize the computer as a means of facilitating that learning.

Word Processing

The Word Processor and the Writing Process

Hypertext, the Internet, the World Wide Web, Interactive video games, CD Rom disks—these are all wonderful computer applications with a great deal to offer to writers. My own feeling, though, is that the most important computerized assistance in writing is provided by word processors, since they promote ease in invention and revision, and foster a collaborative spirit between writers and among writers and tutors (see Jennings 1987). When students write in a computer lab, they often assist one another, not only in the mechanics of using the machine but in the production of text as well. Somehow, when text is printed on a screen, it doesn't seem as "private" as it does when it is written by hand on a piece of paper, so students feel more comfortable about sharing their work with others and receiving feedback from fellow students. When a text is written on a word processor, students can work in groups to examine texts in progress, as the screen can be viewed by several students at a time (or even projected onto a wall screen by means of a video projector).

Another advantage to using word processors is that because they make revision so easy, students can develop a more flexible, fluid model of text production. Because students can move text and work with it in different versions, they do not feel as *attached* to every word they have generated—they are more willing to *play* with their texts—to move sections around by cutting and pasting, develop weak sections with additional examples, rewrite introductions and conclusions, without the nuisance of having to retype the entire paper.

In her book, *Writing Technology,* Christina Haas reports on interviews she had with writers ranging in age from 18 to 52, who had been working with computers from three months to twenty years. Evenly divided according to discipline, the humanities, science, and engineering, all felt positive about working with computers, citing the following reasons for their enthusiasm:

- text generation is easier;
- texts are neater;
- there are a variety of formatting options;
- the computer provides ready access to other writers;
- the computer provides systems for accessing and managing large amounts of information;
- the computer facilitates revision, both global and local.

All of these advantages are provided by word processing.

Of course, some people also cited the following disadvantages:

- small screens make it difficult for writers to reread their texts;
- it is often hard to find specific places in the text;
- it is hard to get a sense of the structure of the text;
- one loses the sense of the history of the text, because revision occurs instantly;
- the ability to plan is diminished.

Awareness of these difficulties will help you work more insightfully with word processed papers in the writing center. Structural problems, repetitions and omissions may be a function of students' lack of ease with working at the screen. For such students, focusing on the paper copy can be helpful.

Word Processing and Tutoring

If students bring in their papers on disk to the writing center, you can work directly at the screen, enabling students to revise their papers on the computer and then talk further with you about additional revision. Although word processors do not specifically teach students how to write, they make it easy for students to write multiple drafts and to experiment with different models of the writing process. It therefore seems likely that a student who writes and revises frequently is going to develop a more effective writing process than one who does not. Of course, no study has as yet demonstrated definitively that word processing has a positive effect on student writing ability; however, one must also recognize that measuring the effect of *any* tool or teaching method on a process as complex as writing is quite difficult to accomplish.

If you are fortunate enough to work in a writing center in which students have access to word processing, here are some general suggestions you might find useful:

1. Become familiar with the particular word processor in your writing center so that you will be able to answer students' questions about the mechanics of the program.

2. Encourage students to become familiar with the program. If students have to spend a great deal of time thinking about how the program works, they will be distracted from composing. The mechanics of the program should become automatic.

3. Whenever possible, the student's, not the tutor's, hands should be at the keyboard. Although sometimes you may wish to show students a particular technique, such as moving a block of text, students should be encouraged to work on the text themselves.

4. Encourage students to print drafts frequently and then mark them up by hand. Although some students have no difficulty reading text on screen, others find it difficult, particularly if the screen is small; moreover, reading a text screen by screen often prevents students from gaining a global sense of the text. A few studies suggest that when students work exclusively at the screen, they are likely to focus on sentence level revision rather on the thesis and structure.

Word-processing and Invention

If a student comes to the writing center with insufficient ideas for a paper, you can suggest that he or she develop materials at the screen. One useful strategy is what is sometimes referred to as "rushwriting," which, as its name implies, means that the student sits at the screen and writes as quickly as possible without stopping. Rushwriting is, of course, another form of brainstorming or freewriting, and if the student is a competent typist, working at the screen usually yields more material than working with a pencil and paper. This method can also be very useful when a student must respond to a text, an essay or a work of literature. The student can begin by writing their impressions of the text as quickly as possible, and they are often surprised by how much information they are able to generate, ideas they didn't know they had.

Then they can print it out and elaborate on a few ideas that they especially liked, and before they know it, they have begun developing ideas for the paper.

Sometimes, students have not developed adequate typing skills, so that the mechanics of typing can interfere with their ability to think. If this is the case, then you, as the tutor, might sit at the screen and the student can dictate ideas to you. Once you have written down what the student has said, print out the text and use it to develop additional ideas. Of course, when you sit at the computer and do the actual typing, you may be concerned that you, rather than the student, are doing most of the work. However, if you resist inserting your own ideas, dictation at the screen can be a very effective method for helping students generate ideas, particularly for students who suffer from writing block.

Sheridan Blau at the University of California at Santa Barbara uses a technique that he calls "invisible writing," which means that students "rush write" or brainstorm with the monitor on the computer turned down so that they are unable to see what they are writing. Blau feels that this technique is especially useful for students who are so anxious about surface correctness that they are unable to write freely. Because invisible writing does not allow them to see their text, they cannot focus on editing at the time they are generating ideas. You might try using this technique for students in the writing center who suffer from writing block.

Because the computer can have a liberating effect on student idea generation, it is sometimes helpful to list a set of questions on screen for students to respond to. Some computer packages that focus on writing provide a variety of prompts to which students respond, thus helping them generate ideas. Such prompts can be very useful for some students, although, of course, since no author or programmer can anticipate every possible question for every possible topic, the prompts tend to be fairly general. However, for many students, responding even to a set of general questions on the computer can lead to the discovery of ideas.

Word Processing and Revision

The word processor is ideal for revision, as chunks of texts can be moved, additional material can be developed, and words and sentences can easily be manipulated. One model for incorporating the computer into your tutoring is that you and the student first discuss the draft in conference, decide what needs to be done, and then work with the student at the screen to begin the revision (or else students can revise the draft on their own and then return for additional discussion). If the paper requires a great deal of revision, construct a sequential plan, so that the student does not become overwhelmed and discouraged. Begin with one section of the paper at a time, perhaps the refinement of the thesis or a particular paragraph which needs development, and work on one task at a time. An important point to remember is that revision does not have to begin at the top of the paper and then continue down until the conclusion is reached. If a student is having difficulty with an introduction, then he or she might begin revising some other section. **Remember, though, to caution students to save their work and keep back-up copies on disk and in hard copy of everything they write.**

Word Processing and Organization

Working at the screen with a word processor can be very useful for helping students work with a disorganized paragraph. You might have the student type a paragraph onto the screen and then work with it, rearranging and revising sentences to attain greater coherence within the paragraph, an activity that the computer enables students to do very easily. Sometimes it is also useful to have the student type all of the sentences in a paragraph in the form of a list and then examine how these sentences could be rearranged or connected through the use of transitions.

When you do your own writing, you may have discovered methods of using the computer that work especially well for you. It is therefore useful to reflect on your own composing method and apply it when you tutor—by experimentation and exploration, you may be able to create an individualized approach that is particularly effective.

A Caution About Students and Word Processors

One potential problem with writing on a word processor is that even the roughest of drafts emerges from the printer looking neat, clean and ready for submission; therefore, even if the text is undeveloped, stylistically ineffectual, and filled with grammatical errors, students sometimes regard it as a completed draft. In working with word processed drafts in the writing center, then, remind students that clean print does not mean that the paper is finished. Have students read their drafts aloud and mark the hard copy to call attention to the necessity for additional work.

Information Literacy

Some of the material in this section appears also in "Information Literacy and the Writing Center." Computers and Composition. V 12, No.2 (1995): 203–211.

In addition to word processing, a very useful way in which the writing center can utilize computers is to help students acquire what is known as "information literacy," a term that encompasses the variety of skills needed for accessing, evaluating, and utilizing outside information. When students are assigned to write research papers, they are frequently unaware of when they need information from outside sources, have not developed effective search strategies for locating appropriate material, don't know how to evaluate the material once they locate it, and are unfamiliar with techniques for integrating information smoothly into their own texts once they have decided that they wish to use it. But when computers are located in or near the writing center, tutors can work with students during the process of accessing information for their papers, thereby helping them acquire "information literacy."

Political Implications of Information Literacy

Why should tutors in the writing center get involved in helping students acquire information literacy? One important reason is that because we live in an increasingly information oriented age, those who can access and work with information will have a significant advantage over those who cannot. According to the American Library Association Presidential Committee on Information Literacy (1989), the acquisition of information literacy is crucial not simply because of its traditional role of enabling students to locate information for college research papers, but, more significantly, because it will ultimately become a primary determiner of life quality and economic independence. The committee report makes the case that because "information is expanding at an unprecedented rate and [because], enormously rapid strides are being made in the technology for storing, organizing, and accessing the ever growing tidal wave of information . . . how our country deals with the realities of the Information Age will have enormous impact on our democratic way of life and on our nation's ability to compete internationally (1). The report further suggests that information literacy is "needed to guarantee the survival of democratic institutions. All men are created equal but voters with information resources are in a position to make more intelligent decisions than citizens who are information illiterates" (5).

The concept of an information age implies not only the ability to work with existing technology, but also the power to determine the form and shape of that technology as it evolves in the coming century. In an essay written in 1994, Haas and Neuwirth critique several misconceptions concerning the relation of literacy to technology, two of which are relevant in this context. The first is that literacy exists independently of technology and is therefore unaffected by it—that is, technology is viewed merely as a tool that makes reading and writing more efficient but has no impact on the nature of literacy. This assumption presumes that "the essential processes of reading and writing are universal and unchanging: writers and readers simply exchange their pens and books for word processors, replace their face-to-face conversations with computer conferences, and continue to produce texts and construct meanings in the ways they always have" (321). The second misconception is the notion that "computers are not our job," which distances the field of composition from technology by presuming a division of labor and produces a vast gulf between those who create literary technology and those who use and teach it. Composition scholars and teachers who adhere to this view tend to "see themselves as users, but not as shapers of technology"(327). Both assumptions, Haas and Neuwirth maintain, are flawed and dangerous—flawed, because they do not recognize the dynamic interaction between literacy and technology, dangerous because they condone a passivity that usually results in powerlessness. Those of us in writing centers who have long been concerned with literacy must recognize that technology impacts literacy as much as literacy impacts technology and that we must become involved with technology so that we can contribute to its creation. Although tools are not always used as they were intended to be, "those who fund, design, and build computer tools exert a powerful control over what kind of activities those tools facilitate" (Haas and Neuwirth 329). When writing centers make information literacy an important goal, they foster "interaction between those who know about literacy and those who know about computers," an interaction that, according to Haas and Neuwirth should occur not "after the artifact but during its shaping" (329).

Topic Knowledge and the Writing Process

An additional rationale for writing centers to focus on information literacy is based on the important role that topic knowledge plays in the writing process. Nancy Stein, maintains that "topic knowledge" is "probably the most essential knowledge for the production of discourse" (247), and most of us would agree that writers must have adequate knowledge about a topic before they can successfully write about it. Nevertheless, many compositionists, including some of us in writing centers, tend to underplay the role that topic knowledge plays in determining the quality of a piece of writing, thereby reducing writing acquisition to learning what Landis refers to in her essay as "patterns and processes, steps and strategies" (107). Such a view erroneously assumes that students already have all the information they need in order to write—composing thus becomes simply a matter of arrangement and style.

Students who visit the writing center, however, "are generally inexperienced writers writing on topics about which they are **not** already knowledgeable. That is, their writing process takes place alongside an 'acquisition of knowledge' process—a parallel that occurs not only in freshman composition but in other college courses and in 'real life' writing tasks as well" (Landis 108). Accessing information is a key component of this 'acquisition of knowledge' process, but information without context and coherence does not result in knowledge, but remains an overload of undigested facts. John Naisbitt, in his popular 1983 book *Megatrends* bemoans this phenomenon, stating that the world is "wallowing in detail, drowning in information, but is starved for knowledge" (24). Part of the research process involves learning to transform information into knowledge, something that writing centers can emphasize when they have access to computers.

Implementing Information Literacy in the Writing Center

When computers are located within or very near to the writing center, tutors can help students acquire a workable research, as well as a writing, process. At the University of Southern California, for example, the writing center includes a computer lab that is linked to the library and the Internet via Ethernet, which enables students and tutors to explore the world of the Internet and conduct searches just as they would in a library. Within the comfortable environment of the writing center and under the guidance of a tutor, students can access the university library catalogue, various magazine and periodical indexes, and a myriad of additional informational resources via Gopher, the World Wide Web, and hundreds of news groups. The writing center has thus assumed an important role in helping students learn to work with electronic resources, scheduling whole class workshops and small group sessions, as well as incorporating search strategies into tutor-student conferences held directly at the keyboard. Moreover, the computer room in the writing center has also become a place for tutors to congregate when they are not on duty—helping one another learn to use e-mail and navigate various information sources—thus acquiring expertise that they can pass along to students.

With access to information resources within the writing center, tutors can work with students directly at the screen, demonstrating how search terms can be manipulated to narrow and expand a search, and helping them understand that different search words may yield very different possibilities and choices, even if their definitions are almost identical. Moreover, as soon as a new information tool is added to the university system, everyone in the writing center can become immediately aware of it and can then pass that awareness on to students. Because the writing center fosters a collaborative environment and tolerates a higher level of noise than do most libraries, both students and tutors can ask one another questions freely and help each other learn, keeping abreast of the technology as it develops and changes. Moreover, access to electronically generated information enables the writing center to work with students on assessing the quality, reliability and appropriateness of the resources they have discovered, helping them to become readers who question, readers who do not accept everything that is either printed or published electronically. Such readers will ask questions about the sources available to them, questions such as "How do you know that? What evidence do you have for that? "Who says so? and "How can we find out?"

The World Wide Web

When computers are located in or near the writing center, tutors can also work with students when they "surf" the World Wide Web, a burgeoning information source that has been doubling every two to three months. According to Reddick and King, "in the spring of 1995 there were more than 4 million Web sites on the WorldWide Web. By August there were more than 6 million" (66), and the numbers continue to grow. The Web provides access to all sorts of information, from academic research to directories of local bars, and it is very easy and entertaining to browse from site to site, using a browser such as Netscape. What can writing center tutors do to help students who are using the Web to obtain information for a paper? I suggest the following forms of assistance:

1. Writing center tutors can help students understand what sort of information the Web can and cannot provide. The Web can provide valuable information about many topics, but it is unlikely to have **all** the information students will need to write research papers, particularly if the topic is unfamiliar to them. Students should first think through their topic and access information through library materials before they begin to search for information on the Web.

2. Writing center tutors can help students find search engines to begin a search. Some good places to begin are

    ● Infoseek (http://www.infoseek.com)
    ● Lycos (http://lycos.cs.cmu.html)
    ● Webcrawler (http://webcrawler.com.html)
    ● Yahoo (http://www.yahoo.com)

3. Writing center tutors can help students choose appropriate key words on which to search.

    Search engines work through the use of keywords that describes the information one might want. By entering keywords, one obtains a list of sites from the Web in which the title of the site or some of the key information provides a match. Because every entry is matched to a site, a user can jump from site to site, looking for information. The problem is that finding the proper keywords is not always easy; moreover, the major search engines are often busy, sometimes too busy to respond to a student's request.

    An important source of information about selecting keywords is the campus library; most librarians are now experts in accessing electronically generated information resources. If a student is having trouble finding information and if you suspect that he or she is not inputting the proper key words, a librarian can probably be of assistance. It is a good idea, then, for writing center tutors to develop an on-going, working relationship with campus librarians.

4. Writing center tutors can help students evaluate the quality of the information they find. Because information on the Web is not subject to expert review, and because anyone can (and does) create a Web page, a lot of the

information available on the Web may not be useful because it doesn't have the necessary credibility for inclusion in an academic essay. Help students develop a critical, questioning approach to information they find on the Web (or anywhere else) by asking questions such as the following:

- What is the source of this information?
- Was this information created by an expert in the field?
- Was the author motivated by a particular bias or agenda?
- Is the information presented credibly?
- Can the information be validated?

5.   Help students behave responsibly with the information they obtain from the Web.

Because the Web provides easy access to a great deal of information, students may be tempted to cut and paste information they find directly into their own texts. Writing center tutors can help students understand that although the Web is a new technology, fundamental academic values are the same as when students access information from paper sources— that is material that is not their own work must be quoted and properly cited. Otherwise, the student is guilty of plagiarism.

6.   Writing center tutors should encourage students when they get impatient and discouraged. Trying to find information through the Web can be a frustrating experience for anyone and it is important to assure students that everyone has trouble some of the time.

The Internet

The Web is part of the Internet, but the Internet can also enable students to contact others through electronic mail and provides access to new groups and various forums for discussion. If students have access to the Internet through the writing center, they should understand that although it is relatively easy to obtain outside help on a paper, students are expected to do their own work and to acknowledge any help they receive. Writing center tutors should help students understand what is legitimate and illegitimate assistance when they obtain information through the Internet.

On-Line Writing Labs (OWLS)

Many writing centers have their own Web sites that provide on-line writing assistance through electronic mail. Others provide all sorts of useful handouts freely available to anyone. If your writing center has an on-line computer, you should investigate these materials and OWLS. Some possibilities are as follows:

http://www2.rscc.cc.tn.us/~jordan.jj/OWL/OnlineOWLs.html

This provides an annotated list of OWLS which offer handouts and e-mail consultations.

http://www2.colgate.edu/diw/NACAOWLS.html#Handouts

This is the National Writing Centers Association home page.

Writing Center Websites

All of these sites offer materials you might find useful. However, because the Web is constantly in flux, you may discover that some of their addresses have changed.

Rensselaer	http://www.rpi.edu/dept/llc/writecenter/web/home.html
University of Texas at Austin	http://uwc-server.fac.utexas.edu/
University of Southern California	http://www.usc.edu/dept/expo/
St. Cloud State University	http://leo.stcloud.msus.edu/
University of Florida	http://www.ucet.ufl.edu/writing/nwe.html
University of California, Santa Barbara	http://humanitas.ucsb.edu/
Ball State University	http://www.bsu.edu/english/wc.html

Computer Assisted Instructional Packages

Some writing centers have purchased computerized instructional packages that can aid students in a variety of ways: prompt and respond in preprogrammed dialogue to the writing of a student user, analyze a student text for certain kinds of surface errors, or provide opportunities for drill and practice. Some of these programs address not only idea discovery, but also organization through outlining programs, and style analyzers, including number counts of words and sentence length, a report of "to-be" verbs, and feedback on passive constructions, undesirable word choices, grammatical error, and more. Many students find programs of this sort quite useful, and you may discover that your writing center computers use such a program.

If your writing center has or is considering purchasing a computer assisted writing program and you are wondering about how to maximize its potential benefits, I offer the following suggestions: Begin by reviewing the program thoroughly yourself, thinking about how you might find it useful in your own work, and considering what philosophy or model of writing the particular program supports. Nancy Kaplan points out that "all of our practices are shot through with ideological statements" (13) and suggests that you ask yourself what statements a particular tool—a stylistic program or set of programs make about the nature of writing and the relationship between the writer, the text, and the reader. Similarly, Kaplan points out that "introducing computers into the writing curriculum . . . reintroduces old and familiar issues in new and sometimes unrecognizable forms" (28). Programs that focus on error correction and sentence level feedback, for example, reflect the notion that correctness and style are very important and students who work with such programs may consequently concentrate disproportionately on surface, rather than global aspects of writing. Therefore, if students work with programs adhering to what you believe is an incomplete or incorrect model of the writing process, you, as the tutor, can compensate for its limitations by helping students understand what response from such programs actually means and pointing out its limitations. For example, some style analyzers provide readability levels of the student's text or counts up instances of "to be" verbs or instances of abstract nouns. When students receive this kind of feedback, they often don't know how to apply it to their own writing (any kind of feedback is useful only if it also implies an application). Thus, if students in the writing center receive feedback about "to be" verbs or excessive abstract nouns, you, as a tutor, can teach students strategies for reformulating passive sentences or making abstract nouns more concrete (See chapter 6). You can also help students understand that stylistic analysis is only one facet of the writing process, one which should be addressed only after the student has generated ideas and addressed the writing task on a more global level.

In working with packaged programs the point to remember is that you, as the tutor, should help the student use the program and compensate for its limitations with your own ideas and comments. Do not assume that the program by itself can help a student learn to write. No computer program has the insight into text that a tutor has.

Programs for the Discovery of Ideas

Several programs on the market contain sets of questions aimed at helping students discover ideas. For some students, these can be very useful, sometimes more useful than having a tutor ask the questions, because students feel a sense of privacy and ease when a computer, rather than a human being, is hearing their first attempts to deal with a topic. The computer will not laugh at their ideas or indicate that it thinks they are foolish or incompetent in any way. Moreover, the act of actually writing responses to questions often serves as a catalyst for generating additional ideas. As Ellen

Nold pointed out many years ago, "the computer provides a patient and non-threatening, fluid and provocative backboard against which to bounce ideas (271).

These programs can be useful, although they have been criticized as being overly generalized and oversimplified. Students will sometimes enter wisecracks instead of exploratory discourse, and since the computer has no way of evaluating the quality of the response, it has no way of responding appropriately. It will still say "Good, John. Anything else?" no matter what the student writes. Hashimoto criticizes such programs as "optimistic" and "oversimplified" (73) in that they cannot accommodate individual learning and writing styles. Sirc similarly observes that structured discovery programs can exclude the serendipity that less structured, more associative methods of prewriting can facilitate.

As a general principle, then, computers can serve as a valuable tool in the writing center if they foster enlightenment about the writing process and facilitate the generation and revision of text. However, despite general enthusiasm about computers and composition, despite numerous articles, conference presentations, and new software development, we are only at the beginning of discovering how computers can be applied to the teaching of writing. As a tutor in the writing center, you are in an excellent position to participate in that discovery.

For Further Exploration

Burns, Hugh. "Recollections of First-Generation Computer-Assisted Prewriting. In *The Computer in Composition Instruction: A Writer's Tool.* ed. W. Wresch. Urbana, Ill: NCTE, 1984.

Collier, R.M. "The Word Processor and Revision Strategies." *College Composition and Communication 34* (1983): 149–155."

Haas, C. "How the Writing Medium Shapes the Writing Process: Effects of Word Processing on Planning." *Research in the Teaching of English 23* (1989): 181–207.
—"Seeing It On the Screen Isn't Really Seeing It. Computer Writers' Reading Problems." in G.E. Hawisher and C.L. Selfe (Eds) *Critical Perspectives in Computers and Composition Instruction* (pp. 16–29): New York: Teachers College Press, 1989.
—*Writing Technology.* Mahwah, New Jersey: Lawrence Erlbaum, 1996.

Haas, C. and Hayes, L.R. "What Did I Just Say? Reading Problems in Writing with the Machine." *Research in the Teaching of English 10* (1986): 22–35.

Hawisher, Gail E. "Electronic Meetings of the Minds: Research, Electronic Conferences, and Composition Studies." In *Re-Imagining Computers and Composition: Teaching and Research in the Virtual Age.* Eds. Gail E. Hawisher and Paul LeBlanc. Portsmouth, New Hampshire: Boynton/Cook, 1992.

Hawisher, Gail E. and Cynthia L. Selfe. Eds. *Evolving Perspectives on Computers and Composition Studies.* Urbana, Illinois: NCTE, 1991.

Hawisher, Gail E., et al. *Computers and the Teaching of Writing in American Higher Education, 1979-1994: A History*. Norwood, New Jersey: Ablex, 1996.

Holdstein, Deborah H. and Cynthia L. Selfe. *Computers and Writing: Theory, Research, Practice*. New York: MLA, 1990.

Jennings, Edward M. "Paperless Writing: Boundary Conditions and Their Implications." In L. Gerrard (Ed) *Writing At Century's End: Essays on Computer Assisted Composition*. New York: Random House, 1987. 11–20.

Lanham, Richard. "Foreword." *Computers and Community: Teaching Composition in the Twenty-first Century*. Ed. Carolyn Handa. Portsmouth: Boynton/Cook, 1990.

Rodrigues, R.J. and Rodgriguez, D.W.. "Computer Based Invention: Its Place and Potential." *College Composition and Communication, 35* (1984): 78–87.

Rodriquez, D.W. "Computers and Basic Writers." *College Composition and Communication, 36* (October 1985): 336–339.

Selfe, Cynthia and Gail Hawisher, eds. *Critical Perspectives on Computers and Composition*. New York: Teachers College Press, 1989.

Selfe, Cynthia, and Susan Hilligloss. Eds. *Literacy and Computers*. New York: MLA, 1994.

Schmersahl, Carmen B. "Teaching Library Research: Process, Not Product." *Journal of Teaching Writing* 6.2 (Fall/Winter 1987): 231–239.

Spitzer, Michael. "Incorporating Prewriting Software into the Writing Program." in C.L. Selfe, D.W. Rodriguez, and W.R. Oates (Eds) *Computers in English and the Language Arts*. NCTE: Ubana, Ill., 1989. 205–212.

Standiford, Sally N., Kathleen Jaycox, and Anne Auten. *Computers in the English Classroom*. Urbana: NCTE, 1983.

Wresch, William, ed. *The Computer in Composition Instruction: A Writer's Tool*. Urbana: NCTE, 1984.

Wresch, William, Donald Pattow, and James Gifford. *Writing for the 21st Century*. New York: McGraw-Hill, 1988.

Works Cited

American Library Association Presidential Committee on Information Literacy. Washington, D.C.: January 10, 1989.

Haas, Christina, and Christine M. Neuwirth. "Writing the Technology That Writes Us: Research on Literacy and the Shape of Technology." In *Literacy and Computers: The Complications of Teaching and Learning with Technology*. Eds. Cynthia L. Selfe and Susan Hilligoss. New York: MLA, 1994.

Hashimoto, I. "Structured Heuristic Procedures: Their Limitations." *College Composition and Communication.* 36 (1985): 73–81.

Kaplan, Nancy. "Ideology, Technology, and the Future of Writing Instruction." In Gail Hawisher and Cynthia L. Selfe (Eds.) *Evolving Perspectives on Computers and Composition Studies: Questions For the 1990's.* Urbana: NCTE, 1991. 11–43.

Landis, Kathleen. "The Knowledge of Composition." *Ilha do Desterro* 29 (1993): 107–118.

Naisbitt, John. Megatrends: *Ten New Directions Transforming Our Lives.* New York: Warner Books, 1983.

Nold, Ellen. "Fear and Trembling: The Humanist Approaches the Computer. *College Composition and Communication* 26 (1975): 269–273.

Reddick, Randy, and Elliot King. *The Online Student.* Fort Worth: Harcourt Brace, 1996.

Sirc, Geoffrey. "Response in the Electronic Medium." In Chris M. Anson (Ed.) *Writing and Response: Theory, Practice and Research.* Urbana: NCTE, 1989. 187–205.

Sommers, Nancy. " I Stand Here Writing." *College English* 55.4 (April 1993): 420–28.

Stein, Nancy L. "Knowledge and Process in the Acquisition of Writing Skills." In *Review of Research in Education.* Ed. Ernst Z. Rothkopf. Washington, D.C., 1986.

SPECIAL ASSIGNMENTS: THE RESEARCH PAPER AND THE LITERARY ESSAY

This chapter is concerned with a few of the special assignments that students often bring to the writing center. In particular, I will address the "research" paper, including difficulties students have in working with sources, and papers concerned with literature, including book review assignments. Of course, in one chapter, I cannot discuss these genres thoroughly; however, I can give you some ideas that may help you work with students more effectively, and I will also include a list of references so that you can pursue these topics more thoroughly on your own.

Undergraduate "Research" Papers: Some Common Problems

When students are assigned what has traditionally been called the "research" paper, they often bring in some depressingly unsatisfactory writing. Because they are confused about what is expected of them—that is, about the *genre* of the research paper— students simply find a lot of quotations and paste them together, rather than using them to support a well-developed thesis. Thus, their papers are often excessively long and pointless, overly generalized, disorganized, unfocused and occasionally plagiarized. The main reason these papers are so poor is that many students don't realize that research oriented essays, like other essays, should have a main point, and thus they use sources, not to support that main point, but simply to show their instructors how much information they have found. Consequently, their papers are a collage of quotations that often don't connect coherently to a central idea.

Writing center tutors who are aware of this problem can begin to work with students on research papers in the same way they would on other types of assignments—

on developing and shaping a thesis, on addressing audience, and on fulfilling purpose. As in working with other unfocused papers, I suggest that you begin by asking students what their papers are about, have them tell you what their thesis is, and summarize their main supporting points. Then, when you read the paper, you will be able to compare what is written to what the student has stated as the main point. You can also have students write down a thesis statement while you read the paper. You can also ask them about their audience and how the paper is intended to influence that audience. These approaches will emphasize that the "research" paper is supposed to develop a thesis, and once students understand the purpose of their research paper assignments, they often have less difficulty with them.

However, even when students understand the purpose of research paper assignments, they may encounter additional problems—typically, the ability to plan time, take and synthesize notes, and incorporate sources smoothly into their papers. You may find some of the suggestions in this chapter useful for helping students with these difficulties.

The Research Paper Time Management Form[1]

If students come to the writing center as soon as they receive their research paper assignment, you can help them plan their time, because papers involving research usually require some library work, outside reading, and notetaking, as well as time for drafting and revising. Below is a form you may wish to use with students when they begin to work on their research papers:

---

[1]This form is adapted from: Clark, Irene L. *Taking a Stand: A Guide to the Researched Paper With Readings.* New York: Harper Collins, 1992.

Research Paper Time Management Form

Research Activity	When?	Where?
Reading assignment		
Writing Exploratory draft		
Reading sources		
Brainstorming		
Developing preliminary topic		
Creating an outline		
Writing First draft		
Getting Feedback on first draft		
Writing second draft		
Revising second draft		
Editing second draft		
Checking documentation		
Printing and copying		

Taking and Synthesizing Notes[2]

You can also work with students on their research papers by helping them develop note taking and note synthesizing strategies. Many students are unaware of *why* one takes notes, and they, therefore, take notes on everything they read. Then, when they start actually writing the paper, they have a set of copious notes but don't know which ones they ought to include and have difficulty organizing them. The two sheets on the following pages are useful for helping students record and synthesize their notes.

The **Source Notesheet** is used to record notes about a single source and contains information only from that source. The first piece of information the student records is the author's last name, so that these sheets can be alphabetized to create the bibliography. There is also a place on this sheet for a brief summary of the source, to help the student remember what the overall purpose of the source was.

In working with this sheet, point out to students the section marked "Idea About Note." That section can be used to record ideas that student might have for actually using the note in the paper—for example, the student might write, "This would make a good argument against the general viewpoint" or "This is a good example of _____." The Source Notesheet provides a place to help students jot down ideas, so that they don't lose interesting thoughts as they occur.

The **Note Synthesis Sheet** helps students organize notes around a particular aspect of a topic and allows them to combine information from several sources. One advantage of using the Note Synthesis Sheet is that the column marked "Reason for Using" focuses student attention on *why* they may choose to incorporate a particular quotation or paraphrase. For example, does the quotation or paraphrase provide an example? Does it support the thesis? Does it establish authority? Does it contradict someone else's point of view? These are important questions for students to ask themselves, so that they don't fill their papers with too many quotations simply to display how many sources they have found. The Note Synthesis Sheet thus emphasizes the importance of using the opinions of others for a particular purpose. However, if a student brings in a draft which consists simply of a string of quotations, a useful strategy is to have them highlight all of the quotations with a marker. This will illustrate in living color what percentage of the paper is quotation and how little of their own writing there actually is. Point out that papers without a personal voice and are usually lifeless and uninteresting to read.

---

[2]Both the Source Notesheet and the Note Synthesis Sheet may also be found in: Clark, Irene Lurkis. *Taking a Stand: A Guide to the Researched Paper with Readings.* New York: Harper Collins, 1992.

Source Note Sheet

Author(s)
Title
Journal
Publisher
Date, Place
Pages

Page#	Note	Idea About Note

Note Synthesis Sheet

Subject of Paper
Sub-Topic

Source	Page#	Note	Reason For Using

Common Student Problems in Using Quotations

The "Crouton" Effect

One common problem exhibited in research papers brought to the writing center is that of incorporating quotations and paraphrases smoothly into the text. Often students seem to just sprinkle them in, like croutons in a salad, so that they never seem to blend in. Here is an example:

> Although many people are under the impression that smoking marijuana has had no effect on them, some recent research studies indicate that it has an effect on the heart, lungs, and brain. "All the subjects had significant lung function impairment in several areas. These impairments were similar to those found by other researchers studying people who had smoked tobacco moderately to heavily for many years" (Mann 115).

In this example, the quotation is not framed by a reference to where the study was done, nor does it indicate how the study illustrates the writer's point. In working with students on incorporating quotations, you can suggest that they **refer to the source in some way,** usually by mentioning the author or title, indicating the source's attitude or position by using a verb, or showing the source's relevance to the point being made. Some useful verbs to suggest are as follows:

> indicates, exemplifies, observes, argues, explains, suggests, describes, advocates

Here is a possible revision of the above paragraph:

> Although many people are under the impression that smoking marijuana has had no effect on them, some recent research studies indicate that it has an effect on the heart, lungs, and brain. A study of marijuana smokers conducted at UCLA suggests such an effect. In fact, as Peggy Mann points out, "All the subjects had significant lung function impairment in several areas. These impairments were similar to those found by other researchers studying people who had smoked tobacco moderately to heavily for many years" (Mann 115).

Another problem students often have with using quotations is that of framing them gracefully. They will write a sentences such as this:

> In Peggy Mann's discussion of a marijuana research study, she says . . .

Students should be taught that it is not necessary to repeat the word "she" in this construction, that there are other ways of saying "says," and that framing or contextual references can appear in the middle or end of a sentence, not just at the beginning.

Thus, the above sentence could be rephrased in many possible ways, such as:

> In her discussion of a marijuana research study, Peggy Mann says (indicates, suggests, maintains, states, points out, reveals, shows, etc.)
>
> or
>
> Research on marijuana smoking indicates its effect on the lungs, heart, and brain, an effect, which, as Peggy Mann points out, is "similar to those found by other researchers studying people who had smoked tobacco moderately to heavily for many years" (115).

Difficulties in incorporating quotations can often be detected if either you or the student reads the text aloud.

 ## For Discussion

A student has come into the writing center with a draft of his research paper, reprinted below. Read the paper and then, in small groups, use the discussion questions to examine how you would work with this student.

Writing Assignment

> *Our culture's attitude toward science and technology has its roots in the Enlightenment, a period in which reason and observable fact were believed to hold the answers to any questions we could think up. Being steeped in these beliefs, we have difficulty imagining any other way of thinking: questions about the limitations and risks of scientific knowledge seem to threaten our most fundamental principle that to know more is always better. But the controversies surrounding new discoveries and technological developments, from the atomic bomb to gene splicing, computers to threshing machines, suggest that we are not as comfortable with this principle as we thought. In the introduction to* Jurassic Park, *for example, Michael Crichton suggests the need for scientists to be monitored. He points out that a major problem associated with current research in biotechnology is that there are no "watchdogs" among the scientists themselves, because most have a commercial stake in their research.*

Writing Topic

Working in your tutorial group, select an area of scientific research that has the potential for having a profound impact on humanity. Then write a five to six page essay that addresses the following question:
Are there dangers inherent in this type of research that scientists ought to consider?

 **How Far Should We Go?**

The modern world has been taken over by the continuous progression of science and technology. It seems that these days we can accomplish anything through science, but in fact we have only begun to solve many mysteries. Through scientific research, we have been able to perform many operations which we had previously thought were impossible. One particular area which is currently being researched for future use is the practice of manipulating genes in undeveloped embryos that have resulted from artificial fertilization.

Genetic manipulation in artificial fertilization is a complex concept. First sperm must be introduced to an egg in a petri dish, therefore creating an embryo. Once the embryo has formed enough cells the doctors can remove one. Into this single cell, a virus can be injected. This virus could carry genes that would work to correct any faults that may be present in the original genome code.

Genetic manipulation in artificial fertilization has many potential benefits, such as the detection of genetic defects and the cures for these defects. But we must not be blinded by the possibilities. We must recognize that there are also many possible repercussions which could occur. We must realize that although science has bettered the quality of life in innumerable ways, the balance of nature is very delicate. If we keep trying to push further, we could very easily destroy the natural balance of life. Therefore it is imperative that we take extreme caution when experimenting with the manipulation of the genes in undeveloped embryos.

With the knowledge that scientists are gaining rapidly these days, it is conceivable that in a few short years we would be able to determine the complete genetic makeup of people for the rest of their lives. This means that if they had any latent diseases in their genes that would develop later in their life the doctors would know about it before they were born. Basically, with the studies of the genome codes in the human body, it is possible that our entire genetic lifespan could be mapped out for us.

All of this recent information opens many doors to the medical and scientific worlds. With the information obtained through the studies of genome codes and the recent studies of genetic manipulation it might be possible to create cures for many genetically caused defects in young embryos. Already, genetic manipulation is being used in many current experiments in which doctors are altering the genes in new embryos in order to treat genetically based diseases, such as diabetes or AIDS.

One such project is that of Dr. Flossie Wang Stoal, a doctor at the University of California at San Diego who has been working on an experiment to counter act the effects of the AIDS virus on young children. How this operation works is first they extract blood cells from the umbilical cord. Then these stem cells are injected with a new gene which produces an enzyme called hairpin ribozyme. This enzyme destroys the RNA cells which HIV uses to duplicate it's genes therefore preventing AIDS from establishing itself in the body. This is just one example of the many possibilities there are for the use of genetic manipulation in the field of medicine.

Dr. Stoal's experiments are used with newborns, not with new embryos, but they do give us an idea of the type of operations that could be performed regularly with more research and experimentation. We are learning that it is possible for doctors to inject foreign viruses into the cells of the embryo. These non-harmful viruses would carry therapeutic genome codes which would spread to the other cells of the body and eliminate the faulty genes which would cause disease to occur.

Being able to perform such operations seems to be a marvelous breakthrough in the quest for health. But, we must realize that there are far too many dangers which could occur if there aren't strong enough restrictions placed on the experimentation. It would be too easy for things to get out of hand with the knowledge that could be acquired through the the studies of genome codes.

Although doctors may be able to create cures to genetic diseases by uncovering people's genome codes, they might also uncover diseases that they can not cure. If this were to happen, peoples lives could be ruined. For example, there would be no more life insurance for people who knew that they are going to die. Also it would be very unlikely that people who are going to die soon would be able to get jobs and support themselves while they are alive. These are just a couple of immediate social problems. There are other natural and ethical problems which would occur.

There are many ethical problems which arise such as 'do we have the right to tamper with genetic codes?' Since who a person is is determined by his or her genetic code, then by altering that code we are in turn altering who that person is. In a way, this would be acting like God. There is also the law of nature which states that the strong shall survive. This may seem to be a cruel and un-humane concept, but there are people who were meant to die and people who were meant to live.

If we were to create cures for all people who have genetic defects then there would be even greater over crowding in the world then there already is. This particular argument is an especially touchy one. If I were in a situation in which I had a hereditary genetic disease and it could be diagnosed and cured before I was even born, then of course I would want to be cured. But, objectively I would have to say that genetic research should be strictly guided in order that it does not get out of hand.

Works Cited

Glass, Bently. *"The Ethical Dimensions of the Biological Sciences.* Eds. Ruth Ellen Bulger, Elizabeth Heitman, Stanley Joel Reiser. New York: Cambridge University Press, 1993. 51-55.

Klepner, Daniel. "Thoughts on Being Bad." *Physics Today.* 46.8 Aug. 1993: 9-11.

Moore, Pat. "Genetic Manipulation." *New Scientists.* 141 13 Nov. 1993: 1-4.

Vines, Gail. "How Far Should We Go?" *New Scientists.* 142 12 Feb 1994: 12-13.

Questions For Discussion

1. What do you feel are the student's strengths and weaknesses as a writer? How can you use these to determine your approach to revision?

2. What area of the paper will you focus on during this session? Will you suggest a revision strategy that the student might be able to use in a subsequent writing task?

3. How can the concept of audience and purpose help focus the revision?

4. Do you feel this student is comfortable incorporating outside material into his own text? Is there a way that the student could have used sources more effectively?

You may also find it helpful to use the **Worksheet For Examining Sources in a Text,** reprinted on the following page.

Worksheet for Examining Sources in a Text

Adapted from Margaret R. Kirkland. "Intertextuality in Discourse Community Culture: An Analytical Tool" *Conference on College Composition and Communication*

1. What types of source material are used in this paper (journal articles, encyclopedias, books, etc.)

2. Where is the source material located (primarily in one or two sections or dispersed and integrated in the argument?)

3. How is the source material incorporated into this paper? (paraphrased? summarized briefly or at some length? densely synthesized, material from several sources "stacked?" quoted? given a reference only?) Are there croutons in this text?

4. What context/introduction is provided for each type of source material? (none, the writer's name only? name and identity? explanation of the context of the previous work?)

5. What is the function of the references? (as proof/evidence? to support a position or interpretation? to establish authority? to contradict another position?)

Essays about Literature

Two common assignments concerned with literature that students frequently bring to the writing center are those of the book review and the literary essay. Both types of assignments cause problems for students, partly because they may be unfamiliar with strategies for analyzing literature but also because they may not understand the nature of the tasks they are being asked to fulfill. Of course, the requirements of these two genres are too complex to address adequately here; however, the information discussed below will enable you to work with students in the writing center who are assigned essays concerned with literature.

The Book Review

The book review is a particularly confusing assignment because the models students see in newspapers and magazine often contain a great deal of plot summary, when, in actuality, the aim of the academic book review essay is to convince an intelligent readership that a particular book is or is not worth reading—that is, the review should have an argumentative thrust. Because students do not understand this, they often write plot summaries instead of developing a thesis about the book, supported with evidence from the text. In helping students write book reviews, then, find out if the student really understands what the assignment requires. Point out that some form of plot summary should be included in order to give the reader a sense of what the book is about, but that the primary purpose of the review, usually, is to convince an audience that the book is or is not valuable in some way. Here are some questions you might find useful:

1. Are the characters believable? Are they well developed?

2. Does the plot keep your attention? How does it do so?

3. Does the book raise important questions about our society? About relationships?

4. Is it well-written? How would you characterize the author's style? Is it descriptive? Evocative?

5. Does the book address an important controversy? Does it take an unusual position?

In responding to these questions, students should find examples in the text that illustrate their ideas. They can use the Note Synthesis Sheet to record quotations they might wish to use.

The Essay About a Work of Literature

Students have difficulty writing about works of literature for the same reason they do when they are assigned to write book reviews—they often don't understand what sort of essay they are supposed to write and therefore simply write a plot summary. In working with students on these types of assignments, then, you should emphasize that the essay about literature aims to persuade readers of an idea or point concerning the particular literary work and that they will be using evidence from the text and sometimes the opinions of others to support their views. Point out that there must be a definable focused thesis that ties together all the specific claims made in the paper. A.M. and Charlene Tibbetts (*Strategies of Rhetoric with Handbook*. Fifth edition. Glenview, Illinois: Scott, Foresman and Company, 1987) suggest that students should think of themselves as writing for an audience who has read the work but may not have thought of the idea that the writer is presenting. They sum up the writer's relationship with their reader as follows:

> I have read a work (that you also have read), and I have an idea about it that may have not occurred to you. I am going to explain this idea, giving you examples from the work to prove my point, and I hope when I am through that you will agree with me (449).

Helping Students Understand a Literary Work

When students come to the writing center with an assignment to write about a work of literature, you can help them understand the work by asking them the following questions:

1. *What happens in the work?*
    Ask students to summarize the plot and tell you about the characters. Ask them which character they think is the main character and whether that character faces any conflict. Perhaps that conflict is physical; more often it is psychological or or emotional. Ask students if they can find the climax or turning point within the story or if there is a point where loose threads are tied together or when a decision is made.

2. *What is the "theme" of the work? Or what does the work say?*
    Point out that many writers of poetry, drama, and fiction have ideas about society or about human relationships and that works of literature often raise issues or themes for the reader to consider. Some works of literature clearly emphasize a particular idea, and the author's idea of right and wrong are clearly presented, perhaps even one-sided. But others often show that human nature and human decision making is complex and that

it is difficult to determine absolute right and wrong. In fact, most important works of literature do not have clearly defined heroes and villains, and concepts of right and wrong are presented as complex.

3. *Does the author have a clear voice in this work?*
Ask students if they can trace a narrative voice that tells a story or if they can determine the author's point of view. Sometimes works of fiction are presented from a first person viewpoint, in which case, the writer functions almost as a character within the story. At other times, the writer assumes an omniscient viewpoint, in which case he or she can present thoughts and feelings of all characters and summarize all actions which pertain to the story. Sometimes the author attempts to be completely objective in the telling of the story and presents "facts" without authorial comment.

4. *Where is the author physically, socially and temporally located in this work?*
Often, the narrator stands outside the narration—he or she is simply an observer of the events being related. This distance may be the result of actual physical or social separation (the narrator is an outsider, as in *Gulliver's Travels*) or because the narrator is telling about something that happened a long time ago, in which case, time has created the narrator's distance from the narrated events. Asking students about the location of the narrator to events being narrated or described is also helpful when helping students to analyze a poem. Since many poets write about particular scenes or landscapes, it is helpful to ask students if they can see the poet and view what is being described through his or her eyes. This can help the student understand the perspective of the work.

5. *How is the work organized? What is the structure of the work?*
Ask students how the literary work is shaped or how it gets its form. If it is a play, does it have scenes and acts? If so, how do these divisions create the shape of the story? If it is a fictional work, is it divided into chapters or episodes? Do different sections deal with different perspectives? If it is a poem, is there a pattern of stanzas or sections? Can the student locate any repetition or patterns within the work?

6. *Are there problems in the work? Is the work unsuccessful in some way?*
This question is very helpful in enabling students to think of ideas, since they can focus their papers in exploring where the work may not have succeeded. Is a character poorly developed? Are the characters too "black and white," or unbelievable? Is the action improbable? Is the tone too uneven (too hysterical or too flat)? Is the value system completely dated?

Questions such as these can help students clarify for themselves their overall reaction to the work and can enable them to think about a possible thesis.

Finding "Evidence" for the Literary Paper

Another reason that students encounter difficulties in writing about literature is that they may not know how to provide evidence for the claims they make. They assert something, refer briefly to the plot and assume that they have proven a case. Therefore, one important way that writing center tutors can help students with literary papers is to teach them how to take notes from or mark a text in order to gather evidence for their essays. Suggest that students read the text more than once, the first time to get a sense of its major themes and structure, the second with the aim of seeking out puzzles or anomalies, to mark passages that confuse them or contradict what they previously believed the work to be about. Have them question the actions of the characters (why do they do the things they do? What do they notice about the narrator?) Assure students that few literary critics read a work only once, and that they will perceive the text with greater complexity if they read it several times, gathering "evidence" for the points they wish to make. The Source Note Sheets and the Note Synthesis Sheets discussed above can also be useful for gathering this type of evidence. Learning to incorporate quotations into the text also pertains to assignments concerned with literature.

Other Problems With the Literary Essay

In addition to writing plot summaries and not knowing how to gather evidence, students often attempt to cover too many possibilities—characters, settings, plots, symbols, themes—everything they can think of. Urge students to narrow their focus—perhaps to concentrate on the effect of a particular character on the plot, to trace a change in a character, to examine the role of the setting on a character's decision, or to find patterns of imagery that help the story to unfold or which provide a counterpoint to the apparent mood of the story. Another common misunderstanding is that there must be one "right" interpretation to a literary work, as if it is a puzzle that must be solved. Students should aim for an interpretation which they can support with evidence, one which is not simply a matter of opinion.

A Handout on the Literary Essay

The following handout can be reproduced and distributed to students who are writing essays concerned with literature.

Writing About Literature

This handout was developed by John Bruns at the University of Southern California

When you write about a literary work, you are offering other readers your particular interpretation. Since a good piece of literature will lend itself to a number of possible coherent interpretations, your particular reading offers yet another possibility in opening up work to further insight and investigation by readers. The literary work actually invites readers to make sense of it. Thus it offers readers the opportunity and the challenge to acknowledge one possible reading.

The Argumentative Literary Essay

There are many different forms an essay about literature can take (book report, personal responses, etc.), and the instructor will usually give specific directions for the kind of essay required. The aim of the argumentative essay, however, is to persuade the reader of an idea or point of a particular interpretation. Because most students are probably more familiar or comfortable with other forms of essays about literature (such as those mentioned above), they often don't understand what sort of essay they are supposed to write and therefore focus primarily on character exposition or plot summary.

For this reason, it is important that you understand that the argumentative essay tries to persuade your readers that your ideas about the literary text are valid. Your writing, then, will use evidence from the text and sometimes the opinions of others to support these ideas. Unlike the book report or the personal response essay, however, the argumentative essay is driven by a definable focused thesis that ties together all the specific aims of the paper. The book report, for instance, may be structured according to the plot of the text (what happens in the beginning, the middle, and the end). The argumentative essay, on the other hand, subordinates plot and character to a central idea about what the text "means" or how it functions culturally. As the authors of *Writing Worth Reading* put it, *Let the structure of your argument take priority over the structure of the text.*

How you summarize important events in the story or how you discuss what a certain character represents depends entirely on a central thesis. For instance, if I choose to argue that Joseph Conrad's *Heart of Darkness* is about humankind's fear of its own primitive unconscious, then I may wish to focus largely on the relationship between the narrator, Marlowe, and Kurtz. As evidence of this idea, I will draw on passages from the text in which these two figures play a part. If, on the other hand, my interest is in demonstrating how the story is a product of British colonialism, I may wish to emphasize the racist language and images Conrad uses to describe Africa. What evidence I bring from the text (how I discuss the book) depends on what argument I wish to make.

Reading Carefully and Critically

Although it is good advice to read everything carefully, literature especially requires close reading. To read a work of literature closely, you might begin by deliberately seeking out puzzles in the text. Mark passages that confuse you or contradict what you previously believed the text to be about. Don't be afraid to recognize multiple interpretations of a particular passage or of the text as a whole. Although it may be true that an interpretation of a text depends a great deal on what the author *intended,* it is important to be aware of differing perspectives of just what this intent *is.* No writer can control the diversity of effects that combinations of words and images have, especially as those combinations require personal meaning supplied by individual readers. Perhaps it is useful to think of the writer of an argumentative literary essay as having a much more *active* role as a reader.

Tips for Reading Carefully and Critically

These are simply suggestions of ways that may help you look more closely at a passage, and are by no means, exclusive. Each passage is different and, accordingly, different things will need to be emphasized.

> I. *Literal Reading:* This is simply designed to make sure that you understand, on a literal level, what is going on in your passage. Try paraphrasing a passage.

> II. *Grammatical Structures:* This includes looking at things like: syntax, grammar, subordinate clauses, parallel structure, punctuation, length and structure of the sentence, ambiguous pronouns, word order and choice, the overabundance of nouns, verbs, adjectives, etc.

> III. *Figures of Speech:* This category would include: metaphors, similes, personification, ellipsis, alliteration, chiasmus, etc.

> IV: *Images and Themes:* Some words can have more than one meaning (it's good to look them up in the dictionary). Moreover, words within the passage can evoke previous scenes, images or ideas that have occurred earlier in the text.

> V. *Context:* When you are analyzing a passage, you are taking is out of context. Make sure that you put it back in its context. Remember that you experience a novel cumulatively and that your feelings and impressions of characters, themes, etc. change.

> VI: *Putting it All Together:* After you have looked at literal meaning, grammatical structure, figures of speech, themes and ideas, and context, you need to decide what all of these say about your passage. Sometimes there won't be clear distinctions. For example, the use of metaphor in a sentence might be dependnt upon the sentence's syntax.

Gathering Evidence for Your Argument

Careful reading should result in providing you with sufficient evidence to begin formulating an opinion about the literary work. The evidence you gather to support your thesis may require you to return again and again to the text to isolate passages that clarify your meaning. This is what is meant by "textual evidence" and it is crucial to arguing anything where interpreting the words and ideas of others is involved. This evidence can assume the form of dialogue, events, descriptive details, key words, images, themes and metaphors. Do not be afraid to scrutinize evidence that possibly contradicts your present thesis. Although it can be frustrating, you can view this conflicting evidence as an opportunity to help you not only refine and clarify your work, but enrich your understanding of the complexity of a particular literary work. An awareness of a literary work's complexity is always encouraged in the literary essay. It is what helps make the argumentative literary essay argumentative.

There are many bases for interpretation. The authors of *Writing Worth Reading* describe two types of interpretation. One type is **factual analysis.** Some feel that interpretations can be persuasive if one starts with the facts of the text and stays close with them. Such readings are plausible when the insights are grounded in the text.

Often, however, interpretation can go beyond the facts to what could be called **informed speculation.** It is informed because it *involves* the text, *engages* it; it is speculation because it goes beyond the facts to the possibilities they imply.

We do not mean to simplify textual interpretation by reducing it to only two possibilities. Usually, writers of literary essays employ a combination of both, and certainly no one type of interpreations is more important than the other. What is imporant (and/or interesting) is the argument that can be persuasively made from an interpretation.

Tips for Developing a Clear and Compelling Thesis

When evaluating an early draft of your essay, examine the thesis statement to determine whether it makes a point.

- Is the argument worth making?

- Would the statement provoke reactions?

- Can someone legitimately disagree with it?

Read your thesis aloud and then ask yourself whether an intelligent member of the audience would respond to your point with "So what?" or "Big deal!" If they can, look for a more significant idea, present a more interesting facet of your original thought, or modify it to say something that sparks interest or raises expectations.

Tips for Gathering Evidence

There is no question that careful reading is crucial to gathering evidence for a literary essay. Even if one has a firm grasp of the fundamental elements of a text (plot, theme, author's voice, etc.), this does not ensure that these elements will provide adequate support for any claim made about the text. Not only are these elements sometimes unreliable, they are often subordinated to other, less clear elements (such as language, imagery, or character dialogue). For example, at the end of Shakespeare's *The Taming of the Shrew,* the otherwise independent and ferocious Kate finally marries Petruchio. Because of this, we might be led to ignore ambiguity in dialogue (double meaning, irony, wit, etc.) in and choose instead to base out argument on plot only ("Kate is, like all women, ultimately submissive to her man"). This would be a shame, however, for it is precisely the ambiguity which makes for interesting argumentation. This is not to say that things such as plot and theme aren't essential to argumentation—indeed, there is no reason to suggest that an argument cannot be built and supported by these elements alone. Just be aware that the richness of a good text is seemingly fathomless—the basic elements of storytelling need not be your sole source of evidence.

Tips for Using Quotations

When you quote an author, be sure to address all the pertinent issues (i.e., thematics, language) raised by that quote. Any quotation, if accompanied by some analysis, could prove useful in supporting your thesis. What does it mean, however, to say "if accompanied by some analysis"? Is the quote itself sufficient enough to support whatever point you need to make about the text? Obviously not. As a general rule, you might remember that the commentary you make about a specific quote or passage should, invariably, be substantially longer than the quote itself. For instance, Roland Barthes, a French literary critic, wrote an entire book entitled *S/Z* about a single short story. In this book, the analysis Barthes makes is considerably longer than the short story itself, which is included in its entirety. The lesson here is *not* to be as ambitious as Barthes. Rather it is to take your time with the text. Get your hands dirty. Wrestle with individual words and confusing phrases. Not only will this make your essay more interesting, but it will also challenge you to interact with the text more and to come up with your own analyses, instead of falling into the trap of dealing with a text on too general a level, or by simply repeating what has been said by your professor.

Be sure to write in the present tense. By convention, one writes as though the events of the poem, play, novel, or story are taking place in the present (for example: "Hamlet says to himself. 'To be or not to be, that is the question.' he means that . . ."). We write about a work of literature in the present tense precisely because that is exactly how we experience it as a reader. When we write without using the present tense (for example: "When Hamlet said 'To be or not to be' he meant that . . ."), we do so because we are recalling what we *have read*. For this reason, it seems natural to use the past tense. The literary work, however, has its own space and time—however fictional it may be.

A Checklist for reading and writing about literature:

- Give yourself to the reading the first time through and make your notes on the second reading

- Remember that theme, symbolism, and language are concerns in nearly all literary works.

● When reading fiction, think about plot, character, setting, and point of view.

● Read poems aloud, and, as you do, think about meter and rhyme.

● Try to employ both factual analysis and informed speculation about the meanings in the work.

● Identify what interests or confuses you most, and use that as the basis of your analysis.

● Develop an essay on literature as you would other argumentative essays, with a thesis, evidence, warrants.

● Avoid mere plot summary and character analysis.

● Let the structure of your argument take priority over the structure of the text you are interpreting.

● Write in the present tense.

(From Writing worth Reading)

Thanks goes to Anne Thrope and Andrew Durkin for providing supplementary material

The discussions that take place in the writing center about literature are, unto themselves, extremely useful in enabling students to understand works of literature. Even if the tutor has not read the work (and no tutor can have read every work a student may be assigned), the questions discussed in this section can generate a great deal of enlightenment. Actually, after you work with several students on the same work of literature, you will feel as if you have already read it, even if you hadn't previously!

For Further Exploration:

Writing about literature is a study unto itself about which a great deal has been written. Here is a list of some additional sources which you might find helpful:

Barnet, Sylvan. *A Short Guide to Writing About Literature*. 7th Edition. New York: Harper Collins, 1996.

Minot, Stephen. *Reading Fiction*. Englewood Cliffs, New Jersey: Prentice-Hall, 1985.

Perrine, Laurence. *Sound and Sense: An Introduction to Literature*. Fort Worth: Harcourt Brace, 1992.

Petrosky, Anthony R. "From Story to Essay: Reading and Writing." *College Composition and Communication*. 23 (1982): 19–36.

Roberts, Edgar. *Writing About Literature*. 8th Edition. Englewood Cliffs, New Jersey, 1995.

Rosenblatt, Louise. *Literature as Exploration*. New York: Noble, 1965.

Suleiman, Susan R. and Inge Crosman, Eds. *The Reader in the Text: Essays on Audience and Interpretation*. Princeton: Princeton University Press, 1980.

Tomkins, Jane P. Ed. *Reader-Response Criticism: From Formalism to Post-Structuralism*. Baltimore: The Johns Hopkins University Press, 1980.

Working with Non-native and Dialect Speakers in the Writing Center

John R. Edlund
California State University, Los Angeles

Introduction

Immigration patterns and demographic changes have dramatically increased the numbers of non-native speakers of English attending American universities and colleges. At California State University, Los Angeles, more than 60% of the students report that their first language is not English, and other institutions across the country have similar populations. These students have generally attended English as a Second Language (ESL) programs either in high school or in special programs designed to prepare them for college admission, but college-level academic writing puts increased demands on their English writing ability. Cultural and linguistic differences combine with the normal difficulties of acquiring new information and concepts to create unique problems, problems that the writing center is often expected to solve.

Faculty have generally not been trained to deal with the problems of non-native speakers. Left to their own devices, faculty members come up with a wide range of strategies. Some try to ignore the errors they see. On our campus the Philosophy professors continue to assign written exams because they do not believe they can test

203

knowledge of philosophy with multiple choice tests, but they cannot always understand the writing of their students. One of them said, "If the philosophy's ok, I'll give it a good grade no matter how bad the writing is. But if I can't understand the writing, I don't know how to evaluate it." On the other hand, we have an anthropology professor who can't leave an error unmarked. When told it is a waste of time to mark up final drafts he said, "I know. I can't help myself."

The School of Business has the least tolerance for error. One Business professor called our Writing Center to complain "My student met with one of your tutors and there are still three errors in her paper. What's wrong with you guys?" In business, a grammatical error can lose a customer or a contract. In this case, however, writing center pedagogy and our desire to be more than a proofreading and editing service are in conflict with the understandable desire of the business professor for error-free writing.

Ann Johns describes an interview with some Political Science professors who call their ESL students "academically illiterate," because from their point of view they lack background knowledge, have trouble understanding the purposes of texts, don't plan reading or writing tasks well, lack "conceptual imagination," and lack essential vocabulary (Johns 168). These professors ask "Why can't they write like political scientists?"

The best thing about what Johns' political scientists have to say is that they do not reduce the problems they perceive to a simple lack of grammatical knowledge. While the tone of their comments is less than charitable, their analysis of the problems is quite accurate as far as it goes. However, it would be a mistake to attribute these shortcomings to a lack of ability or motivation. In "Assessment by Misconception: Cultural Influences and Intellectual Traditions" Ballard and Clanchy map out a continuum of attitudes toward learning that ranges from conserving to extending knowledge, and identify three learning approaches: reproductive, analytical, and speculative. They note that all of these patterns are found in all cultures, but do argue that Asian cultures, following a Confucian pattern of social value, tend to focus on the reproductive forms of knowledge, where the emphasis is on memorizing and imitating what is already known rather than criticizing or speculating. This cultural difference is, I believe, at the root of what these political scientists are calling a "lack of conceptual imagination."

Ballard and Clanchy also made a study of the marginal comments made by instructors on 500 first-year essays from Australian colleges. They found that instructors expected the essays 1) to be clearly focused on the topic and deal fully with its central concerns, 2) to be the result of wide and critical reading, 3) to present a reasoned argument, and 4) to be complete.

Ballard and Clanchy note that when the teacher and the student do not share the same language and culture, there are problems with all of these concerns. Focus is problematic because different cultures have different standards of what is relevant and what is not, and because standards of etiquette in some cultures require indirection. Wide reading on a topic presents problems when the sources disagree—the student who is interested in memorizing received wisdom wonders which authority to agree with. Argumentation perhaps causes the most difficulty of all, because even different academic disciplines have different standards about what constitutes a valid argument and what counts as evidence, and varying cultural standards also apply. However, Ballard and Clanchy argue that in reading ESL papers, even when there are major problems in other areas, teachers focus most of their attention on the linguistic aspects of the presentation, because these matters appear to be the most objective, and because there is an erroneous sense that the linguistic errors are the key to solving the other problems.

We will take up some of these cultural differences in greater detail later in the chapter. However, it is clear that while grammatical problems may be the most visible sign of ESL writing, they are often only a symptom of other underlying problems. As we explore the issue of ESL students in the writing center, consider the following questions:

1. What is known about language acquisition and its development that can be useful to you as a writing center tutor?

2. What should you, the writing center tutor, be doing to help ESL students?

3. To what extent should you take responsibility for helping to educate faculty members about dealing with ESL students?

Second Language Acquisition and the Writing Center

Let's take up our first question: "What is known about language acquisition and its development that can be useful to you as a writing center tutor?"

Stephen Krashen's language acquisition theory is a good starting point for understanding the implications of this question. First, Krashen distinguishes between language *acquisition* and language *learning*. For Krashen, second language *acquisition* is a natural unconscious process similar to first language acquisition. Language *learning*, on the other hand, is the development of conscious knowledge about a language-rules, forms, etc. (*Principles* 10-11). Krashen's view is that conscious learning has *no* effect on unconscious acquisition, a position that has generated considerable controversy. However, let's accept this extreme position for the moment, and consider the implications for teaching.

Comprehensible Input

According to Krashen, acquisition occurs when *comprehensible input* in the target language is available. Just as babies acquire language from the surrounding environment without studying grammar books and dictionaries, second language learners acquire language from interacting with other language users. Krashen argues that we acquire by understanding language that contains structure a bit beyond our current level of competence through the help of context or extra-linguistic information. We acquire best by "going for meaning" first, and as a result, we acquire structure and vocabulary.

In Krashen's view, simplified codes-caretaker speech, foreigner talk, teacher talk—facilitate acquisition by making input more comprehensible. In fact, for Krashen, because direct teaching of rules and forms is not useful, the main task of a language teacher is to facilitate language acquisition by creating the proper linguistic environment (*Principles* 20-25).

The Affective Filter

Sometimes acquisition does not appear to occur even when comprehensible input is available. Krashen proposes that input is blocked by what he calls an "affective filter." Motivation, self-confidence, and anxiety are three factors that influence this filter. A student with low motivation, low self-confidence, and high anxiety will not acquire the second language in spite of the presence of comprehensible input. Krashen discusses two types of motivation: *Integrative,* the desire to be *like* those who speak the language, and *instrumental,* the need to use the language to accomplish some purpose, like obtaining a college degree. Integrative motivation is much more powerful than instrumental (*Principles* 30-31).

Another way to look at the issue of motivation is to say that the input must not only be comprehensible, but also socially meaningful. An individual may live and work in an environment rich in input in the second language, but if this potential input is defined as being directed toward some social group the individual does not belong to, it may not be attended to. For example, an instructor working to improve the literacy of a group of California Conservation Corps employees noticed that the two Vietnamese members of the predominantly African-American and Chicano group paid little or no attention to the social interaction of the other members. The only English language interactions they attended to were direct orders and instructions from the supervisor.

The Monitor

Krashen does admit that conscious learning can be used to modify output to some degree, if the following conditions are met: If the speaker or writer has the *time* to apply such knowledge, if the situation calls for or triggers a *focus on form,* and if the speaker or writer has *knowledge of the rule.* He calls this function the *monitor* (Principles 15-18).

Implications for Teaching Writing

In writing there is more opportunity for monitoring and revising output than in oral speech, so Krashen's "monitor" hypothesis could be seen as a justification for teaching grammar in the writing class. Indeed, a process approach to writing generally emphasizes separating the proofreading process from composing and revising, thereby providing the time and the focus on form required for monitoring. However, rules are notoriously given to exceptions, and ESL writers often engage in hyper-correction—changing correct forms they have acquired to incorrect ones generated by the misapplication of a rule. Rules, while useful on occasion for proofreading concerns, are a poor substitute for a strong basis in acquisition.

Because reading is the source of comprehensible input in written English, Krashen's theory also implies that students who read more will write better, and that teaching writing in isolation from substantial amounts of reading is likely to be unproductive, especially for non-native speakers. How students go about this reading is also important. For example, a Business professor from China told me that when he was studying accounting in Canada, he wondered why his English reading ability was not improving. He was reading so many books in English! He opened one of his textbooks and discovered that in his extensive marginal notations he had essentially translated the book into Chinese, and that when he studied it he was reading Chinese, not English. He decided to throw his English-Chinese dictionary away and read only in English, and his reading ability quickly improved. This is not to say that bilingual dictionaries are necessarily bad, but it is true that translation is a different process from reading.

Alternative Second Language Acquisition Theories

Rod Ellis's *Understanding Second Language Acquisition* provides a useful overview of competing theories of language acquisition (248-82). One of the most interesting of these is the "Acculturation Model," which takes the concerns addressed by Krashen's Affective Filter and makes them the central issue of language acquisition. Ellis quotes John Schuman, who states that "the degree to which a learner acculturates to the target language group will control the degree to which he acquires the second language" (251). Thus the degree of psychological and social distance between the learner and the target language culture will determine the success of the second language acquisition process. We will take up these issues of motivation and social distance again later in this chapter.

Krashen's insistence on the lack of connection between conscious learning and unconscious acquisition, characterized as the "non-interface" position, has been the most controversial hypothesis in his version of language acquisition theory. Other linguists posit some kind of interface between acquisition and learning. William Rutherford, for example, stakes out a compromise position in which acquisition is still the most powerful factor in second language mastery. However, Rutherford believes that conscious attention to grammatical forms or other features can produce "consciousness raising" which can guide acquisition.

Interlanguage

Essential to Rutherford's position is the concept of "interlanguage." An "interlanguage" is a structured grammatical system, constructed by the learner, which approximates the grammatical system of the language being acquired. As acquisition proceeds, the interlanguage system evolves into a better approximation of the standard system. In Rutherford's model, this evolution proceeds through "hypothesis testing," and thus highlighting or focusing on specific differences or mismatches between the learner's interlanguage system and the standard grammatical system can facilitate hypothesis formation and testing (Ellis 47, Rutherford 40). However, not every learner progresses to the end of the interlanguage continuum. When acquisition stops before the grammatical system is entirely standard, "fossilization" is said to have occurred.

In practice, language acquisition theory means that reading and listening to a large amount of comprehensible English is essential to improving a student's English language ability. Rutherford's revision of this theory means that highlighting specific points at which the student's interlanguage system is at variance with a native-speaker's grammatical system can help that student form a better hypothesis about how that particular part of the system works, and thus facilitate acquisition of the proper forms. This is pretty much what current composition pedagogy recommends anyway. It is important to note, however, that although Rutherford's theory does not preclude the teaching of grammatical rules, it does not require such teaching either. The tutor's job is simply to call attention to non-standard forms.

Exercise

> *Write an account of your own efforts to learn a second language. Do your own experiences tend to support or contradict the language acquisition theories recounted above?*

Contrastive Rhetoric: Cultural Differences Regarding Discourse Structure

Occasionally in the writing center you will encounter a paper written by a non-native speaker that is difficult to read or understand, but more because of its organization and argumentation than because of grammatical or idiomatic problems. You may find the paper unfocused, contradictory, illogical, or vague, even though the writer seems intelligent and well-informed. In this case it is likely that the rhetorical patterns of the writer's culture—stylistic preferences, organizational expectations, standards of evidence and argument—are significantly different from American patterns.

Robert Kaplan first took up the problems of what he called "Contrastive Rhetoric" in a 1966 article called "Cultural Thought Patterns in Intercultural Education," and later in a 1972 book entitled *The Anatomy of Rhetoric: Prolegomena to a Functional Theory of Rhetoric.* Kaplan analyzes numerous examples of foreign student writing in English, and represents his findings as a series of five simple diagrams. "Semitic" writing is represented by a series of parallel lines with dotted connections, "Oriental" by a spiral, "Romance" by a crooked single line, and "Slavic" by a similar crooked, but dotted, line. The English pattern is represented as a single, direct, vertical line. These "squiggles" have provoked both interest and controversy. Clearly they are simplifications of complex factors; even Kaplan calls them superficial.

It is clear, however, that cultural differences in rhetorical patterns exist. What is less clear is how they develop, how they are transmitted, and how much they influence writing in English. Tutors should at least be aware that an essay that appears to be illogical or incoherent by American standards may in fact be well-crafted by the standards of another culture. This is not to say that the foreign pattern should simply be accepted as a cultural difference, but on the other hand, calling the paper "illogical" or "incoherent" probably won't help the student improve.

Culturally-based rhetorical patterns can range from stylistic preferences at the sentence level to global organizational structures. Kaplan argues that modern Arabic writers prefer elaborate parallel structures connected with coordinating conjunctions to the subordinating constructions preferred in English since the Elizabethan period. This style is based on the style of the Koran, but can be seen in the English of the King James version of the Hebrew Old Testament (*Anatomy* 34-40). In my experience, Arabic speakers do tend to produce long sentences in English, connected with "and," "but," and often simply with commas.

American teachers often ask students to write "in your own words." However, Feng-Fu Tsao reports that Chinese writers have "an extraordinary fondness for quotation and allusion," because it is the mark of an educated person to quote from the literature of past ages (*Contrastive Studies* 109). Chinese classic literature and history are considered to be part of the context of the writing itself, an essential source for idiom and elegant language, and such quotations and allusions are usually undocumented, because it is assumed that any educated reader will recognize them. However, a Chinese writer who relies heavily on undocumented sources when writing in English for an American teacher is likely to be accused of plagiarism.

The patterns and rhetorical strategies that are taught in school are the most persistent. Linguist John Hinds presents an organizational pattern from a Japanese textbook on writing that is roughly analogous to the five-paragraph essay formula in English:

ki First, begin one's argument.

shoo Next, develop that.

ten At the point where this development is finished, turn the idea to a sub-theme where there is a connection, but not a directly connected association [to the major theme].

ketsu Last, bring all of this together and reach a conclusion.

(K. Takemata in Hinds, 80) Hinds points out that the *ten* and *ketsu* sections are especially problematic for English readers.

> In *ten*, an abrupt shift takes place in which information only indirectly relevant to the major point is brought up with minimal syntactic marking. This obviously causes problems for English readers who do not expect "digressions" and "unrelated information" to come up suddenly. . . . In *ketsu*, the major difficulty involves the Japanese definition of this term and the difference between that and the English definition of "conclusion." Takemata (1976:26-27) states that a Japanese *ketsu* "need not be decisive [*dan-teiteki*]. All it needs do is to indicate a doubt or ask a question."

I have read numerous papers by Japanese ESL students that were four paragraph essays in which the third paragraph seemed to be entirely off topic. If you know this pattern, you expect the third section to make some kind of turn away from the topic; otherwise, you are confused. Is it a good idea to counteract this Japanese formula by teaching the five-paragraph essay? It may help, but I would be cautious, because some students will overgeneralize the formula to all writing situations in English.

Hinds also proposes a typology of language based on relative reader/writer responsibility, and classifies Japanese as a reader-responsible language, English as writer-responsible, and Mandarin as a language in transition from reader-responsibility to writer-responsibility (Kaplan "Contrastive Rhetoric" 291). This means that in Japanese the reader is expected to read between the lines, to supply missing connections and information, and in general to tolerate far more ambiguity than an American reader would be comfortable with. Thus Kaplan argues "the fact that a student understands audience in one language does not mean the student understands audience in any other language system" ("Contrastive Rhetoric" 296)

Just as American teachers have difficulty understanding foreign rhetorical patterns, many foreign students have similar troubles with American patterns. One student wrote on her Writing Proficiency Exam:

> My friend and I read an article. Although my English-speaking friend thought it was very good convincing article, I, on the other hand, did not agree with him. What I thought was that it was very pushing one way argument . . . . Most of native-speaker agreed with him. Some foreigner agreed with him, some agreed with me . . . all Asian who have strong Asian background agreed with me.

This writer has conducted her own survey research on an important issue in Contrastive Rhetoric, and found American patterns to be one-sided and narrow from an Asian point of view. Many non-native speakers would agree with her.

Exercise

> *Replicate the experiment described by the student above. Take an editorial or an opinion piece from a newspaper or news magazine, and ask students from various cultural backgrounds to respond to the argument and the evidence. Do they think the article is persuasive? What do they think of the writer? How would a writer from their own culture handle a similar issue? Write up your results and share them with your fellow tutors.*

Who Are Your Non-native Speakers?

Because issues of comprehensible input, literacy, cultural discourse patterns, motivation, affect, social distance, and other personal and cultural factors have such a powerful influence on second language acquisition and the development of writing skills, it is useful to know who your students are, where they are from, and what they are trying to do. This is not to say that you should confront each ESL student with a battery of personal questions the first time he sits down with you, although many writing centers routinely gather some of this information with a first-contact questionnaire. However, as you encounter certain kinds of writing problems, you may be better able to help the student if you tactfully ask some background questions.

What Is the Student's Native Language?

Native language is a more reliable indication of cultural affiliation than name or ethnicity. However, don't be surprised if this question is difficult for some students to answer. I once tutored a student who was literally a Hindu from Hong Kong. He looked like he was from India, but his paper exhibited all the problems typical of Chinese writers. He told me most of his friends were Chinese, and he spoke Chinese more often than English or his native Indian dialect. Similarly, you may encounter Chinese students from Latin America, who typically can speak Chinese to some extent, but for whom Spanish is dominant. Some students may feel that they have more than one "native" language. Asking this question will at least begin a discussion of language background.

Is the Student Literate in His or Her Native Language?

Refugee students often have serious gaps in their educational careers, due to war or political persecution. I once taught a Cambodian student who had had no education at all during the Khmer Rouge years, escaped from Cambodia and spent two years in a Thai camp, immigrated to Germany and had two years of high school, and then moved to California after he discovered that family members were living here. I have also taught Chinese from Vietnam for whom English was their first literate language. On the other hand, some students are highly skilled writers in their native languages, and are frustrated with English because they can't achieve the same level of skill. In my experience, expatriate poets can be among the most difficult of students.

Is the Student an "International" Student?

Students with visas who intend to return to their own countries after completing their degrees have a different motivation for learning English than immigrant students who are citizens or permanent residents. Often, but not always, their motivation is instrumental rather than integrative, and they want to get through the English requirements as quickly and efficiently as possible. In some cases, however, the fact that they have chosen to study here while still firmly defining themselves as part of a different culture actually appears to make them more open to acquiring English.

If the Student Is an Immigrant, How Long Has He or She Been in This Country?

The process of language acquisition takes time, and length of time in the United States is clearly a factor. Many teachers think that six years in this country is a significant benchmark. However, there is considerable variation. I have hired non-native speaking tutors who were fluent enough to work in our writing center after having been here only three years. I once taught a Venezuelan military helicopter pilot who had become a very fluent writer in English after seven months. On the other hand, some students live in communities where all daily business is conducted in a language other than English, and where it is possible to live an entire lifetime without acquiring much English. If a student has been here a long time, yet his or her English ability is weak, you may want to talk about opportunities to increase the amount of input in English the student is exposed to.

How Much Does the Student Read in English? How Much in His or Her Native Language?

Because reading provides comprehensible input in the written language, students who read a lot generally write better. Krashen cites a number of studies that show that good writers do more pleasure reading, read the newspaper more often, and have more books in the home (Krashen, *Writing* 6). It is interesting to survey how many pages of English, excluding textbooks for classes, a student reads per week, and how many pages in another language. A student who does no pleasure or personal interest reading in any language is likely to be a poor writer. Students who read a lot in English often develop fluency quickly. The above-mentioned helicopter pilot was always carrying around books by Henry Kissinger and other political writers. One of my most impressive students was a Chinese woman from Vietnam whose first literate language was English, which she began acquiring at age twelve. On her survey she wrote that she was reading more than 100 pages of English per week, "but trying to cut down." She felt that all of the fiction she was reading was interfering with her studies.

Students who read a lot in their native language, but little in English, often have much to say, but struggle to express it. For these students, switching some of their reading to English will help. You might suggest that they read an English language newspaper once a week. In our writing center we address this problem by requiring some students to write three short summaries of newspaper and magazine articles per week, plus a personal response to one of them.

Why Did the Student Come to This Country, and How Does He or She Feel About Being Here?

These questions often get to the heart of serious problems in language acquisition. As noted above, the attitude of the language learner toward the target language group is perhaps the most important factor in the learner's progress. I once had a Chinese student in a Basic Writing course whose accent was very difficult to understand and whose writing, although well-developed and full of interesting ideas, was riddled with grammatical and idiomatic problems. He had taken the same course several times without success. When I asked him, "How do you feel about living in the United States," he said that no one had ever asked him that before and that he would have to think about it. When he came to the next class he told me that politically and economically he liked the U.S., but as far as culture was concerned he wanted to go back to Shanghai.

One's language is a personal matter; learning a new language involves acquiring new perspectives, new habits and behaviors, perhaps even a new self, or self concept. A resistance to the new culture can become a barrier to language acquisition, and not all immigrants have chosen to come here. Sometimes war or politics has made it necessary, and sometimes whole families immigrate and one member doesn't adjust well. A writing center tutor who listens to the student's honest feelings about living in a new culture can help change those attitudes and aid language acquisition in ways that have nothing to do with comprehensible input.

In our post-colonial world there is a political dimension to this conflict as well. Judith Rodby, in her book *Appropriating Literacy: Writing and reading in English as a Second Language,* outlines a dialectic of "Universalism" versus "Ethnicity." The universalist argues that English mediates between language minorities and the rest of the world, opens pathways to science, technology, education, and democracy, and serves well as an international language because of its "objectivity" and "plasticity." From the ethnicist viewpoint, English is a colonizing influence that destroys the voice, the literature, the culture, the integrity, perhaps the very existence of the ethnic group (30-41). If we ask, "Is the writing center a tool of empowerment or an instrument of oppression?" in the context of this dialectic, we can see that it can be both.

The writing center tutor may find him or herself in the middle of this psychological, cultural, and political conflict. This is quite appropriate-the writing center exists at the borders of academia, of disciplines, of discourse communities. The tutor's role is to help the student negotiate whatever border crossing is necessary and make decisions about what to do, what to take, and what to leave behind. The student needs to construct a self, or a voice, that works in the new context but is comfortable for the writer. The tutor's role in this negotiation is perhaps best represented by a subtle distinction: Do you teach your students to write *like* Americans or to write *for* Americans?

Exercise

Create a survey based on the questions above. Administer it to the non-native speakers who come to your writing center, or who attend your writing classes. Analyze the results and share them with your classmates or fellow tutors.

Strategies for working with Non-native Speakers in the Writing Center

Finally, we have gotten to the point where we can answer our first question: "What should you, the writing center tutor, be doing to help ESL students?" ESL students who come to the Writing Center often have all the writing problems of inexperienced native-speaking writers, in addition to the problems of second language acquisition and cultural assimilation. Your major role for these students is to function as a native-speaking (or fluent-speaking) informant about American language, culture, and rhetorical patterns. Here are three major points to remember about tutoring non-native students:

Language acquisition is crucial. As noted above, language acquisition is a natural on-going process. Many students speak their native languages at home and with their friends. Even if you feel that you lack the technical terms to explain the various grammatical and syntactical problems you observe in their papers, your conversations with them about the meaning of their papers are a significant and important part of their English language input.

Conscious knowledge of grammar is not necessary. Because language acquisition is an *unconscious* process, you yourself as a native speaker (or fluent-speaker) of English may not have conscious knowledge of a grammatical terminology or grammatical rules. You know what the correct forms are, but you do not know why they are correct or how to talk about them. This is *not* a serious detriment to your ability to tutor these students. In fact, you may be a better tutor because of it, as you will be naturally inclined to discuss meaning rather than grammatical forms. In time your knowledge of grammar will increase and you will learn to recognize when grammatical intervention is helpful.

A conference with a non-native speaker is not essentially different in goals or procedures from any other. Whatever the visible problems are, the basic rule is this: Deal with global issues—focus, audience, argument, organization—first; deal with grammatical and syntactical problems last. Find out what the writing is about and what it is intended to accomplish before you make suggestions about grammatical changes. Make sure you know what the writer intends to *mean* before you recommend altering the structure of any sentence.

It is best to sit side-by-side with the student so that you can read and edit the paper together, which is hard to do if the student is sitting across from you. It is a good idea to have scratch paper available for explaining concepts, but it is generally better to **avoid making any marks on the student's paper.** If the *student* takes notes on the conference and marks revisions and corrections on her own paper, she retains control and responsibility for the content and expression. Use your finger to point out problems. If you have trouble following this advice, try putting your pen back in your pocket and tutoring with empty hands. Your role is to identify rhetorical and communicative problems and possible solutions; it is up to the writer to decide what to do.

Ask the student what he or she wants to focus on in the conference. Let the student define the agenda, at least at first. Whatever strategy you ultimately take in the conference, it should address the student's main concerns.

Listen carefully to everything the writer says. The writer's attitudes, intentions and beliefs are important to the tutoring process. It is easy to talk too much and miss important clues.

Establish the context in which the writing is occurring. Ask what course the writing is for, and ask to see the assignment. Ask what the instructor has said he or she wants. Find out if it is an individual assignment or a group project. Ask when the paper is due, so that you can get an idea of what scale of revision is possible or appropriate.

Keeping the student's priorities in mind, skim the draft quickly to find the major problems or areas of possible improvement. With ESL writing, it is especially easy to fall into the practice of reading the paper sentence by sentence and marking errors as they are encountered, but the usual result is an overwhelming, disheartening, and contradictory morass of corrections and notations, with no clear plan for improvement. It is therefore important to skim the paper first to get a general impression of the purpose, the audience, and the nature of the most important problems, and make a tutoring plan. Of course in many tutoring situations you won't have more than three or four minutes to ask the student what she wants, skim the paper, and devise a rough agenda or plan for the session. Still, even the briefest of plans is preferable to the correct-as-you-go approach. Consider the three possible levels of response identified below:

1.   *Global/Rhetorical* (The paper as a whole)
     Considering the audience and format required by the assignment, and the purpose for the writing:

     ● Do the content, organizational scheme, tone, and other characteristics serve the writer's intention?
     ● What fairly simple changes could be made in the paper that would immediately improve its readability or effectiveness? (Such changes might

include supplying missing information, deleting irrelevant information, sharpening a thesis, reorganizing a paragraph, or writing a conclusion.)

2. *Syntax/Style* (Readability or sentence-level negotiation of meaning)

    ● Is the text "readable," easy to process? If not, what is the problem? (You may find problems with pronoun reference, missing relative pronouns, phrases that don't fit together grammatically, word order problems, etc.)
    ● Are any sentences awkward, unclear, or incomprehensible? (Here you can say "I don't understand what you mean." and have the student explain. When the writer says something that makes more sense than what she has, get her to write it down.)

3. *Grammatical Systems* (Long-term language development)

    ● What consistent language problems appear that are likely to be problems in future papers?
    ● Are there consistent problems with particular grammatical forms?
    ● Can "consciousness raising" (as in Rutherford, above) facilitate acquisition of these forms?
    ● What would you put on a "personal proofreading checklist" for this student?

In making your tutoring plan you should weigh and balance all three types of response. In some conferences the emphasis will be on global issues, in others the main concerns will be at the syntactic or grammatical level, but it is best if every conference addresses all three levels in some way. In most cases you will not be able to deal with all of the apparent problems in the available time. That's ok, however, because the writer can't cope with all the problems at once anyway.

Ideally, the student should leave feeling positive about you, himself, and the Writing Center. The paper you worked on should be better than it would have been if the writer had not come in to see you, but it doesn't have to be perfect or error-free. The writer should have some insight into long-term problems, and a plan for working on them, which may include coming back to see you again.

Exercise

Choose a paper written by a non-native speaker and create a three level plan for working on it. What would you address on the global/rhetorical level? What sentences would you select for discussion? What grammatical forms would you highlight for "consciousness raising"? Discuss your plan with your fellow tutors.

Typical ESL Problems

Non-native speakers have problems with features of the language that never trouble native-speakers. For example, until recently, most standard handbooks did not even address problems with articles or prepositions, because native-speakers rarely get them wrong. These are major problem areas for ESL students, however.

When conferencing with students about grammatical problems, keep in mind the language acquisition issues related above. When you put your finger under a problem with a grammatical form, one student may simply say "How silly of me!" and correct it. Another might come up with several incorrect solutions before finally giving a satisfactory one. Yet another might have literally no idea what the problem is, and in this latter case it is cruel and unusual punishment to try to force the student to correct the problem. Your conferencing technique depends on how far along the interlanguage continuum the writer has progressed. In the latter case, supplying the correct forms may facilitate language acquisition more than playing a "What form should this be?" guessing game.

The examples below illustrate problems that you might address at the sentence level, in terms of meaning, or at the systematic level, in terms of grammatical forms you want the student to acquire. As you will see, it is rare that particular problems occur in isolation. Generally, different kinds of problems appear in the same sentence, interacting to further confuse the meaning and make simple explanations impossible. For this reason, it is best to have a plan concerning which problems you are going to foreground with close attention and explanations, which you will handle in a "by the way" fashion, saying something like "This really should be like this," and which problems you will ignore for the present. Your first move should be to make the meaning of the sentence comprehensible. Your second move might be to make it grammatical, though perhaps still awkward or not quite idiomatic. Your third move might be to help the writer shift elements around to make it read better. It is up to your own judgment how far to go.

These examples are not intended to be a comprehensive overview of all of the grammatical problems a tutor might encounter in an ESL paper, but instead represent a sample of issues the tutor is likely to face, and illustrate modes of thinking that will be helpful to the student.

Third Person Singular "s"

One of the most common errors in ESL writing is omitting the third person singular present tense "s," e.g. writing "He say" instead of "He says." The most likely cause of this problem is that fact that regular verbs remain uninflected in the present tense except in the third person singular. We say *I speak, we speak, you speak* and *they speak,* but *he/she/it speaks.* Another source of confusion is the fact that in plural constructions the "s" is on the noun but not on the verb, but in singular constructions the "s" is on the verb. We say "the horses jump" but "the horse jumps." Although the third person singular is usually one of the first things taught in a grammatical syllabus, research in the natural order of acquisition indicates that it is one of the last forms acquired, and fluent non-native speakers may continue to make this error indefinitely.

Although omitting the third person singular "s" rarely causes confusion of meaning, for native-speaking readers it is an obvious and distracting error and writing center tutors should call attention to it.

Articles and Determiners

Articles, which are part of a class of words called "determiners," are the little words "a," "an," and "the." The rules for article use are surprisingly complex and subtle, and there are so many exceptions that approaching articles through rules is entirely impractical. One problem is that most grammatical analysis does not go beyond the sentence level, but article usage often depends on the context of the whole discourse. For example, the first mention of an object will generally have an indefinite article, but subsequent occurrences will have a definite one. (Yesterday I bought a car. The car is red with black upholstery.)

Chinese, Japanese, Korean, most Slavic languages and most African languages, do not have articles, and those languages that do have them use them in ways that are very different from English (Celce-Murcia and Larson-Freeman 171). Speakers of Asian languages who are acquiring English tend to leave articles out entirely at first. In English a lack of articles creates a very odd effect. For example, the difference between "the man" and "Man" is the difference between an individual and a philosophical abstraction.

In the following example, the writer simply doesn't use articles at all:

> However, to boy or girl in adolescence, children, or other people who
> have psychological problems, it is very different story.

If a tutor pointed a finger in front of "boy," the writer may or may not be able to supply the articles. In this case, either "a" or "the" would do. Of course, the sentence as written implies that all children and adolescents have psychological problems, which is another issue.

In the next example, the writer overgeneralizes a rule based on the fact that we say "the United States of America."

> Today, in the United States of America, the most of people came from
> other countries like the Mexico, the India, the China, and the Vietnam.

It is true that we use a definite article in front of the names of some countries. The Soviet Union is another (now defunct) example. These exceptions tend to be names that are also descriptions of the political organization of the country invoked. This writer also writes "the most of people." It is a common pattern to omit all articles at first, and then begin overusing them.

In the second sentence of the following example the writer needs "a" in front of "very."

> I arrive there and interviewed with the director, Kim. She was very pleasant and happy person.

Note, however, that if we leave off "and happy person," the article is unnecessary because "pleasant" becomes a predicate adjective and there is no second noun in the phrase. It is this sort of complexity that makes articles difficult for non-native speakers to understand.

Noun Plurals

At the early stages of acquisition many non-native speakers will simply leave off plural markers, writing things like "two student." Fluent students in later stages will still have trouble with the distinction between count and non-count (or mass) nouns. What is a count noun in one language may be non-count in another. "Information" is non-count in English but countable in French and Spanish. ESL students will often talk about doing "a homework," or how many "vocabularies" they have to learn.

> The assignments were based on computer work and many researches from net work and CD's.

By the time ESL students get to the college level they are usually very familiar with the count/non-count problem, but they are still uncertain about which words are count and which are non-count.

Prepositions

Prepositions are another source of difficulty. These little words define relationships rather than referring to objects or meanings. In many languages this kind of information is coded in an inflection on a noun. English has more prepositions than most languages, and if you look a preposition up in a dictionary you are likely to find twenty or thirty meanings, all rather vaguely defined. The use of prepositions is largely idiomatic, meaning that logical explanations are not very helpful. We ride "in" a car, but "on" a bus. I am "on my way to school," but you are "in my way," as I climb the stairs. It doesn't make sense—you just have to know. Here is another example:

> In the other hand, some group members were very quiet with no opin-
> ion, so we just took time to end of class or just talked each other.

"In the other hand" actually makes more sense than "on the other hand," but no na-tive-speaker would say it. We also need a preposition at the end between "talked" and "each other." "To" or "with" would serve, but there is still a problem—this is a group so there are more than two people talking. "Among ourselves" would be a more satis-factory phrase, but do we want to get this subtle with a student at this level? Ultimately, it is a judgment call for the tutor. Sometimes almost right has to serve for the moment.

On occasion, the wrong preposition can create an amusing effect:

> My specialty is to test buildings of Asbestos, Lead, and Radon.

Buildings constructed of these materials must be very dangerous to live and work in. It is clear that the writer needs to use "for," but if he or she asks for a rule about this, most teachers would be unable to supply a rule concise and accurate enough for use. And how do native-speakers know whether "for" in this sentence means "test for" or "buildings for" in the sense of "constructed to store asbestos, lead, and radon?" Context and world-knowledge often have far more influence on how a word is interpreted than gram-mar and dictionary meanings. The tutor's role here is to check the writer's intention by getting him or her to talk about it, and then supply the appropriate preposition.

Preposition problems are often mixed up with idiomatic problems regarding the confusion of the infinitive, which looks like it has a preposition because it starts with "to," and the gerund, as in this example:

> People work hard for making more money.

Although the sentence as written is comprehensible, most native-speakers would write "to make." Another alternative might be "People work hard for their money." In situ-ations where there are two or more slightly different idiomatic possibilities, many non-native speakers will combine them. Some non-native speakers might even write "to making" in this sentence. The following sentence is a similar combination of id-iomatic possibilities:

> In the Christmas season, I will buy some presents to my parents and my
> brother.

We can say "buy for" or "give to" but not "buy to." Two word verb combinations like this are a big problem for non-native speakers because the writer doesn't always realize that when she gets to the preposition, the choice has already been dictated by the verb chosen earlier in the sentence.

Tense

The English tense system is another source of confusion. In English we pay a lot of attention to the order of events—what happened first, what happened before that, what is happening now, and what will happen. On the other hand, Chinese dialects don't have tense at all, although time is represented in other ways. Here a Chinese writer uses "was" as a past tense marker:

> I was open the restaurant in Killeen Texas.

This looks like a passive to a native speaker, but it is intended simply to mean "opened."

Simple Past

ESL writers often believe that things expressed in the past tense are no longer true. A student may write "Mr. Williams was my math teacher in high school. He is a very strict no-nonsense teacher." If we point out that "is" in the second sentence should be "was," the student might respond, very logically, "But he still *is* a strict teacher!" However, in this context, "was" does not indicate that the teacher has changed, or no longer exists. "Was" simply indicates that the condition existed *at that time* in the past. Here is a more complex example of that problem:

> That morning I came to work and met Cheryl. She was a very nice person. She seems to be a very happy person.

Here the second sentence uses the past tense correctly. However, the third sentence veers into the present.

When English teachers see students switching from past to present indiscriminately, they often tell them to stick to one tense. Some students overgeneralize this admonition and are afraid to switch tenses in a document, even for good reasons. Some will even add past tense markers to infinitives, which shouldn't take tense or person markers of any kind. The following sentence is an interesting example:

> But it took him about six hours to fixed, and it give us enough time to start a relationship.

Here the form "to fixed" is probably an attempt to stay in the past tense. It is clear that the student is struggling with past and present forms. However, the form "to fixed" may also be the way the writer hears "to fix it," which would make sense in this context. In this case it is possible that overgeneralized instruction from a teacher, incomplete language acquisition, and misunderstood aural input all combine to create the observed grammatical problems.

Generalizations also create past tense problems. In order to respond to the following sentence we need to know what kind of statement is being made. It all depends on whether the statement is rooted in a specific past or is intended as a universal observation:

> They feel people are free to dress how they wanted to dress.

Do we change "feel" to "felt" and "are" to "were"? Or do we change "wanted" to "want"? Only the context, and the writer, can tell us.

The following example contains problems related to both universal generalizations and overgeneralizing the past tense:

> We should realized that the first impression is the base point to judge people. We should understand people well, then we could make a judgment to people.

Students often put past participles (or simple past tense) after past modals (could, should, would, might), again probably in an attempt to stay in the past tense. Thus we get "should realized" above. The correct form is the base form of the verb, i.e. the infinitive without "to." The second sentence avoids saying "should understood," but because the writer is generalizing the second verb phrase should be "can make." Here is another example of incorrect past tense forms after past tense modals:

> That was a very difficult decision for me whether I should stayed in my country or came to U.S.

ESL writers often have trouble with parallel structures like "whether I should stay or come." This could be written "whether I should stay in my country or should come to the U.S." but the second "should" is elided, masking the need for a parallel structure. If we want to we can venture beyond grammar into idiom and style in our corrections; this whole phrase probably should be the subject for the sentence: "Whether I should stay in my country or come to the U.S. was a difficult decision for me." Notice that if we change the viewpoint from the past to the present we have to use present perfect, which to a non-native speaker is a very subtle change: "Looking back on that time, it is hard to know whether I should have stayed in my country or come to the U.S." Tutors have to use their own judgment about how much complexity to discuss at a given time.

Perfect Tenses

As noted above, the present perfect and past perfect tenses also cause problems. Most Americans avoid the perfect tenses in their spoken language. If someone asks us "Are you hungry?" we respond, "No, I already ate." However, technically the present perfect should be used in this situation, because what happened in the past has current relevance—if you hadn't eaten in the past the questioner is likely to feed you. Thus the correct response is "No, I have already eaten."

For most of us this sounds too formal for ordinary conversation, but perfect tenses are still essential for academic discourse, especially *written* discourse. Native-speaking students tend to write like they talk and stick to simple present and simple past. Non-native speakers have generally been taught all about perfect tenses, but have not become fluent enough to use them correctly. Here is a simple example of the misuse of present perfect:

> I have bought my car as grand new six years ago.

If the student wrote "I have driven my car for six years," it would be correct because the activity started in the past and continues to the present. In this example, however, simple past is appropriate because the action of buying the car began and ended at a specific point in past. English is very concerned about these distinctions, and if making them doesn't come naturally to you because your native language doesn't make them, you are going to struggle with them. ("Grand new" is a wonderful example of an attempt to make sense out of an idiom that no longer makes sense even to most native-speakers. One explanation I have read is that in the past when you bought an axe handle the maker's name was "branded" into the wood. As you used the tool the handle would wear away and the brand would become illegible.)

The following example has simple past where present perfect is required, along with numerous other problems we have already discussed:

> In modern society, teamwork became very important in workplace.
> Many schools also give group projects or works students to cope with
> the modern society that need a lot of group works in workplace.

If the student wrote "In the nineteenth century, teamwork became . . ." simple past would be appropriate. However, the phrase "in modern society" means that the writer is talking about a process that began in the past and continues up to the present, so he should write "teamwork has become." Of course there are also problems with non-count nouns, missing prepositions and articles, missing verb endings, etc. In addition, the writer seems to be recycling the same words and ideas in an effort to fill up space when words and ideas are in short supply. This is a common pattern when language acquisition is weak.

Vocabulary

Finally, after the problems noted above, lack of vocabulary probably causes more syntactic difficulties than any other single problem. When you don't know the word for something, you are forced into one of two strategies: to use a bi-lingual dictionary and choose a word you have not acquired and therefore have no feeling for, or to "write around" the gap, describing the concept you are groping toward. The first strategy usually ends up with a word with inappropriate connotations, and the second often produces a complex and tangled sentence structure. When these problems are mixed with tense and word form problems, the result can be incomprehensible, or at least puzzling.

> I am considered that the bad weather was so bad, because the cloudy were shining above on the ground covered the traffic signals. I have opened my eyes as wider enough to focus on traffic signals, but I could have looked it was very hard to read it. In addition, bad weather was caused the head lights were flamingly becoming dim. Due to the fact, it was bad weather had neither thunderstorm nor humidity. It was a cloud.

A lot of the problems this writer has with this passage would have been solved if he had known the word "fog."

Providing Grammatical Explanations: Participle Problems (and the Passive Voice)

Grammatical conundrums that nearly defy logical explanation often lurk just below the surface of perfectly common and ordinary English sentences. The typical native speaker is generally unaware of this complexity until he or she corrects an ESL writer's language, and the writer innocently asks "why?" The unsuspecting tutor launches into an explanation, quickly realizes that she doesn't really know, and reaches for a handbook. However, the handbook probably won't help, because the student's question goes beyond usage and convention into the deep structure of the language. Marianne Celce-Murcia and Diane Larsen-Freeman attempt to deal with such questions from the ESL point of view in *The Grammar Book: An ESL/EFL Teacher's Course*, but their explanations, though solidly (if somewhat eclectically) grounded in both linguistic theory and teaching experience, are usually far too complex for the average student. However, the book should be on the resource shelves of every writing center with an ESL clientele because sometimes neither student nor tutor will be comfortable without some kind of explanation, and the very complexity of the rules and exceptions can have the effect of making both parties feel better about not having known why.

We will explore one of these conundrums as an example. We tend to think of passive voice as a fairly simple matter. To transform a sentence from active to passive you invert the subject and object, add "by," and add the appropriate form of the verb to be with the past participle. "The dog bit the man" becomes "The man was bitten by the dog." Real problems with passive voice, as in the following example in which the causality of the event is reversed by the grammar, are rare.

> I had an auto accident, but it was my fault because the bad weather was caused by having an auto accident.

Here dropping the negative combines with reversing the passive construction to create an unintentionally humorous effect. ESL students often have more complicated idiomatic difficulties that appear to involve passive constructions, such as when a student writes "My mother worries me," when he intends "My mother is worried about me," or "Disneyland locates in Anaheim" instead of "is located."

In English we can use both past participles and -ing participles as adjectives. When these appear after the verb to be, they look like passive or progressive constructions. This causes multiple layers of confusion. Compare these two examples:

> I am learning in this class.
> I am boring in this class.

The second statement often appears in student evaluations of ESL classes. If we rewrite it as "I am bored in this class," is it a passive construction or is "bored" a predicate adjective? Celce-Murcia and Larsen-Freeman suggest adding an intensifier such as "very" to the phrase (449). If you can add it, it's an adjective; if not, it's a verb. If we do that to the original pair of sentences we get:

> *I am very learning in this class
> I am very boring in this class.

(The asterisk is a convention in linguistics that indicates an example that is not grammatically correct.) Thus, the first example is a verb phrase and the second an adjectival construction. However, because we can also write "I am very bored in this class," we can see that that structure is also adjectival, and we haven't solved our writer's problem. We still can't explain why it doesn't mean what our writer thinks it means. Sentences such as "I am boring in this class" and "I am interesting in computers" are common in ESL writing.

Celce-Murcia and Larsen-Freeman note this difficulty and say that it happens most often with what they call "emotive" verbs. Their list includes *amuse, annoy, bother,* and *puzzle,* along with *interest* and other words. They say,

> In such cases it must be made clear that if the adjective refers to the *experiencer,* i.e. the animate being or beings that are *feeling* the emotion, then the *-En* participle [past participle] should be used. If, on the other hand, the adjective refers to the *actor,* i.e. the thing or person that is *causing* the emotion, then the *-Ing* participle should be used. (451)

Native-speakers know this unconsciously through acquisition, without working it out. Eventually, as acquisition proceeds, your student will also acquire this rule, unless "fossilization" occurs before that happens. Rather than giving a rule, however, it is generally easier and more effective to tell the writer what the sentence as written *means,* for example, "You are saying that you are a boring person and you make other people in your class bored. Is that what you mean?"

If you offer feedback on the meaning of grammatical forms in context rather than rules for choosing the "correct" forms, you will keep the focus on communication, facilitate natural acquisition, and spend far less time consulting your grammar books and attempting to untangle exceptions and contrary views. And if you try to provide a rule, you are likely to get yourself confused too. (What if we write "I am bored *by* this class"? Is that a passive?)

Exercise

Pick one of the typical problems discussed above, and do some research. Look at various handbooks for explanations and examples. Do some Internet searches and look at handouts and other materials offered by On-line Writing Labs. Create your own handout to help students acquire the correct forms. Test your handout carefully. Work with students and decide: Does it help or does it cause more confusion? When you are satisfied, share your handout with your fellow tutors.

Some Notes about Non-standard Dialects of English

Speakers of non-standard dialects of English are often placed in Basic Writing classes with non-native speakers. Although the rhetorical problems and grammatical errors of these writers often appear similar to those of ESL students, there are some significant differences. First, some background from Sociolinguistic theory.

As with many linguistic problems, there are contradictions between the way linguists conceptualize the issues and the way lay people such as teachers, students and other language users think about them. Even the terms we use are slippery. Hudson, for example, concludes, "there is no real distinction to be drawn between 'language' and 'dialect' (except with reference to prestige, where it wold be better to use the term 'standard language' or just 'standard' rather than just 'language'). He points out that Norwegian and Swedish are considered to be separate languages, but are mutually intelligible. He also employs the term "dialectic continuum" which describes "a chain of adjacent varieties in which each pair of adjacent varieties are mutually intelligible, but pairs taken from opposite ends of the chain are not," and notes that such chains exist from Amsterdam through Germany to Vienna, and from Paris to southern Italy (*Sociolinguistics* 35-37).

Linguists argue that there is no inherent grammatical superiority in any dialect. All dialects are grammatically equal. When we discuss prestige dialects such as "standard English," we are talking about social meaning, not objective scientific judgment. However, in the writing center, we must deal with the entire rhetorical effect of the writing, which includes the impression the writer creates on the reader, and the problems of communication across social groups. Again, the writing center exists on a border between those who speak the standard dialect as native-speakers, and those who are members of other groups that wish to participate in the mainstream academic, political, and economic institutions of our society. Social meaning is important.

The linguistic concept of "register," which is used to explain the fact that the same individual will produce different lexical forms and grammatical structures in different social situations, is important to our discussion. "Register" usually refers to levels of formality. Hudson notes, "one man's dialect is another man's register." He continues

> The items which one person uses under all circumstances, however informal, may be used by someone else only on the most formal occasions, where he feels he needs to sound as much like the first person as he can. This is the relation between 'native' speakers of standard and non-standard dialects. Forms which are part of the standard speaker's 'dialect' are part of a special 'register' for the non-standard speaker (51).

The normal processes of language acquisition apply to a non-standard dialect speaker acquiring the standard dialect. Comprehensible input in the form of oral interaction and reading can lead to acquisition of standard forms. Calling attention to non-standard forms can facilitate this acquisition. In this sense, tutoring second dialect speakers is similar to tutoring non-native speakers. However, the affective issues involving membership in the new group and loyalty to the non-standard speaking group can seriously inhibit the acquisition process. As for ESL students, the attitude of the learner toward the standard-speaking group is an important factor. One way of addressing this problem is to ensure that the writing center staff is ethnically and culturally diverse, and trained to be sensitive to cultural and linguistic diversity.

A major difference between second language acquisition and second dialect acquisition is that in the former, the non-standard forms that are part of the learner's interlanguage should disappear from use as standard forms are acquired. In the case of the dialect speaker, the non-standard forms continue to be appropriate in many social interactions the speaker will engage in, and thus standard forms become an addition to the speaker's linguistic repertoire, not a replacement for incorrect ones that are to be abandoned. The student should not be forced to leave his old group, his family, friends and peers, as a price to be paid for joining the new discourse community. Thus it is important not to label non-standard forms as "incorrect" except in a specific context.

Recently there has been controversy about the teaching of "Ebonics," otherwise known as "Black Dialect"or "Black English Vernacular." When a school system in Oakland, California announced plans to give its teachers training in the grammar of this dialect, many people became upset because they assumed that the school district was planning to teach students in Black English. However, this was not the case. School officials later said that they wanted teachers to understand the grammatical features of Black English so that they could better teach standard English. This knowledge can be useful to writing center tutors as well. The section below is a comparison of common Standard English and Black English forms for the same meanings.

Black English Consistencies

Based on material by SF. Braxton

- *Total elimination of "to be" in present tense*
  He a nice man.   He *is* a nice man.

- *"Be" or "be's" used to indicate a habitual condition*
  The soup be (be's) hot.   The soup *is* (always) hot.

- *"Was" with plural nouns*
  They was at the park.   They *were* at the park.

- *The future "be" with helper (will)*
  He be graduating soon.   She *will* be graduating soon.

- *"Been" without helpers "have," or "had"*
  He been sick.   She *has* been sick.

- *Third person singular, present tense "s" omitted*
  He play ball.   He *plays* ball.

- *Past tense "-ed" omitted*
  Jane bag is on the table.   *Jane's* bag is on the table.

- *Omission of plural "s"*
  I have three dog.   I have three *dogs*.

- *Pronoun forms*
  Them kids.   *Those* kids.

- *Comparatives*
  This table is more better.   This table is better.

- *"Ain't" replacing "isn't," "aren't," "hasn't," and sometimes "didn't"*
  This ain't my house.   This *isn't* my house.
  You ain't going with us.   You *aren't* going with us.

● *Multiple negatives*
  Nobody don't work here.   Nobody works here.
  Don't nobody ever do nothing.   Nobody ever does anything.

● *"Going to" becomes "gon" with no helpers.*
  You gon' get sick   You*'re going* to get sick

● *Loss of final "l"*
  She's a foo'   She's a *fool.*

● *"It" as a dummy subject*
  It was two people there.   *There were* two people there.

● *Elimination of final and middle "r"*
  He wants mo'   He wants *more.*
  He woke up do'ing the night.   He woke up *during* the night.

● *Dropping of final consonant*
  He passed the tes'.   He passed the *test.*

● *Substitution of "d," or "f" for "th"*
  Dey ran home.   *They* ran home.
  She hurt her mouf.   She hurt her *mouth.*

The differences outlined above range from significant variations on the tense system and other important grammatical structures, to minor differences in pronunciation. The point is that the dialectal formations constitute a consistent and meaningful grammatical system. A student who speaks naturally using these forms can acquire standard forms as a formal, academic register, without abandoning these forms in the home and community context.

Exercise

Read a short story or a novel written at least partially in a non-standard dialect. Why did the writer choose to use non-standard English? What effect do the non-standard forms create? Select some of the most common non-standard locutions in the work and discuss what they mean and how they compare with standard ways of speaking. Share your insights with your fellow tutors.

Faculty and ESL Writers

Now to take up our final question: "To what extent should you take responsibility for helping to educate faculty members about dealing with ESL students?"

The traditional view is that the writing center operates as a supplement or an adjunct to regular instruction, and that the classroom instructor is ultimately responsible for the student's performance. Lil Brannon argues that it is time for the writing center to abandon this subordinate role and that we should see ourselves as an integral component of writing instruction in all courses, and activists for teachings strategies grounded in the best composition theories our field has produced. Furthermore, she argues that if we are forced to choose between serving the student and adhering to the specifications of the instructor, it is "the student to whom we owe our support" (11).

Without a doubt, writing centers should actively seek to improve both writing instruction and student performance. However, in my view, if we get to the point where we have to choose sides between instructor and student, we have already lost most of our power to induce change. We must work with faculty from many disciplines, each with its own genres, standards, vocabulary, and modes of thinking. We cannot expect them all to understand our theories or agree with our conclusions. But if we are willing to learn from them-about their discourse, the goals of their assignments, the problems of their students-most will be willing to learn from us.

At one level the answer is very simple. If instructors feel that writing center tutors are going to criticize their assignments and question their judgments, they will not be comfortable sending students to us for help.

The instructor is part of the rhetorical situation in which the student operates, and the instructor has the right to define the standards. The tutor's job is to help the student understand the instructor's standards and to help him or her meet them. However, instructors sometimes misjudge the capabilities of their students, or do not realize that students may misunderstand or misinterpret their assignments. When a student comes into the center with a paper that has been very harshly judged, it puts the tutor in a delicate situation. We want to build the writer's confidence, and show them what they can do to improve their writing ability. The instructor's response to the writing may have had the opposite effect, and the instructor may or may not be aware of this. However, even in cases like this the safest role for a writing center tutor is to help the student understand the comments and marks the instructor has made on the paper, and what sorts of concerns or standards lie behind those marks.

In general, it is difficult for tutors to "educate" faculty. Faculty members are used to educating others. On the other hand, a little information about the causes of the problems ESL students and dialect speakers have in producing academic writing can make life easier for both students and instructors. Writing center directors often make presentations to faculty groups about designing writing assignments and responding to student writing, and information about language acquisition theory, contrastive rhetoric and other relevant concepts can be included in these. Most faculty are happy to receive tips that will make teaching and grading papers easier.

However, such insights are most easily grasped in the context of individual cases. Ongoing dialogue between tutors and instructors is extremely important. One way of facilitating and structuring this exchange is to create a tutor/instructor dialogue form which contains spaces for instructors to describe or check off the problems they see, and a place for tutors to describe what they worked on. Students sometimes have questions that they need to ask instructors but which they have trouble articulating; the tutor can help the student formulate these and write them down on the form.

In talking with faculty, it is important to listen carefully. Often they are unfamiliar with the terminology of composition and linguistics. Listen to the words they use to describe the problems they see in student writing, and pay close attention to the types of problems that are important to them. It may be best to discuss the problems in the instructor's terminology, at least at first. If you have a chance to discuss a paper that has been given a judgement that you feel is overly harsh, acknowledge the problems and discuss how you will work on them, but also point out what the student has done well. Diplomacy is important. Over time, in a good working relationship, trust will build, and more risks can be taken.

Often the disagreements between faculty and compositionists have more to do with pedagogy than standards. No one wants to argue that grammatical errors are acceptable in the business memo, or that it should be written in non-standard dialect. What is at issue is how to go about getting to that goal. If this distinction is made clear, most faculty will be more open to your suggestions.

Exercise

> *Interview one or more faculty members about ESL writing. Do they encounter ESL problems in student writing? How do they respond to these problems? What do they think should be done? How do they think the writing center can help? What do they need to know about language acquisition theory and contrastive rhetoric?*

Works Cited

Ballard, Brigid, and John Clancy. "Assessment by Misconception: Cultural Influences and Intellectual Traditions." In Hamp-Lyons, Liz, ed. *Assessing Second Language Writing in Academic Contexts*. Norwood, N.J: Ablex, 1991, 19–35.

Celce-Murcia, Marianne, and Diane Larsen-Freeman. *The Grammar Book: an ESL/EFL Teacher's Course*. Cambridge, Mass.: Newbury House, 1983.

Ellis, Rod. *Understanding Second Language Acquisition*. New York: Oxford Univ. Press, 1985.

Hinds, John "Linguistics and Written Discourse in English and Japanese: A Contrastive Study (1978-1982)" *Annual Review of Applied Linguistics*. 1982 Ed. Robert B. Kaplan. Rowley, Mass.: Newbury House, 1983. 78–84.

Hudson, R.A. *Sociolinguistics*. Cambridge: Cambridge Univ. Press, 1980.

Kaplan, Robert B. *The Anatomy of Rhetoric: Prolegomena to a Functional theory of Rhetoric: Essays for Teachers*. Language and the Teacher vol. 8. Philadelphia: Center for Curriculum Development, 1972.

———"Contrastive Rhetoric and Second Language Learning: Notes Toward a theory of Contrastive Rhetoric." *Writing Across Languages and Cultures: Issues in Contrastive Rhetoric*. Ed. Alan C. Purves. *Written Communication* Annual Vol. 2. Newbury Park: Sage, 1988. 275–301.

Krashen, Stephen. *Principles and Practice in Second Language Acquisition*. Oxford: Pergamon Press, 1982.

———*Second Language Acquisition and Second Language Learning*. Oxford: Pergamon Press, 1981.

———*Writing: Research, Theory and Application*. Oxford: Pergamon, 1984.

Rodby, Judith. *Appropriating Literacy: Reading and writing in English as a Second Language*. Portsmouth: Boynton/Cook, 1992.

Rutherford, William E. *Second Language Grammar: Learning and Teaching*. London; New York: Longman, 1987.

Tsao, Feng-Fu. "Linguistics and Written Discourse in Particular Languages: Contrastive Studies: English and Chinese (Mandarin)." *Annual Review of Applied Linguistics*. 1982 Ed. Robert B. Kaplan. Rowley, Mass.: Newbury House, 1983. 99–117.

ARE WRITING CENTERS ETHICAL?

Irene L. Clark
Dave Healy

The ethics of writing center assistance have often been subject to question. Even at the present time, when more writing centers exist than ever before, colleagues from a variety of academic departments continue to express concern that the sort of assistance students receive may be inappropriate, perhaps even verging on plagiarism. "The problem is my dean," someone in the process of establishing a new writing center recently confided. "He worries that tutoring students in a writing center will result in plagiarized papers, so he thinks that we should stick to grammar instruction."

The writing center's response to such suspicions has been to embrace a pedagogy of noninterventionism that precludes both the appropriation of student texts and any challenge to teachers' authority occasioned by questioning their judgment of a writer's work. Writing center personnel are cautioned against writing on clients' texts or suggesting specific wording or performing primarily as proofreaders, and with instructors, the writing center has generally accepted Stephen North's dictum: "[W]e never play student-advocates in teacher-student relationships. . . . [W]e never evaluate or second-guess any teacher's syllabus, assignments, comments, or grades" ("Idea," 441). Precepts of noninterventionism have thus become what Shamoon and Burns refer to as a writing center "bible," an orthodoxy that has attained the force of an ethical or moral code.

However, although these precepts arose out of ethical concerns, a noninterventionist policy as an absolute must ultimately be judged ethically suspect, increasing the center's marginality, diminishing its influence, and compromising its ability to serve writers. Writing centers thus need a new ethic that acknowledges the theoretical, pedagogical, and political facts of life.

Origins of Established Writing Center Policies

Current writing center policies—whether referred to as a "bible" (Shamoon and Burns), "mantras" (Blau), or "dogma" (Clark)—began to be articulated in a public forum in the seventies and early eighties, when open admissions policies precipitated the growth of writing centers as separate university entities and when the *Writing Lab Newsletter* in 1977 and *The Writing Center Journal* in 1980 provided a medium for publication. Before that time, as Peter Carino notes, many writing centers consisted of "labs," located within writing classrooms, that utilized an individualized instructional approach designed to help students master a specific content; frequently that content focused on grammar and surface correctness. Carino's purpose is to redeem the bleak picture of early writing centers as "current-traditional dungeons where students were banished to do grammar drills" (113), and he therefore stresses that not all early centers were the same. In many of them, heuristic and global concerns of writing were recognized as important pedagogical goals. Nevertheless, he also acknowledges that "drills were part of the methods of early centers" (113), certainly more so than they are today, and that whatever instruction actually took place, most writing centers were conceived of within the university as centers of remediation where less proficient students labored to master surface correctness. The writing clinic at Stephens College, for example, was set up for "[t]he student who finds it very difficult to spell correctly or who makes gross errors in English usage. Here causes are determined, exercises under supervision are given, and practical applications to everyday writing are made" (Wiksell 145).

This emphasis on remedial education and on the mastery of a specific grammar-based content was a "safe" function for writing centers to assume because it was deemed by the academy an unfortunate but necessary supplement to the more important scholarly instruction that occurred in the classroom. When other departments on campus conceived of a writing lab as a center for remediation, they could easily understand and accept what presumably occurred there—skill and drill did not generate either suspicion or controversy. However, as writing centers developed into autonomous entities, and as interest in composition as a discipline led to a rejection of the current-traditional paradigm in favor of a process/collaborative, student-centered approach, skill and drill in the writing center was supplemented. In many instances, it was replaced by a greater emphasis on helping students figure out what they wanted to say in response to a writing assignment, or on providing assistance with the shape and content of an actual text. Many writing centers took to heart James Moffet's conviction that teachers must shift their gaze "from the subject to the learner, for the subject is the learner" (67). As a result, instruction in the writing center became what Steve North calls

> a pedagogy of direct intervention. Whereas in the "old" center instruction tends to take place after or apart from writing, and tends to focus

> on the correction of textual problems, in the "new" center the teaching
> takes place as much as possible during writing, during the activity being
> learned, and tends to focus on the activity itself. (North, "Idea" 439)

This shift in approach, however, was not greeted with unqualified enthusiasm by faculty members in other departments on campus, who were concerned about the "ethics" of this type of writing center instruction and alarmed that it represented a form of plagiarism.

Plagiarism, Intellectual Property Rights, and the Rise of Writing Center Orthodoxy

Writing centers' concern with defending themselves against charges of inadvertent or even deliberate plagiarism reflects western culture's emphasis on intellectual property rights, an emphasis manifested in the number of lawsuits concerned with issues of copyright and authorship. Although postmodern theorists have problematized the conception of authors and authorship, the teaching of literature and composition, as Woodmansee and Jaszi point out, "continues to enforce the Romantic paradigm" (9) of the solitary author whose work is absolutely original. In a presentation concerned with writing centers and ethics given at the Conference of College Composition and Communication several years ago, Karen Hodges discussed the wide diversity in attitudes toward collaborative effort among various disciplines. She concluded that English Departments, in particular, were concerned about the shaping of the text and were thus least likely to favor collaborative writing or writing assistance. Hodges's perspective is supported by Bruffee, Trimbur, and Lunsford and Ede, who trace the concept of the solitary author to the eighteenth-century concept of individualism and a nineteenth-century romantic notion of the solitary creative genius that eventually manifested itself in a twentieth-century emphasis "on writing as an individually creative act, and on 'objective' testing as a means of evaluating the intellectual property of solitary writers" (Lunsford and Ede 418).

Departments of literature are particularly concerned with the issue of plagiarism in terms of style and text structure, in contrast to departments of science and social science, who tend to focus primarily on the originality of an idea. One particularly amusing but unfortunately apt portrait of English departments' attitude toward plagiarism is depicted in Bernard Malamud's novel *A New Life*, whose hero, an English teacher named Levin, has to deal with a suspected plagiarist, Albert O. Birdless, a "D" student who has turned in an "A" paper. Warned by his colleagues that his duty is to locate the original source in order to trap the culprit, Levin spends many evenings in the library, reading "with murderous intent, to ensnare and expunge Albert O. Birdless" (164). But he never finds the source and is compared unfavorably with another instructor, Avis Fliss, who has earned a reputation for her unfailing ability to detect suspected student plagiarists:

> [Avid] has a knack of going straight to the *Reader's Guide*, looking over the titles of articles on the cribbed subject for a couple of years past or so, and just about right away putting her finger on the one she needs. Her last incident she had this student nailed dead to rights an hour and a half after she read his theme. We had him suspended by his dean and off the campus before five o'clock of the same day. (161).

Although this portrait is humorous, a concern with avoiding plagiarism, coupled with the second-class and frequently precarious status of writing centers within the university hierarchy, generated a set of defensive strategies aimed at warding off the suspicions of those in traditional humanities departments, who feared that students were receiving assistance that strained the boundaries of ethics.[1] As a result, precepts associated with noninterventionist tutoring became not only the preferred, but often, in fact, the only writing center approach.

Reflecting what may be viewed as a pedagogy of self-defense, articles appearing in early issues of the *Writing Lab Newsletter* delineated strategies aimed at ensuring that tutors did not provide excessive help, thereby averting suspicion of plagiarism. For example, in 1981, Larry Rochelle warned: "We must keep in mind that some 'enemies' of the Center are overwrought English professors, our own colleagues, who really do not like students or teaching, who are very demanding in their classrooms for all the wrong reasons, and who really think that Writing Centers are helping students too much" (7). A 1984 article by Patrick Sullivan contains the similarly suspicious observation that the close relationships which develop between tutors and students sometimes generate their own "special set of problems. The instructor may not be aware that a student has received help with a writing assignment. In this case, instructors may feel that matters related to the policy on plagiarism obtain" (2). The following year, in a subsequent article for the *Newsletter*, Sullivan discussed the results of a survey asking faculty whether or not they "object to tutors assisting your students," admittedly a loaded question. Although many were pleased, even enthusiastic, about this sort of assistance, a significant number regarded it with great mistrust. "I don't approve of them editing final drafts," one respondent observed. Another indicated his strong disapproval, particularly for non-native speakers:

> My Vietnamese student who came in to see you received much too much help with his composition—even suggestions for ideas to be incorporated into the paper. In cases where a student has serious grammatical and organizational problems, I would even prefer he or she not take a draft of the paper to the center at all, but rather get help through the use of verb exercises. (6)

To forestall suspicion, then, the concept of tutor restraint became a moral imperative, dictating a set of absolute guidelines for writing center instruction. For Suzanne Edwards that means training her staff "not to write any portion of the paper—not even one phrase" nor to "edit the paper for mechanical errors. This includes finding or labeling the spelling, punctuation, or grammar mistakes in a paper or dictating corrections" (8). Evelyn Ashton-Jones argues that tutors must engage in a version of "Socratic dialogue" and not "lapse into a 'directive' mode of tutoring." Quoting Thom Hawkins, she labels the directive tutor as "shaman, guru, or mentor," and Socratic tutors as "architects and partners" (31), labels that leave no doubt as to which group is on the side of the angels. More recently, Jeff Brooks, in arguing for "minimalist tutoring," warns: "When you 'improve' a student's paper, you haven't been a tutor at all; you've been an editor. You may have been an exceedingly good editor, but you've been of little service to your student. . . . The student, not the tutor, should 'own' the paper and take full responsibility for it" (2). Finally, Thomas Thompson describes how tutors at The Citadel's Writing Center easily work within the constraints of a military honor code:

> [T]utors try to avoid taking pen in hand when discussing a student paper. They may discuss content, and they may use the Socratic method to lead students to discover their own conclusions, but tutors are instructed not to tell students what a passage means or give students a particular word to complete a particular thought. (13)

An encapsulation of what eventually developed into the writing center credo is an oft-quoted statement from Stephen North: "[I]n a writing center the object is to make sure that writers, and not necessarily their texts, are what get changed by instruction" (438). In that article, North was reacting against the "fix-it shop" concept of writing centers prevalent at that time, and his intention was to enlighten a non-writing center readership about what writing centers really do—that is, help students become writers, not simply clean up their papers. However, another, perhaps less obvious intention was to assure colleagues in the English department that the help students receive in writing centers does not constitute a form of plagiarism. After all, if it is the writer and not the text that improves as a result of a writing center visit, then surely no textual property has been unfairly appropriated.

Theoretical Limitations of Writing Center Orthodoxy: The Complexity of "Owning" Texts

Despite the salutary influence of North's "The Idea of a Writing Center," both inside and outside writing centers, its philosophy of textual noninterventionism has not served writing centers well. As we have noted, such a philosophy perpetuates a limited and limiting understanding of authorship in the academy. By privileging individual responsibility and accountability and by valorizing the individual writer's authentic "voice," the writing center has left unchallenged notions of intellectual property that are suspect at best. Furthermore, as Lisa Ede, Andrea Lunsford, Marilyn Cooper, and others have argued, the idea that writing is fundamentally a solitary activity and that individual writers can and should "own" their texts relegates the writing center to a limited bystander's role, even as it limits writers' understanding of their options and of their relationship to others.

Ede notes that some collaborative learning theorists, such as Bruffee, seem to view collaboration as a compensatory strategy for inexperienced writers. The implication is that accomplished writers won't need to "interrupt" their essentially solitary writing process with dialogue. If writing centers adopt such a view, says Ede, they implicitly limit their clientele and their mission: "[A]s long as thinking and writing are regarded as inherently individual, solitary activities, writing centers can never be viewed as anything more than pedagogical fix-it shops to help those who, for whatever reason, are unable to think and write on their own" (7).

Lunsford labels those writing centers that view knowledge as individual either "storehouses" or "garrets." The former locate knowledge outside the knower, "stored" in texts or other repositories, while garret centers "see knowledge as interior, as inside the student, and the writing center's job as helping students get in touch with this knowledge, as a way to find their unique voices, their individual and unique powers" (5). Storehouse and Garret centers are limited, says Lunsford, by their epistemologies—positivistic, Platonic, and absolutist. To "enable a student body and citizenry to meet the demands of the twenty-first century . . . we need to embrace the idea of writing centers as Burkean Parlors, as centers for collaboration" (9).

Cooper, too, critiques epistemologies that are based on "a preexisting coherent and rational self," that see writing as "a matter of subduing the text to the self by achieving personal control over it" and "achieving an authentic voice" (101). Writing centers founded on such epistemologies, says Cooper, will tend to focus on helping students "fix" papers rather than concentrating on "what students know and need to know about writing" (99). Writing centers will be more effective and their clients better served by a different view of textual ownership:

> [T]utors can best help students become agents of their own writing by helping them understand how and the extent to which they are *not* owners of their texts and *not* responsible for the shape of their texts, by helping them understand, in short, how various institutional forces impinge on how and what they write and how they can negotiate a place for their own goals and needs when faced with these forces. (101)

Ironically, the same fix-it mentality that these theorists see as the legacy of a limiting epistemology prompted Stephen North's apology for writing centers in a recent article that itself helped perpetuate that very epistemology. In fairness to North, it should be observed that in "Revisiting 'The Idea of a Writing Center,'" the passage about not second-guessing teachers is one of four that he singles out to revisit. He acknowledges that in the writing center we see "what we at least construe as the seamier side of things," which "in cumulative form puts a lot of pressure on the sort of tutor-teacher détente proposed by the [original] passage" ("Revisiting," 13). However, North's second article provides no suggestion that writing center personnel should directly challenge the pedagogical status quo. Instead, it argues for a new curricular state of affairs wherein the writing center would work primarily with students enrolled in a "Writing Sequence," a "program—a four-year sequence of study—that values writing" (16). Such a program presumably minimizes conflicts between the writing center and instructors "because the classroom teachers are directly involved with, and therefore invested in the functioning of, that center" (16).

Pedagogical Limitations of Writing Center Orthodoxy

Textual noninterventionism is suspect not only on theoretical grounds, as we have been arguing; it also overlooks the possibility that for some students, an interventionist, directive, and appropriative pedagogy might be more effective—as well as ethically defensible. Deborah Burns, for example, points out that her thesis director, who supervised the writing of her master's thesis using directive intervention, was the person most helpful to her in her graduate studies. Yet everything he did violated entrenched writing center policy. He "was directive, he substituted his own words for hers, and he stated with disciplinary appropriateness the ideas with which she had been working" (Shamoon and Burns 138). As a compositionist, Burns puzzled over the effectiveness of her director's interventions. Moreover, she observed, he was equally effective with other graduate students:

> [H]e took their papers and rewrote them while they watched. They left feeling better able to complete their papers, and they tackled other papers with greater ease and success. . . . His practices seem authoritative, intrusive, directive, and product-oriented. Yet these practices created major turning points for a variety of writers. (138)

Shamoon and Burns cite other similar examples from faculty workshops in which professors, acting like tutors, were equally directive:

> Over and over in the informal reports of our colleagues we find that crucial information about a discipline and about writing is transmitted in

> ways that are intrusive, directive, and product-oriented, yet these behaviors are not perceived as an appropriation of power or voice but instead as an opening up of those aspects of practice which had remained unspoken and opaque. (139)

This type of directive tutoring is consistent with Vygotsky's concept of "the zone of proximal development," which is defined as "the distance between the actual development level as determined by the independent problem solving and the level of potential development as determined through problem solving under adult guidance or in collaboration with more capable peers" (86). In terms of writing center pedagogy, Vygotsky's view of learning suggests that tutors should work on "functions that have not yet matured, but are in the process of maturation, functions that will mature tomorrow, but are currently in an embryonic state" (86). Such functions might require the tutor to assume a more directive role until the student can assume the function alone. As Vygotsky points out, "what children can do with the assistance of others might be in some sense even more indicative of their mental development than what they can do alone" (85). However, inflexible precepts against directive tutoring preclude this sort of assistance and overlook variation in student need and tutorial context. In an essay concerned with tutoring strategies for learning disabled students, for example, Julie Neff points out that orthodox tutoring practices are often not very effective because such students require a great deal more specific and directive assistance. For students from nonwestern cultures as well, non-directive tutoring may be insufficient, particularly since many of them are unfamiliar with the western conceptions of academic discourse and have little understanding of the purpose or components of the essays they are expected to produce. Harris and Silva refer to the "sometimes bewilderingly different rhetorical patterns and conventions of other languages" (525) sometimes manifested in a "seemingly meandering introduction or digressions that appear irrelevant" (526). In dealing with these students, Harris and Silva point out that

> [i]n terms of the tutor's role, there may have to be adjustments in their pedagogical orientation. Tutors who work with ESL students may have to be "tellers" to some extent because they will probably need to provide cultural, rhetorical, and/or linguistic information which native speakers intuitively possess and which ESL students do not have, but need to have to complete their writing assignments effectively. (533)

In terms of fostering the best environment for assisting student writing, then, it's important to recognize the virtues of flexibility since "one tutoring approach does not fit all" (Shamoon and Burns 139).

Illegitimate Collaboration and Imitation

Of course, deciding just how much and what kind of assistance to provide is not an easy task, often requiring tutors to walk a fine line between legitimate and illegitimate collaboration. Tutoring is "a balancing act that asks tutors to juggle roles, to shift identity, to know when to act like an expert and when to act like a co-learner" (Trimbur 25), and when we say that writing center foster the spirit of "collaborative learning," it is sometimes difficult to define exactly what we mean. True collaboration occurs between colleagues who are both members of the same discourse community. True colleagues collaborate without fear of text appropriation; in its ideal form, collaboration between colleagues involves mutual assistance and mutual learning.

Collaboration in writing centers, however, often involves a writer who is not a full-fledged member of the academic discourse community. In fact, the purpose of the tutoring is often to help the author attain that status. Moreover, although practitioners frequently use the term "peer tutor" to refer to undergraduate tutors in the writing center, many tutors are not peers in any sense of the word. Some of them may be graduate students or composition teachers who are considerably older than the students seeking their assistance, and all of them young or old, even those who are, indeed, undergraduates, were selected to be tutors because they have demonstrated an ability to write. By definition, then, writing center tutoring takes place in a hierarchical context in which there is danger that a tutor might assume an unethically dominant role in creating and developing a text. Hence the rationale for a nondirective pedagogy.

Blind adherence to any absolute principles of tutoring, however, can be counterproductive to student learning because it precludes other instructional possibilities, in particular the role of imitation. In his discussion of the history of plagiarism, St. Onge points out that "in the vast arrays of animal behaviors, mimicry is a fine art. The mocking bird plagiarizes the calls of any one of its peers and has been known to tease human whistlers" (17). Vygotsky similarly implies a key relationship between imitation and learning. Yet, as Anne Gere has pointed out, our culture, in its privileging of original creation, is predisposed to distrust imitation as a learning tool, even though imitation was once considered a method of choice. In her discussion of the development of oratory, Gere cites Isocrates' concept of the teacher who "must in himself set such an example that the students who are molded by him and are able to imitate him will, from the outset, show in their speaking a degree of grace and charm greater than that of others" (8). Gere also refers to Cicero and Quintillian, who recommended "paraphrase because of its challenge to achieve expression independent of the original" (8).

Muriel Harris advocates modeling, even for novice writers, pointing out that imitation can be useful for teaching composing skills and writing behaviors such as invention and editing. Harris cites a case study in which she used modeling to help a student improve his composing process, working through the process herself as the student observed, helping the student decide what topics to choose, what information to gather, and what writing behaviors to engage in. "And what better way is there," Harris asks, "to convince students that writing is a process that requires effort, thought, time, and persistence than to go through all that writing, scratching out, rewriting, and revising with and for our students?" (81)

Concern With Plagiarism

Let us suppose, however, that as a result of Harris's use of imitation and modeling, her student had appropriated a few of her "ideas" or phrases for his own paper. Should Harris's approach then be regarded as unethical? Would the results be considered "plagiarism"? Would the student need to acknowledge Harris in a full citation or else be guilty of a moral offense? Some faculty members would probably answer "yes" to all of these questions. But one might also argue that few of us can know with any certainty how or where we obtained our own ideas in the first place, a view expressed by many writers. Accused of plagiarism at a young age, Helen Keller, for example, characterizes her writing as a mixture of assimilation and imitation: "It is certain that I cannot always distinguish my own thoughts from those I read, because what I read becomes the very substance and text of my mind. Consequently, in nearly all that I write, I produce something which very much resembles the crazy patchwork I used to make when I first learned to sew" (67–68). Similarly, Virginia Woolf writes in her diary that "reading Yeats turns my sentences one way: reading Sterne turns them another" (119). A poststructuralist perspective "does away with origins. . . . Thus, writing can be nothing more than a tissue of quotations, a pastiche of passages possessing no authorial affiliation and therefore belonging to no one" (De Grazia 301).

Moreover, as Woodmansee and Jaszi point out, "studies of writing practices from the Renaissance to the present suggest that the modern regime of authorship, far from being timeless and universal, is a relatively recent formation" (2–3). In fact, "quotation marks were not used on a regular basis until the end of the eighteenth century" (De Grazia 288). Before this time, they were used for the antithetical purpose of highlighting a commonplace or statement of truth that could be appropriated by all readers, "facilitating the 'lifting' of the passages they marked. . . . In brief, rather than cordoning off a passage as property of another, quotation marks flagged the passage as property belonging to all—'common places' to be freely appropriated (and not necessarily verbatim and with correct authorial ascription)" (289). Our conception of plagiarism as a reprehensible moral offense, then, is a relatively recent notion.

In the context of writing center pedagogy, however, that notion suggests that because nondirective tutoring has the smallest risk of becoming a form of plagiarism, it is, by definition, the most effective and hence "ethical" approach. Yet, as Barry Kroll suggests, it is not necessarily true that plagiarism is counter-productive to student learning. What would happen, Kroll asks,

> if one comes to suspect that plagiarism (particularly the familiar case of copying a paragraph or so from a source) does not inevitably damage learning—at least, no more seriously than quoting the same passage would damage learning[?] In fact, from the view of consequences to oneself, there would seem to be no morally significant difference between quoting and copying without acknowledgment; neither is more or less likely to lead to creativity, to learning, or to independent thought. And what if one could show that copying a passage from a source sometimes leads to learning or improved writing? (5)

This is not to say, of course, that writing centers should write students' papers for them or relinquish their insistence that students take responsibility for their own work. However, as the Internet becomes an increasingly common means of communication and facilitates easy access to texts of various sorts, it is important that the writing center begin to question the absolutism of its noninterventionist policies in favor of a more flexible "rhetorically situated view of plagiarism, one that acknowledges that all writing is in an important sense collaborative and that 'common knowledge' varies from community of community and is collaboratively shared" (Lunsford and Ede 437).

Political Limitations of Writing Center Orthodoxy

Writing center practitioners who let ethical concerns drive a noninterventionist, nonappropriative praxis suffer not only pedagogically; they suffer politically as well. An ethics based on defensiveness is ill-suited to challenge the prevailing order. If writing centers limit themselves merely to fixing what comes in the door, they run two risks. First, as Nancy Grimm has observed, in the interest of conforming to a perhaps flawed standard of academic writing, they may end up trying to fix what isn't broken. Second, by accepting what comes in the door as given—including the assignments, pedagogies, assumptions, and epistemologies that lie behind clients' texts—writing centers abandon the ground from which they are in a position to contest the larger political reality of which all of us—teachers, students, and tutors—are a part.

For the fact is that writing centers are well positioned to question the status quo. Writing centers occupy what Harvey Kail and John Trimbur have called "semiautonomous" institutional space located "outside the normal channels of teaching and learning." By providing a place where students can experience some distance from "official strictures," the center can help them "reengage the forms of authority in their lives by demystifying the authority of knowledge and its institutions" (11). Writing centers can be sites of what Nancy Welch calls "critical exile," from where we can encourage students to "reconsider the kinds of conversation we value in academia" and to "resist the pressure of perfection" (7). "Writing centers," argues Marilyn Cooper,

> are in a good position to serve as a site of critique of the institutionalized structure of writing instruction in college, and . . . as a consequence of this, the role of the tutor should be to create useful knowledge about writing in college and to empower students as writers who also understand what writing involves and who act as agents in their writing. (98)

Too often, though, the writing center's "service ethic" silences its potentially revolutionary voice.

> [B]ecause writing centers are represented in positions of uncritical service, writing center practice often focuses on fixing students who have nothing wrong with them, supporting a literacy curriculum that is often out of sync with the needs of today's students, and talking about assignments with students as though these assignments were not implicitly loaded with one culture's values. Even more troubling is that the close contact writing centers have with students provides a special kind of knowledge, a knowledge that challenges the wisdom of mainstream practices, a knowledge that forms the stories we tell each other. Yet as writing centers are currently theorized, faculty are protected from this knowledge. (Grimm 11)

Because of its location in "semiautonomous space," its status as "critical exile," and its access to "a special kind of knowledge," the writing center is uniquely positioned to challenge business as usual in the academy. Centers may resist making that challenge for a variety of reasons, including their sometimes tenuous institutional standing and the typically untenured status of writing center directors. But political timidity may also result from ethical naiveté, from a conviction that the center's proper role is narrowly responsive rather than initiatory. By being so careful not to infringe on other's turf—the writer's, the teacher's, the department's, the institution's—the writing center has been party to its own marginality and silencing.

Another political danger confronting the orthodox writing center is a kind of classism or elitism. By holding clients to a standard that writing center practitioners and educators in general do not observe, the center may relegate them to an inferior role. In refusing to write on a student's paper or supply occasional phrasing or suggest specific lines of inquiry, writing center personnel are withholding from clients precisely the kind of directive, appropriative intervention that is routinely offered to publishing academics by colleagues and editors. The authors of this article frequently show their writing to others who have suggested and sometimes actually make specific, detailed changes in their texts. Do students deserve less than what we expect for ourselves?

Of course, one must qualify that the kind of mentoring performed by a thesis advisor or among colleagues is different from what typically goes on in a writing center. Nevertheless, the difference, we would argue, is one of degree rather than kind. Writing center consultants—whether they are undergraduates, graduate students, or professional staff—have knowledge and expertise that many writing center clients lack. A failure to share that knowledge and expertise inhibits the acquisition of academic literacy by writing center clients. It is ironic indeed if that failure stems from ethical concerns about the appropriateness of directive, interventionist conferencing strategies.

It would be simplistic to demand that writing center personnel practice everything they preach and preach only what they practice. Any of us who teach or tutor writings regularly recommend strategies we ourselves do not use. Teachers or tutors may suggest that a writer try freewriting or looping or outlining even if they never employ those techniques themselves, because they realize that everyone writes differently and that others may benefit from practices they personally have not found especially helpful. Similarly, they may choose not to suggest some method they themselves utilize—out of a conviction that a given writer would not benefit from that particular approach. But it is worse than simplistic to require that writing centers withhold helpful information and refrain from helpful practices out of a misguided sense of what is ethical.

A New Ethics for the Writing Center

So what would an ethical writing center look like? Let us suggest three components:

1. The ethical writing center will be proactive. Though writing centers must, by their nature, be responsive to other people's writing, assignments, and goals, centers must not let responsiveness and a misguided sense of ethics give way to knee-jerk acquiescence and accommodation. The people who work in writing centers should be confident of their own expertise and insight and should be willing to use their unique position in the academy to challenge the status quo by critiquing institutional ideology and practice.

2. The ethical writing center will exercise a broad, encompassing vision. The center will look past individual texts and writers to consider the whole range of literate practices in the academy. Writing centers need to move beyond Stephen North's oft-quoted dictum that "[o]ur job is to produce better writers, not better writing" ("Idea" 438). The center's job encompasses not only individual writers, but also the larger discourse communities of which they are a part. The college and university classroom has

few windows. Because of its one-to-one work with students, the writing center is a window into the classroom, and it ought to show some concern for that realm, just as it does for the individual writers it serves.

3. The ethical writing center will take full advantage of its hallmark: individualized writing instruction. As Roger Garrison has said, "A group, a class, has no writing problems; there are only individuals who have difficulty saying what they mean" (1). Writing centers need to maximize what they do best by consistently treating writers as individuals. Leveling its clientele through rigid policy statements—e.g., "Refuse to proofread," or "Don't even hold a pencil when you're tutoring"—denies the diversity found in any center and stifles the creativity of writing center consultants. Writing centers need to be creative in opening up the world of discourse to their clients and their clients to that world.

Dangers of the New Ethics

This new conception of writing center ethics is not without its dangers. We conclude by suggesting three ways that writing centers might go awry.

1. Although we believe that unfounded fears of appropriation and uncritical notions of textual ownership have limited the writing center's effectiveness, it's clear that writers can and do misrepresent their work and that unwary tutors could be party to such misrepresentation. Writing centers are not likely to become replicas of "Tailormade," the paper-writing business described in a recent Harper's article (Witherspoon), but they can be drawn into questionable practices. However (to risk a shop-worn bromide), their focus should not be on the products their clients produce but rather on the process they undergo in the center. The question "Is this the writer's work?" should be interpreted as "What work has this writer done to produce this result?" We have suggested that writing centers can relax a bit about the question of ownership, but they should not relax about the question of agency. One obvious way that agency manifests itself is in simple volume. If a writer comes to the writing center with nothing written and a consultant writes something, that something is likely to overshadow or unduly influence anything the client might subsequently produce. Interventionist strategies with existing text, on the other hand, run less risk of appropriating agency.

2. Although social-constructionist and collaborative-learning theories are central to the ethical writing center as we have described it, an uncritical

acceptance of those theories could lead, as Christina Murphy has warned regarding social constructionism, to an overvaluation of consensus and to "illusory views of peership" (27) and could blind writing centers to the importance of the individual's emotions in intellectual development. Alice Gillam, in a critique of collaborative learning theory, notes that collaborative learning's critics have suggested that "its emphasis on group process and consensus-building enforces conformity, lowers standards, and denies the importance of the individual mind" (40). Gillam also observes that some versions of collaborative learning theory emphasize social and political goals to the neglect of educational goals. Writing, she suggests, can sometimes get lost in the shuffle.

3. Although we have called for the people who work in writing centers to be less timid in their encounters with writers, teachers, texts, assignments, syllabi, and curricula, they must not let a sense of ethical liberation lead to arrogance or tactlessness. North's maxim of curricular nonintervention cited above ("we never evaluate or second-guess any teacher's syllabus, assignments, comments, or grades") follows a previous observation that writing centers "do a fair amount of trade in people working on ambiguous or poorly designed assignments, and far too much work with writers whose writing has received caustic, hostile, or otherwise unconstructive commentary" ("Idea," 440). We have argued that writing centers do themselves and the larger institutions of which they are a part a disservice by maintaining a complicity of silence about the academy's shortcomings, but how should they go about addressing the sins North enumerates? His observation about bad assignments and teacher commentary, as long as it is generalized and abstract, will offend no one because teachers will recognize only others, not themselves, in his indictment. But what happens when a specific writer brings to the writing center a specific paper based on a specific instructor's poorly designed assignment and already subject to that specific instructor's obviously unconstructive commentary? The ethical writing center must always be characterized by tact and sensitivity, recognizing that although our writing may be initiated by someone else's assignment (and in school it almost always is), for most of us our writing represents our selves and the words on the page seem to be our own words. Intervening in someone else's writing ought to feel perilous and ought to continue to be approached with humility and care.

The "goodness" or "badness" of current writing center policy cannot be judged as absolutes, but must ultimately be evaluated in terms of specific consequences to or behaviors of the clients and institutions it serves. In its current form, the writing center, out of a misguided sense of ethical responsibility, has catered to ill-founded fears and outdated epistemologies, and consequently has not ethically served its clientele. The ethical writing center can and should be a force for change—in writers and in writing and in the academy at large.

Note

1. For a discussion of the writing center's response to faculty suspicions of plagiarism, see Behm.

Works Cited

Ashton-Jones, Evelyn. "Asking the Right Questions: A Heuristic for Tutors." *The Writing Center Journal* 9.1 (1988): 29–36.

Behm, Richard. "Ethical Issues in Peer Tutoring: A Defense of Collaborative Learning." *The Writing Center Journal* 10.1 (1989): 3–12.

Blau, Susan. "Issues in Tutoring Writing: Stories from Our Center." *Writing Lab Newsletter* 19.2 (Oct. 1992): 1–4.

Brooks, Jeff. "Minimalist Tutoring: Making the Student Do All the Work." *Writing Lab Newsletter* 15.6 (Feb. 1991): 1–4.

Bruffee, Kenneth. "Collaborative Learning and the Conversation of Mankind." *College English* 46 (1984): 645–52.

Bruner, Jerome. *Toward a Theory of Instruction.* Cambridge: Belknap of Harvard University Press, 1966.

Carino, Peter. "Early Writing Centers: Toward a History." *The Writing Center Journal* 15.2 (1995): 103–115.

Clark, Irene L. "Collaboration and Ethics in Writing Center Pedagogy." *The Writing Center Journal* 9.1 (1988): 3–12.

———. "Leading the Horse: The Writing Center and Required Visits." *The Writing Center Journal* 5.2/6.1 (1985): 31–34.

Cooper, Marilyn. "Really Useful Knowledge: A Cultural Studies Agenda for Writing Centers." *The Writing Center Journal* 14.2 (1994): 97–111.

De Grazia, Margreta. "Sanctioning Voice: Quotation Marks, the Abolition of Torture, and the Fifth Amendment." Woodmansee and Jaszi 281–302.

Ede, Lisa. "Writing as a Social Process: A Theoretical Foundation for Writing Centers?" *The Writing Center Journal* 9.2 (1989): 3–13.

Edwards, Suzanne. "Tutoring Your Tutors: How to Structure a Tutor-Training Workshop." *Writing Lab Newsletter* 7.10 (June 1983): 7–9.

Garrison, Roger. *One-To-One: Making Writing Instruction Effective*. New York: Harper & Row, 1981.

Gere, Ann Ruggles. "On Imitation." Paper given at the Conference on College Composition and Communication. Atlanta, March 1987.

Gillam, Alice M. "Collaborative Learning Theory and Peer Tutoring Practice." Mullin and Wallace 39–53.

Grimm, Nancy Maloney. "Divided Selves: Exploring Writing Center Contradictions." Address. Midwest Writing Centers Association. Kansas City, 7 Oct. 1994.

Harris, Muriel. "Modeling: A Process Method of Teaching." *College English* 45 (1983): 74–84.

Harris, Muriel, and Tony Silva. "Tutoring ESL Students: Issues and Opinions." *College Composition and Communication* 44 (1993): 525–537.

Hodges, Karen. "The Writing of Dissertations: Collaboration and Ethics." Paper given at the Conference on College Composition and Communication. Atlanta, March 1987.

Kail, Harvey, and John Trimbur. "The Politics of Peer Tutoring." *WPA: Writing Program Administration* 11.1 (1987): 5–12.

Keller, Helen. *The Story of My Life*. New York: Doubleday, 1903, 1954.

Kroll, Barry. "Why is Plagiarism Wrong?" Paper given at the Conference on College Composition and Communication. Atlanta, March 1987.

Lunsford, Andrea. "Collaboration, Control, and the Idea of a Writing Center." *The Writing Center Journal* 12.1 (1991): 3–10.

Lunsford, Andrea, and Lisa Ede. "Collaborative Authorship and the Teaching of Writing." Woodmansee and Jaszi 417–138.

Malamud, Bernard. *A New Life*. New York: Dell, 1961.

Moffett, James. *Teaching the Universe of Discourse*. Boston: Houghton, 1968.

Mullin, Joan A. and Ray Wallace, eds. *Theory and Practice in the Writing Center*. Urbana: NCTE, 1994.

Murphy, Christina. "The Writing Center and Social Constructionist Theory." *Intersections: Theory and Practice in the Writing Center*. Ed. Joan A. Mullin and Ray Wallace. Urbana: NCTE, 1994. 25–38.

Neff, Julie. "Learning Disabilities and the Writing Center." Mullin and Wallace 81–95.

North, Stephen M. "The Idea of a Writing Center." *College English* 46 (1984): 43–446.

————. "Revisiting 'The Idea of a Writing Center.' " *The Writing Center Journal* 15.1 (1994): 7–19.

Rochelle, Larry. "The ABC's of Writing Centers." *Writing Lab Newsletter* September 1981: 7–9.

Shamoon, Linda K., and Deborah H. Burns. "A Critique of Pure Tutoring." *The Writing Center Journal* 15.2 (1995): 134–151.

St. Onge, K.R. *The Melancholy Anatomy of Plagiarism*. Lanhom, MA: U Press of America, 1988.

Sullivan, Patrick. "The Politics of the Drop-In Writing Center." *Writing Lab Newsletter* 8.9 (May 1984): 1–2.

————. "Do You Object to Tutors Assisting Your Students With Their Writing?" *Writing Lab Newsletter* 10.4 (December 1985): 6–8.

Thompson, Thomas C. "'Yes, Sir!' 'No, Sir!' 'No Excuse, Sir!' Working with an Honor Code in a Military Setting." *Writing Lab Newsletter* 19.5 (Jan. 1997): 13–14.

Trimbur, John. "Peer Tutoring: A Contradiction in Terms." *The Writing Center Journal* 7.2 (1987): 21–28.

Vygotsky, Lev. *Mind in Society: The Development of Higher Psychological Process*. Cambridge: Harvard University Press, 1978.

Weiner, Bernard. *Achievement Motivation and Attribution Theory*. New Jersey: General Learning Press, 1974.

Welch, Nancy. "From Silence to Noise: The Writing Center as Critical Exile." *Writing Center Journal* 14.1 (1993): 3–15.

Wicksell, Wesley. "The Communications Program at Stephens College." *College English* 9 (1947): 143–145.

Witherspoon, Abigail. "This Pen for Hire." *Harper's* June 1995: 49–57.

Woodmansee, Martha, and Peter Jaszi, eds. *The Construction of Authorship: Textual Appropriation in Law and Literature*. Durham and London: Duke University Press, 1994.

Woodmansee, Martha, and Peter Jaszi. "Introduction." Woodmansee and Jaszi 1–15.

Woolf, Virginia. *The Diary of Virginia Woolf*. Vol 3, 1925–1930. Penguin: New York, 1982.

LEADING THE HORSE: THE WRITING CENTER AND REQUIRED VISITS

Irene L. Clark
1985

Whether or not students ought to be required to go to the Writing Center has always been a problematic issue, and often those opposed to such a requirement justify their position simply by that old maxim, "You can lead a horse to water, but you cannot make him drink." Steve North, in "The Idea of a Writing Center," asserts that such a requirement usually does not produce the desired results. "Occasionally we manage to convert such writers from people who have to see us to people who want to, but most often they either come as if for a kind of detention or else they drift away" (440). Presumably, students should use the Writing Center when they themselves decide to do so; requiring them to come defeats the purpose.

This argument against requiring writing center visits derives from the prevailing belief that improvement in writing, or in anything, can occur only when the student is motivated intrinsically, and, indeed, few psychologists would argue that "intrinsic factors are more effective in a general learning environment than extrinsic ones" (Williams 102). Moreover, the popular quasi-romantic model of the relationship of motivation to writing postulates that a core of curiosity and excitement about the world exists within all students and that this core must be elicited before students will be motivated to write. The task of uncovering this often deeply buried core is usually assigned to the classroom teacher, and supposedly once the student is properly motivated, he will then visit the Writing Center on his own, use its facilities to maximum advantage, and willingly undertake the necessary work.

The problem with this model, however appealing it might be, is that it is based primarily on anecdotal information and that it presumes that composition students are homogeneous. Perhaps it would make the life of the Writing Center administrator a bit easier if all students functioned according to this mode. However, according to Kolesnic, most of the things that we do cannot be neatly categorized as either intrinsically or extrinsically motivated (180), and the findings of Williams and Alden suggest that students differ widely in their motivational patterns. Certainly some students are intrinsically motivated and write for self-gratification. However, more students than we would like to believe are extrinsically motivated; such students write for grades, not for self-expression or pleasure. Moreover, according to Williams and Alden, even intrinsically motivated students are strongly influenced by the desire to get good grades. For both intrinsically and extrinsically motivated students in the Williams and Alden study, "grade was the single most important reason given for working hard on an assignment" (109).

Awareness that extrinsic as well as intrinsic motivational factors affect students' acquisition of writing skills has important implications for the question of whether or not students ought to be required to visit the Writing Center, a question with which we at the University of Southern California grapple every semester. In our quite large program (3500 students per semester, 155 instructors) the assignment of Writing Center visits are the province of each individual instructor. Some instructors require their students to visit the Writing Center several times a semester, some do not require any visits at all. And each semester, when we reevaluate the program, we consider whether or not required Writing Center visits ought to become a component of program policy. Debating this question, we are of course aware of the "lead a horse to water" philosophy; yet it seems equally sensible that if the horse has not at least been led to the water that he will be even less likely to drink.

Research Design

This year, we decided to conduct a study to assess student attitude toward being required to attend the Writing Center, to investigate the effect of such a requirement on student perceptions of the Writing Center as a useful facility, and to determine the relationship of teacher requirement to student attendance. Three hundred and twenty-nine students enrolled in composition classes at USC during the Fall 1984 semester were interviewed by means of a questionnaire. The sample was drawn from a systematically selected random cluster of class sections. Students from twenty-six of the one hundred and fifty-five class sections were selected to participate in the study.

The questionnaire was designed to assess student attitude toward the Writing Center in relation to motivation for attendance, teacher's requirement for mandatory visits, and perception of the Center's usefulness toward improving both writing skills and grades. Questions pertaining to student attitudes toward various Writing Center factors were asked in a closed-ended, Likert-scale format, which asked for a response in the form of "strongly agree," "agree," "disagree," "strongly disagree," or "does not apply." One half of the questions were written in the negative form to prevent the wording of the question from influencing the response. Questions of particular significance to the focus of this article were as follows:

- The Writing Center is valuable to my overall writing improvement.
- I am too busy to go the the Writing Center.
- I am already a good writer and do not need extra help from the Writing Center.
- I appreciate getting feedback about my paper from someone other than my teacher.
- The tutors in the Writing Center are not helpful.

Two other points surveyed were:

- Teacher requirement of visits per semester (zero, once, twice, three times, or more than three times)
- Actual visits this semester (zero, once, twice, three times, or more than three times)

Thus, the study was designed to assess whether students' attitudes toward the Writing Center were influenced by their having been required to go and to calculate the effect such a requirement had on actual student visits.

Findings

Of the three hundred and twenty-nine students surveyed, eighty-five said they would go to the the Writing Center only if the teacher required such visits, forty-eight characterized themselves as self-motivated, one hundred twenty-eight characterized themselves as both teacher- and self-motivated (the largest group), and sixty-eight said that the question did not apply.

Table 1. Motivation for Visiting the Writing Center.

Reason for attending	
Teacher	85
Self	48
Both	128
Not apply	68
Total	329

Concerning student attitude toward whether the Writing Center helps students improve their writing skills, the survey revealed that three-fourths of the students surveyed felt that the Writing Center does indeed improve their writing skills and that the center is a friendly, helpful, accessible, and needed component of the program. Moreover, over three quarters of the students surveyed disagreed with the statement that they were already good enough writers so as not to require additional help from the Writing Center. The students surveyed were quite aware of their own needs in this regard.

Almost half of the students also believed that the Writing Center improved their grades on writing assignments. One-quarter of the teacher-motivated students believed that visiting the Center improved the grades they received on their papers; nearly half of the self-motivated students felt the same; over half of those motivated by both teacher and self-motivation believed that the Writing Center improved their grades on writing assignments. Apparently, then, a majority of the students believed that going to the Writing Center improved both their writing skills and their grades, whether or not they had been required to come. One would presume, according to these findings, that if most students believed that the Writing Center improved both their writing skills and their grade and recognized their need for help in writing, that they would all flock to the Writing Center, without being required. Yet, as we all know, such is not usually the case.

Concerning teacher requirement, ninety-five of the students surveyed had not been required to go to the Writing Center at all, twenty-seven to go once, eighty-three to go twice, forty-two to go three times, and eighty-two to go more than three times. At the time of the survey, four weeks before the end of the semester, eighty-seven had not gone at all, ninety-seven had gone once, seventy-five twice, thirty-two three times and thirty-eight more than three times.

Table 2. Number of Students Required to Attend the Writing Center Compared with Actual Number of Visits.

Visits	Students Required to Attend	Students Who Attend
0	95	87
1	27	97
2	83	75
3	42	32
more	82	38

What these figures suggest is a strong relationship between teachers' Writing Center requirements and actual visits to the Center. Based upon our experience in the Writing Center, even those students who had been assigned required visits and who had not done so at the time of the survey will eventually fulfill their requirements by the end of the semester, not the best use of the services we offer, yet perhaps better than no visits at all. What the figures also suggest is that unless teachers require their students to visit the Writing Center, the students are unlikely to go or perhaps to go only once.

Why don't students go to the Writing Center on their own if they are aware of their own needs for writing instruction and recognize that the Writing Center can be a source of help? Apparently, because they feel they are too busy. Approximately 65% of those who were motivated only by a teacher's requirement believed that they were too busy to go to the Writing Center, whereas only 40% of those who claimed to be self-motivated (the largest percentage of students) felt this way. Being too busy is apparently a prime reason students claim they do not attend the Writing Center rather than because they do not recognize the worth of going. What seems apparent, then, is that to assign students to visit the Writing Center might indeed lead them to recognize that they weren't quite as busy as they thought.

Conclusions

The study concludes with a recommendation that a Writing Center requirement be instituted as a department-wide policy, with the understanding that the more visits required, the more times the student will be likely to go. And, assuming that the students at USC do not constitute a unique population (and it is unlikely that they do), this recommendation has implications for other colleges and universities as well. Since students already recognize their own need for additional writing instruction and already believe that the Writing Center can improve both writing skills and grades and since the environment in the Writing Center is designed to generate further motivation, it is likely that students will perceive their experiences at the Writing Center as positive. Robert Martin, in *Teaching Through Encouragement*, maintains that through encouragement it is possible to change behavior and that, "when behavior changes, self-image and attitudes are also likely to change." Requiring students to visit the Writing Center at least gives them a chance to be encouraged. And with the right encouragement, even the most recalcitrant horse, aware of his thirst and standing at the water's edge, might bend his stubborn neck and take a drink.

Works Cited

Kolesnic, Walter. *Motivation: Understanding and Influencing Human Behavior*. Boston: Allyn and Bacon, 1978.

Martin, Robert. *Teaching Through Encouragement*. Englewood Cliffs: Prentice-Hall, 1980.

North, Stephen M. "The Idea of a Writing Center," *College English* 46 (1984): 433–46.

Williams, J. D., and Scott D. Alden. "Motivation in the Composition Classroom," *Research in the Teaching of English* 17.2 (1983): 101–113.

Irene L. Clark has published articles in *The Journal of Basic Writing, Teaching English in the Two Year College,* and *The Writing Center Journal.* She is currently the Director of the Writing Center at the University of Southern California. This article appeared in the Spring/Summer 1985 and Fall/Winter 1985 issue of *The Writing Center Journal.*

INDEX

Articles, 219–220
Assertiveness, 33–34
Assignments, 65–92
    Assignment Worksheet, 74–75
    interpreting, 68–70
    problems students have understanding,
        66–68
Attribution Theory, 9–10
Audience, 97–98; 103–107
Authority, issues concerning, 46–50

Book Review, 193; see also Literature

Collaboration, 26–27
    distinction between legitimate and
        illegitimate, 27
Composition theory, 10–16
    Genre theory, 15–16
    process theory, 10–12
    reading theory, 12–13
    social constructionism, 14–15
Computers, 165–178
    Invention and, 177–178
    Word processing, 166–170
Computer assisted instruction, 176
Conclusions, 129–130
Conferences, 43–46
    beginning, 45–46
    conference format worksheet, 109
    focusing, 94–95
Contrastive Rhetoric, 209–211
Crouton Effect, 187–188
Cultural Differences, 31–32

Developing ideas, 176–179
Dialects, 227–230
Dyslexia, 147–149

Ebonics, 228–230
Editing, 138
Egocentricity and writing, 9–10
Ellis, Rod and second language acquisition,
        208
ESL writers, See also Non-Native Speakers
    Faculty Attitudes Toward, 231–232
    Typical Problems, 218–225
Evaluation, ideas about, 25–26
Exploration questions, 90

Five Paragraph Essay, 113–114
Function Outline, 124–128

Genre theory, 15–16
Grammar and Punctuation, 136–138

Heuristics, See Developing ideas

Imitation, 139
Information Literacy, 170–173
    political implications of, 171
Internet, 175
Introductions, 129–130
Invention, see Developing ideas
Involvement with text, 95–97
    Through purpose, thesis, and audience,
        97–98

Krashen, Stephen and second language
    acquisition, 206–208

Language Acquisition, 206–208
Language development, 8–9
    Piaget, Jean, 8
    Vygotsky, Lev, 8
Language Learning, 206–209
Learning Disabilities, 147–163
    Attitudes toward, 149, 152
    Dealing with, 153–162
    Defined, 150
    Identifying, 151
    Questions concerning, 149
    Reading aloud as strategy, 155
    Spatial, 148, 152
    Typical problems of, 161–162
Learning Theories, 8–10
    attribution theory, 9
    Bruner, Jerome, 9
Literature assignments, 181, 193–196
    Argumentative Literary Essay, 197
    Book review assignment, 181
    Checklist for Writing About Literature,
        200–201
    Evidence for, 196, 198
    Problems with, 193, 196
    Quotations, tips for using, 200
    Writing About Literature handout,
        197–201

Narrowing and Focusing, 107
Non-directive listening, 36
Non-native speakers, 203–227
    Faculty attitudes toward, 231-232
    Identifying, 211–215
    Problems of, 218–227
    Strategies for working with, 215–217
Notetaking, 184–186

Organization, 114–124
Outlining, 121–122
OWLS (On-line Writing Labs), 175–176

Prepositions, 220
Prewriting strategies, 79–84
    exploration questions, 90
    intellectual strategies, 86–89
    intuitive strategies, 85–86
    Points to Make List, 88–89
Process theory, 10–12
Purpose, Thesis, Audience, 97–98; 103–107

Quotations, 187–188, 200

Readability, 133–136; 142–145
Reader-Writer Transaction, 13–14
Reading, tips for, 198
Reading Aloud, 95–97
    for students with learning disabilities, 155
Reading Theory, 12–13
Research Papers, 181–188
    crouton effect, 187
    Note Synthesis Sheet, 186
    problems, 181
    Research Paper Time Management Form,
        183
    Source Notesheet, 185
Revision, 108; 111–131
Role Playing, 34–35

Second Language Acquisition, 206–209; See
    also, Non-native Speakers
Sentence Combining, 132–133
Sentence Level Problems, 131–132; 139–141
Silence during conferences, 35
Social Constructionist Theory, 14–15
Students
    Cultural background of, 31–32; 211–215
    Involving in conferences, 55–62
    Putting at ease, 44–45
    Response to, 79–83

Talk-Write Pedagogy, 222
Tense, 222–224
Thesis, revision of, 111–114

Thesis, Purpose, Audience, Interrelationship
    between, 106–107
Transitions, 123–124
Tree diagrams, 121–122
Tutoring, directive versus non-directive,
    62–63
Tutors, See conferences

Word processing, 166–170
    Invention and, 168–169
    Organization and, 170
    Revision and, 169–170

Suggestions for using, 168
Tutoring with, 167–168
Writing Process and, 166–167
World Wide Web, 173–176
Writing block, 77
Writing center
    Definition of, 3
    Language development and, 8–9
    Learning and, 9–10
    Theories, 10–16
    Websites, 176
Writing Instruction, History of, 3–7
Writing Process Report Form, 53